Designing, Writing, and Producing Computer Documentation

Designing, Writing, and Producing Computer Documentation

Lynn Denton

Jody Kelly

McGraw-Hill, Inc.

New York St. Louis San Francisco Blue Ridge Summit, Pa.
Auckland Bogotá Caracas Lisbon London Madrid
Mexico Milan Montreal New Delhi Paris San Juan
São Paulo Singapore Sydney Tokyo Toronto

Library of Congress Cataloging-in-Publication Data

Denton, Lynn.
    Designing, writing, and producing computer documentation / by Lynn
    Denton and Jody Kelly.

        p.   cm.
    Includes index.
    ISBN 0-07-016412-6 (H)   ISBN 0-07-016417-7 (P)
        1. Electronic data processing documentation.   I. Kelly, Jody.
    II. Title.
    QA76.9.D6D46   1992
    808'.066005—dc20   92-20327
                                                        CIP

3 4 5 6 7 8 9 0   DOC/DOC 9 9 8 7 6 5 4

ISBN 0-07-016412-6 (H)   ISBN 0-07-016417-7 (P)

Notices

Apple, the Apple logo, Macintosh, Imagewriter, LaserWriter, MultiFinder, and Stackware are
trademarks of Apple Computer, Inc., registered in the United States and other jurisidictions.
HyperCard, HyperTalk, and MacPaint are trademarks of Claris Corporation registered in the
United States and other jurisdictions.
IBM is a registered trademark of International Business Machines Corporation.

*For more information about other McGraw-Hill materials,
call 1-800-2-MCGRAW in the United States. In other
countries, call your nearest McGraw-Hill office.*

Contents

Acknowledgments

The authors wish to thank International Business Machines Corporation for permission to use the IBM host publishing system, BookMaster 3.0, to produce the final manuscript of this book. To the reviewer of our early drafts, Peggy Newfield, we owe great thanks for making the book much better than it was.

We also wish to thank David McMurrey, Karen K. Travis, Lance C. Amundsen, and Tom T. Beard for special help. Finally, we owe more than can be repaid to our families and friends, especially to Holly Atlas.

Introduction

This book is designed to help writers in the computer industry make their product documentation more useful, attractive, and accessible to their paying customers by building in quality from the beginning.

To produce good documentation, a technical writer has to play many roles: market researcher, library designer, contract negotiator, interviewer, technical researcher, scheduler, financial planner, customer advocate, task analyst, peer reviewer, writer, editor, project manager, moderator of review meetings, planner for translation and foreign distribution, book designer, layout artist, typesetter, legal researcher, usability test coordinator, indexer, glossary writer, distributor, and proofreader.

Writers in one- or two-person writing shops might do all of these jobs and more. Those in larger shops might specialize at first and then rotate into other jobs over time. Mastering all the skills needed to produce quality computer documentation is not easy; this book presents a comprehensive "crash course" in the field.

If you are a new or prospective technical writer, or an experienced writer interested in improving the quality of your documentation, this book is for you. Computer designers, engineers, programmers, and product planners—anyone who writes technical information that others must read and use—will also find many helpful tips and techniques.

Although this book is not designed specifically as a textbook, it includes enough practical examples to serve as a reference for students and instructors of technical writing.

1

Achieving Quality through Library Design

Writers in the computer industry don't set out to produce books that overwhelm, bore, confuse, and irritate customers. When these results occur, writers tend to blame insufficient time, training, or equipment; inadequate audience and market analyses; or red tape of various kinds, including poor communications among people and politically motivated decisions. Some companies, however, produce good books despite these conditions, because their writers understand quality and use a well-defined process to achieve it.

This chapter offers an introduction to task analysis, a discussion of library design, a definition of quality, and a discussion of various influences on the quality of computer documentation.

Support for Customers' Tasks

High-quality computer documentation is designed, first and foremost, to support the *tasks* that buyers of the product want to perform. Customers might or might not take an interest in the details of the various functions, but they always want clear information on how to get their work done when they use the product.

For example, a common task for customers using a word processing or a desktop publishing program is to place the page number on the page: they want to know how to position it at the top or bottom of the page and at the right, center, or left of the line. Good documentation explains in one place all the steps necessary for customers to place the page number exactly where they want it. Less effective documentation might bury the page number under a discussion of running headers and footers, discuss top and bottom placement in a different section from right, center, or left placement, or neglect to mention that page numbering is a built-in function that can't be changed. Flaws like these result from failing to think about how customers are going to use the product and what tasks or jobs they want to do. In a sense, *everything* is a task.

Universal tasks

The following universal tasks associated with software products can accommodate even conceptual and descriptive information:

- *Evaluation.*   Deciding whether to purchase and install the product
- *Planning.*   Deciding on the type, number, and location of the products to install, as well as the relationships among the products
- *Installing.*   Setting up the product for use
- *Administration.*   Managing the resources of the product, including its users
- *Operation.*   Starting, stopping, and maintaining the product
- *Tailoring.*   Tuning the product for specific situations
- *Programming.*   Designing, coding, compiling, running, debugging, and testing programs written for use with the product
- *Diagnosis.*   Recovering from error conditions
- *End use.*   Performing end-user tasks with the product

(from *Information Development Guideline: Task-Oriented Libraries* published in 1986 by IBM)

Using these universal tasks can help you group similar information into one book or, for a one-book library, into the same section of the book. You should also ensure that the subtasks present procedural information that helps customers achieve their objectives. (For an example of a detailed task analysis, see "Detailed task analysis for an installation node" on page 60.)

Library design

A good first step in achieving high-quality computer publications is library design. A *library* is a set of books supporting a computer product. The *design* of a library includes determining how much and what type of information to present, analyzing the audience, dividing the information into books, deciding on the format, providing a design guide to ensure consistency throughout the library, and then developing a publications plan.

Planners, managers, or experienced writers usually design the library for a new product, but less-experienced writers should also understand the principles involved. Even if the product requires only one book, the process of designing a library is still useful because it ensures that the information is organized appropriately.

Determining the information to present

Before you can decide how much and what type of information the customer needs, you must thoroughly understand the product. Study the marketing objectives and technical specifications of the product to find answers to the following questions:

- Is it a new product or an update of an existing product?
- Is it a large-scale product for an entire system, a small single-purpose product, or something in between?
- What is the main function it performs?
- How many subfunctions does it contain and what are they for?
- How complex are the subfunctions?
- Who will use the product and what will be their most common tasks?
- How many ways can the product be used (selecting from menus, clicking on icons with a mouse, entering commands, and writing programs, for example)?
- What makes this product stand out among competitors' products?

With these questions answered, determine how many of the universal tasks listed on page 2 are relevant to the product:

- *Will customers need information on evaluating the product and deciding whether to buy it?* For a new product, describe the features that no competing product provides. For a new release of an existing product, explain the enhancements added since the last release.
- *Will customers need information on planning the number and location of each installation?* For example, most networking and communications products require extensive planning because the interactions among different types of hardware and software are quite complex.
- *Will customers need information on installing the product?* For a simple, automatic install, they might need to know only the command to type, but for a large, complicated product, they might require extensive assistance.

- *Will customers need information on administrative tasks?* Product resources that need to be monitored and maintained might include users, data, memory, programs, network nodes, and workstations.

- *Will customers need information on daily operations?* These operations might include starting and stopping the program, restarting the system after a power failure or some other emergency, maintaining records on the use of system resources, and replacing failing components.

- *Will customers need information on tailoring the product for a specific environment?* For example, a customer might want to speed up access to a resource, protect part of a system from novice users, or enhance a search facility.

- *Will customers need information on application programming?* If user-written programs can interact with the product, customers will need information on writing code in the supported languages.

- *Will customers need information on diagnosing errors and recovering from problems?* You might need to provide only a telephone number to call for service, or you might need to provide extensive problem analysis and resolution information.

- *How much information will customers need for end-user tasks?* Programmers and administrators might require little or no basic information, while general office workers might need only basic information on end-user tasks.

With these questions answered, sort the product information tasks and list all the tasks that different types of users can perform with the product. Duplicate tasks will become apparent. All users, for example, might need to log on, but you don't need to repeat the logon steps in each book in the library.

An important part of library design is deciding where to place common tasks and how to cross-reference these tasks with other books. In general, you'll use a sifting method:

- Tasks everyone must do should go in the end-user information and should be written for the novice user.

- Tasks all technical people might want to do should go in the administrative book.

- Tasks that only specialists do should go in the programming, service, or error-recovery book.

- Reference information usually doesn't contain tasks, so it can go wherever it fits best, sometimes in a book or section by itself.

The sifting method lets you group similar tasks together and keep cross-references to a minimum. It can be a minor annoyance for customers to flip to other sections of a book, but it's a real source of irritation to send them to books they might not have.

Analyzing the audience

Analyzing the audience and dividing information into books should take place at almost the same time, since the two activities are closely related.

Each book should be designed for a specific audience, such as "experienced programmers who write COBOL programs to access a host database" or "network administrators who are responsible for setting up, configuring, and maintaining a local area network." (Tailoring information to a specific group of product users is the subject of Chapter 2.)

Dividing the information into books

The chief library designer is usually responsible for establishing the initial division of product information into separate books. For each book, the designer usually provides an estimate of the length, an audience description, a tentative list of the topics to be covered, and a writing schedule. The designer might also point out relevant source material for the writers and provide a list of technical reviewers for each book.

During the book development cycle, the designer also monitors the books to ensure that the library doesn't contain redundant or inconsistent information. (Chapter 4 contains more information on dividing information into books.)

Deciding on format and design

Good design is *transparent*; it is invisible to the reader. The reader should be able to move comfortably through the book, basically unaware of the design elements.

If you use good design, the reader can focus on the content and on the task at hand—learning, using, understanding, or retrieving information. Your job is to get the reader into the book and out of it as quickly as possible. (Chapters 7 and 8 contain more information on the physical design and production of a book.)

Providing a design guide to ensure consistency

An important step in producing a good book or library is to construct a *design guide*—a document that defines and describes design elements, such as use of color, book components, depiction of menus and screen displays, and page size. You need this information to ensure that the design of your book or library is consistent, and the print shop you work with needs this information to produce exactly the appearance you want.

Your design guide can be very informal, just a collection of notes to yourself, or it can be formalized and circulated—especially if several people are working on your book or on related books in a product library. Close adherence to the specifications described in the design guide is the key to ensuring consistency.

A design guide is different from a *style guide*; you need both to ensure good writing, consistent style, and good design. You might already have an in-house style guide that you follow for each project. A style guide describes how to handle items such as bulleted lists, equations and calculations, abbreviations, units of measurement, paragraph indentations, presentation of artwork, copyright notices, and other stylistic matters.

Your organization might also have its own favorite grammar and writing handbook that the writers should follow. In some cases, sections on writing mechanics are part of a style guide. In addition, some style guides contain elements traditionally found in a design guide, or your organization might have a document called a design guide that includes information traditionally found in style guides. Whatever they are called, you need to be sure to have documents available to address design, style, and writing mechanics. (For an example of a style guide and a design guide, see Appendices A and B.)

Developing a publications plan

A *publications plan* is a set of specifications for the documentation that supports a product. For a small or one-book library, the plan might be brief and informal, but for a large library, the plan might be a lengthy, detailed document. Most publications plans include some or all of the following:

- A description of the product
- The packaging plan for the books—are all the books included with the product diskettes, or are some sold separately from the product? How can the books be ordered?
- Information on whether the books will be translated into other languages
- A list containing the following information about each book in the library:
  - ~ The title of the document
  - ~ The medium of the document (printed or online)
  - ~ The estimated length in pages or panels
  - ~ The writer(s) assigned to the book
  - ~ The purpose of the book
  - ~ The audience for whom the book is intended

~ The schedule for distributing and reviewing the outline and each draft of the book

~ The last date for changes to the book before it is printed

~ The required reviewers of the book

~ A description of the content expected in the book

~ The manufacturing specifications of the book, such as the page size and the binding method

Typically, a publications planner or experienced writer produces the plan and distributes it to all those who might be affected by it: writers, programmers, marketing personnel, manufacturing schedulers, and managers, for example.

Defining Quality in Computer Documentation

The most important indicator of quality is that the information helps customers do their work. Some other characteristics of excellent documentation are that it is easy to understand and use, it enables information to be easily retrieved, its format and visual devices are effective, it is consistent in style and tone, and it is meticulously written.

Technical accuracy and completeness

Technical accuracy means that the product works the way the documentation says it does, as based on actual experience rather than theory. To ensure that your document is technically accurate, carefully check the correctness of each of the following:

■ Text and artwork representing the user interface

■ The functions, commands, and routines of the product

■ Parameters, input and output values, and defaults

■ Error messages and recovery procedures

■ Navigation paths through the product panels

■ User actions and their results

Technical completeness means that the documentation covers everything the customer might want to do with the product or might need to know about it. A technically complete document might also include some or all of the following, if appropriate for the intended audience:

■ Information on the fastest, safest, least expensive, or easiest way to accomplish a task

- Information on how often and when to perform certain tasks
- Reference information
- Information on preventing and recovering from unexpected results

If you can anticipate how customers might use the product in relation to other products, the documentation should give them some guidance on the probable interactions. This kind of information might be difficult for you to find, but it is very useful to customers when you can provide it. (Chapter 3 offers several ways to locate this kind of information.)

Ease of understanding and use

Your documentation should be easy for the intended audience to understand, whether the customers are novices or experts. The writing should be at a level appropriate to the audience, and you should include enough clear explanations, examples, and illustrations to enable customers to understand the information.

Documentation is easy to use only if customers can find what they're looking for and then act upon what they've found. The documentation should ensure customers' success in using the product.

A document that's easy to understand and use employs clear, concise writing that's simple and to the point. It also carefully separates introductory information from procedural information that requires the customer to take some action. Its steps are easy to understand and perform, its logical organization makes sense to the customer, and it provides careful cross-references to related information.

Retrievability

Documentation should be arranged so that customers can find specific information quickly and easily. You can improve retrievability in your documentation by including the following aids:

- A book cover or dust jacket displaying the title of the book
- Table of contents
- List of tables
- List of figures
- Chapter and section headings
- Cross-references
- Glossary
- Index
- Physical devices, such as die-cut tabs, bleeding tabs, and dividers

These retrievability aids should contain effective pointers to the appropriate information. Terms defined in a glossary should be highlighted consistently in the body of the book, so that customers know they can turn to the glossary for more information. The index should contain synonyms for the word actually used in the book. For example, if a particular function is called *discard* in the product, you can also include such words as *remove*, *erase*, *purge*, and *delete* in the index. (See Chapter 6 for more information on retrievability.)

Effective format and visual devices

The format of a book should provide the most effective options for:

- Number of pages in the book
- Size and shape of the pages
- Use of color in artwork and headings
- Captions for tables and illustrations
- Page layout (margins, white space, relationship between headings and paragraphs, number of columns, text justification)
- Fonts (size, shape, and design of the letters)
- Style of illustrations
- Paper and cover stock
- Binding (perfect bound, saddle-stitched, spiral bound)
- Slip cases, boxes, binders
- Covers and dust jackets

Visual devices in a book include almost everything the customer sees, except blocks of text. Visual devices to consider when developing a book include not only illustrations, but also the following:

- Product logo
- Chapter titles
- Headings
- Labeled boxes
- Display screens
- Icons
- Keys and keyboards
- Notes, cautions, and warnings
- Highlighting

- Tables and graphs
- Lists
- Paragraph length
- Margins and other white space

The book should be aesthetically pleasing and physically usable. Ideally, the format and visual devices should be attractive enough to invite readers to pick up the book and use it.

Consistency of style and tone

It's not enough just to select the style and tone used in a document; you must also be consistent in their use. Inconsistency can puzzle, mislead, annoy, and frustrate customers. An excessively formal style can be hard to read, while an excessively informal style might not be taken seriously. A middle-to-formal style is appropriate for most documentation, although information for the novice end user can sometimes be informal. (For more information on style, see the section titled "Using an appropriate style," on page 74.)

Tone relates to how personal or impersonal a book is. The degree of human warmth in a book depends both on the audience it's intended for and the traditions of your organization. Ideally, the tone should be friendly but emotionally neutral. It should never be condescending, pedantic, or cute. (For more information on tone, see the section titled "Using an appropriate tone," on page 78.)

Meticulous correctness

As a matter of course, documentation should contain no misspellings, typographical or formatting errors, unexplained acronyms or terms, punctuation or grammatical mistakes, poor word choices, awkward sentences, unresolved symbols or cross-references, or repeated words (such as *the the*). Correctness must be the writer's responsibility, with the help of editors and peer reviewers.

Other Influences on Quality

A number of additional factors affect the quality of computer publications, including the following:

- Product development schedules (starting when the programmers start)
- Getting the same equipment as the programmers
- Documenting discrepancies between design and implementation

- Reviewing documentation
- Validating a publication with customers
- Testing documentation
- The writing environment

Product development schedules

Writers should start working on a project at the same time as the designers and programmers. They should also match book schedules with product schedules. Concurrent development ensures that the books are integrated into the development process instead of added to the completed product as an afterthought, and that they are reviewed in a timely manner by programmers and designers currently familiar with the product. It also ensures that the documentation is written by the time the code is finished so that it can be revised (if necessary) and made camera-ready for printing shortly after the code is tested. It should be manufactured at the same time as the product diskettes (although printing the books typically takes several weeks longer than reproducing the diskettes).

For a new product, writers can start working at the same time as programmers if all the development teams are staffed at the beginning. For an update of an existing product, however, it's harder to match the programmers' schedules because of the greater manufacturing time needed for books. Part of a writer's time goes to the production process, which might cause a delay in starting on the next release.

Writers still working on the previous release might be too busy to participate in early training. Some product education is informal and communicated by word of mouth; this type of information might not be available except in the early stages of product development. There might never be a list of classes to take. Instead, a programmer who discovers something about the product might mention it to the people who are in the lab at the time, but not think to pass it on to those who aren't present. Missing the early stage of product development might also mean missing opportunities to influence its design and implementation, since late changes to a product might be too expensive to implement, even if the programmers are persuaded that the changes are desirable.

Writers who are behind the development schedule have less time than they need in the early design phase of the writing process—beginning a few weeks later than the programmers tends to compress the information-gathering and library-design stages of the writing process. They might also be slow to develop good working relationships with designers and programmers—by the time a writer begins to collect information for a book, the technical people might have forgotten the earliest details of the product because they're already concerned with the more advanced functions. Also, the technical people are often more pressed for time later in the development cycle as the deadline draws near.

Handling schedule problems. Probably the best way to overcome the problems of scheduling is for a few writers on a project to turn over their books to someone else to complete, so that they can go on to the design and planning of the next release or project. These advance people can accumulate knowledge and source material that they'll share with the others as their books go into manufacturing. They'll also get to know the technical people and their responsibilities, and identify the hardware, software, and training the writers need to catch up with the programmers.

Getting the same equipment as the programmers

In a cost-conscious environment, writers might have to justify their need for the same hardware and software that programmers receive, since one way to save money is to limit equipment to those who actually produce the code. However, if writers don't obtain hands-on experience with the software and hardware they describe, their documentation might not be accurate.

One compromise on equipment is to have a lab with a few machines that the writers can share. As the programmers develop new code, the lab machines can be updated so that the writers always have an accurate picture of what the interface looks like, how the various functions really work, and what the error messages say.

Documenting discrepancies between design and implementation

In some programming shops, programmers might depart from the product specifications as they implement the design. If a specification doesn't seem feasible, they might write the code to work a different way. They might tell the people directly affected by the change, but they might never be required to update the product design document. Writers who rely exclusively on design documents or technical specifications might produce inaccurate books.

Probably the best way to learn about these discrepancies is to spend time talking with the designers and programmers. Although conversation doesn't translate immediately to pages written, it's usually time well spent because the pages you write will be accurate. You'll also acquire expert advice about the product that is never written down. Customers need exactly this kind of information. In general, the more technical knowledge you acquire about the product, the better your book will be.

Documentation reviews

Too many computer publications are written for the designers, implementers, and testers of the code, rather than for customers. These technical people are the main internal reviewers for books, and some might insist on wording or contents that don't serve customers' needs.

The differences are usually a matter of perspectives—technical people frequently want a function-oriented book, one that describes in great detail all the features of the product, while customers usually prefer a task-oriented approach so they can get their work done. Technical people frequently want to include all the technical details; customers usually want just enough information to do their jobs. Technical people sometimes assume that everyone will spend a great deal of time with the product and the book; customers usually want to learn the product in the shortest possible time.

Even when customers are technical people themselves, they like documentation that's concise, easy to read, and easy to learn from.

Validating a publication with customers

One of the best ways to accomplish the task of writing for the customer is to have a book validated by the people who will buy and use the product. As early as possible in the development cycle, talk to or correspond with sales people in your company and with customers. Find out what customers want. Then give it to them through a validation process by including customers as reviewers of the book.

If your company regards products under development as highly confidential, you might need to go through some legal procedures to send your book to customers before the product is shipped. The following are worth considering:

- Find out whether the code is being distributed for early testing to customers who have signed an agreement not to disclose details of the product to the public. If so, you can probably distribute drafts of the books as well. Questionnaires and follow-up telephone calls to these customers can provide valuable information about their satisfaction with the publications.

- If your company makes public announcements about future products several months before they are ready to ship, explore the possibility of making early drafts of the book available to customers who haven't signed an agreement not to disclose details to the public. Your legal department might be able to declassify publications and send them to interested customers.

- Perform your own customer validation using a hypothetical product. For example, write a 10-page passage in two different ways, varying the style (formal vs. informal), level of detail (highly technical vs. summarized), medium (online vs. printed), organization (alphabetized vs. functionally grouped commands), and tone (friendly vs. impersonal). Send the sample passages to as many customers as you can, along with a questionnaire to elicit their preferences and the reasons for those preferences. Follow up with telephone calls as well. As few as a dozen responses can help you understand what customers want.

Validation activities can take time, effort, and expense, but the feedback is worth a great deal. Starting with the library design and continuing through the various drafts of each book, you can get valuable information on customers' preferences.

Developing a close working relationship with customers by taking their suggestions seriously and delivering what they want during the development of a book is important. Keep asking questions to verify that you understand exactly what the customer is saying. Also show the customer that you listened by incorporating as many suggestions as you can into the next draft that you send out.

It's never a good idea, however, to *promise* a particular feature, such as a hypertext system, because you won't be able to deviate much from the schedule and the plan that have been agreed upon. The most you can do is take notes and try to get the feature into the next release.

Testing the information

The best way to build quality into a book is to test the information at several stages of development. Briefly, you ask typical customers to use a publication to perform specific tasks. Then you watch to see how well the customer can accomplish the tasks. This topic is so important to achieving quality that much of Chapter 10 is devoted to showing you how to test a book with its intended audience.

The writing environment

A final influence on the quality of computer publications is the writing environment. In many writing shops, writers labor alone with their books and feel both the pride and the burden of ownership. However, working in teams or partnerships has many advantages.

- Team writing can improve consistency across a library, because team members customarily submit their work to a peer review at every draft level. Peer reviews help team members see any deviations from the approved style guide and fix the errors early.

- Team writing permits more specialization of skills, so that those who like to work in a particular area, such as organizing a book, can do so more often than they can as the sole author of a book.

- Team writing increases product knowledge, because all members of a team must learn how the product functions. Individual writers, in contrast, might find their knowledge limited to the functions they work on.

- Team writing provides backups for writers who are ill or on vacation, or who leave the project before the end.

- Team writing can actually increase a writer's sense of ownership and accountability in a cooperative team environment. Every writer has a built-in appreciative audience for a well-turned phrase or a well-written chapter, and few writers want to let the team down with poor-quality work.

- Team writing can help writers develop leadership skills, since every team must have a leader. Writers can discover, in a safe environment, whether they're effective leaders who should consider moving into management.

- Team writing can increase productivity. Three individuals can produce three books on schedule, but a team of three writers can usually produce four or five books in the same amount of time.

- Team writing can be more enjoyable than writing individually. In a team, you always have someone to turn to for help and support.

In addition to writers, a team might include people with other specialties, such as:

- A manager
- A planner
- A graphic artist or technical illustrator
- An indexer
- A glossary or terminology specialist
- A tools specialist who locates or writes useful programs, such as spelling and grammar checkers
- A person who arranges for the documentation to be translated into other languages and distributed in other countries
- A legal, trademarks, and patents specialist
- An editor
- A production specialist who prepares the camera-ready copy
- A proofreader for the camera-ready copy
- A person who oversees the printing of the books

On a small project, the same person might perform several functions, while on large projects, the team might need several people to perform just one function. These specialists might serve several writing teams or they might support just one writing team for the length of the project.

In setting up a team, you should strive for a cooperative, rather than competitive, atmosphere. Team members need to trust each other's work, respect each other's knowledge, and support each other's ideas for achieving quality. With the focus always on producing better books, teams can be an effective way to achieve better quality with fewer people working on shorter schedules.

2

Analyzing Your Audience and Purpose

An important step in building quality into a book involves analyzing your reading audience so that you can design your book specifically for that audience. Just as you design presentations or arguments for individuals whose traits, likes, and dislikes you know, you want to design your book for a predefined audience.

In addition, very early in the process, you must decide on the purpose of your book. Is it to help a reader learn to use a software program? Plan a systems network? Develop programs? Install and repair a computer system or printer?

You might actually decide on the target audience for a book and on the book's purpose almost simultaneously. Once you establish a need for a book, you quickly begin to formulate ideas about the audience who might need to read such a book; in the same moment, you establish the general purpose of the book—to do any of the following:

- Teach the reader about a program through a tutorial

- Explain how to perform various tasks

- Help the reader easily locate reference information

- Help the user install and customize an operating system or software program

- Help the user install, maintain, and repair hardware

- Describe how to run diagnostics programs to troubleshoot hardware or software problems
- Help the user plan for the installation and maintenance of large or complex systems
- Understand concepts and background before attempting installation or operation

This chapter discusses how to analyze audience characteristics and determine the general purpose of the book. Although this chapter shows how to analyze the audience first, and then how to determine purpose, remember that, realistically, you might perform these steps simultaneously or in the opposite order.

A successful book provides information that people want—in a form they are able to use.

In contrast, some unsuccessful books contain too little useful information; others might contain useful information but confuse readers by presenting the information unsatisfactorily. That is, the information might be difficult to find, wordy, vague, or poorly organized.

Most people read computer books only because they have a task to perform. Being unable to find information about that task creates frustration and stress for your readers. And a frustrated reader might never purchase another hardware or software product from your organization.

To make certain that your readers have a successful experience with books that you write, you must anticipate their needs and present information in ways that minimize their frustration and maximize their success in performing their tasks.

Because matching the contents and presentation of a book with its readers is so important, most computer books identify the target reading audience very early, usually in the preface. In reality, most books are used by a variety of audiences, so you can't always neatly compartmentalize your audience. Instead, you must try to accommodate readers with differing backgrounds and skills.

To learn the identity of your primary and secondary audiences, you should do an audience analysis; that is, you should learn as much as you can about your readers. Even though you might not have the time or resources to do an exhaustive analysis, whatever you can learn can be valuable to you as you plan and write the book. See Fig. 2.1 for some sample statements about target audiences.

What Is an Audience Analysis?

Analyzing your audience is the best way to anticipate your readers' needs. Your audience is the set of all readers who read the final book. Thus, a care-

This book is designed both for those who are unfamiliar with computer systems and for those who have computer systems experience.

If you are unfamiliar with computer editors, read and do Lessons 1 through 4 of Chapter 2. These lessons teach you how to use basic editing functions and then how to perform more advanced tasks.

If you are familiar with computer editors, go to Lessons 5 and 6, which describe editing commands and show you how to customize the keyboard for your convenience.

This book is designed for application programmers who write SIGMA applications for the banking industry.

Figure 2.1 Sample target audience statements.

ful and accurate audience analysis (sometimes called a *user profile*) tells you who your audience is, what their expectations are, and what information they need.

An audience analysis helps you to determine the scope, tone, vocabulary, and organization of your project. It also helps you decide the appropriate style for writing and artwork. In addition, a thorough audience analysis that has been scrupulously integrated into the planning and execution of a book is an invaluable tool for marketing the final product.

For books that are part of a package including a computer or other piece of equipment, the audience usually consists of the customers for the product. Often a marketing analysis contains much of the information you need for an audience analysis. However, if a marketing analysis is not available or complete, you should devote attention to defining the audience. Resist the temptation to gloss over the effort by producing an audience statement such as the following (from an actual publication): "The audience for this book consists of all users (or customers) of the XXXX product."

What does an audience analysis contain?

A complete audience analysis contains a statement of the book and its objectives, a complete description of the audience, and a summary of how the book relates to the projected audience.

Statement of the book and its objectives. To formulate a statement of purpose, you must decide what you want your readers to be able to do as a result of reading or using the book. You might want them to be able to install a software program and use it to do their work. Or you might want them to be able to write an application or set up a complex system. A complete description of these tasks and the subtasks that comprise them is a *task analysis.*

If no task analysis is available and if the book describes many complex and interrelated tasks, you might choose to perform your own task analysis as part of the design process. If an analysis is available but has been compiled by someone else, take time to study it carefully. Talk with those who did the analysis and learn how they arrived at the specific tasks described in their analysis. (See Chapter 1 for more information on task analysis.)

Keeping the statement of purpose in mind helps you determine how to organize the book, as well as what goes into it.

A complete description of the audience. The audience description includes demographic data, occupational data, technical background and expertise, reading grade level, and physical limitations. Sometimes, occupational data can be the most useful information for designing a book. For example, an audience of end users benefits from a user's guide, while an audience of programmers needs a programming guide and reference (explained further in Chapter 4).

A summary showing how the scope, style, tone, organization, and vocabulary of the book relate to the projected audience. The audience description is the core of the audience analysis. The success and usability of the book hinge on your ability to identify and satisfy the audience's needs and expectations. All the decisions you make about the design, scope, and language of your book must be based on the needs of your audience, as identified in the audience description.

Types of audience information

You must determine the level of experience and knowledge that users of the book should have before attempting the tasks described in your documentation. By talking with library designers and planners, you can understand where the book is positioned in relation to other books the customer purchases or receives with the product. You can also determine whether users need information on unpacking the product, setting it up (or installing the program), using the operating system, and so on. Equally important is knowing what items to cover and what items to omit.

Examining books similar to the one you are writing is often helpful. They can help you understand more about the writing style, diction, level of complexity, and appropriate graphics for the audience of your book. Look in the prefaces for statements about prerequisite reading and experience.

A profile of your audience by age, sex, and educational level helps you form the audience description. It might include information about marital status, number of children, years employed, income, and similar data. At first glance, such information might seem useless in the overall scheme of things, but visualize the importance of this information in writing documentation for home video games, home computers, laptops, word processors, highly sophisticated workstations, and so on.

The fact that one individual has been married for 16 years, has three children, and makes $60,000 a year might not seem meaningful to you as a writer. But if you find that profile to be typical of most of your audience, then the information becomes meaningful for the examples you might use, the money you spend on design and production of your book, and the artwork you include.

Determining job function

Are you writing for artists, engineers, medical technicians, secretaries, programmers, or accountants? Certainly each person has different information needs, depending upon his or her profession. The readers' profession often affects how they process information. Programmers look for repeatable patterns, specific descriptions of operating system or programming functions, ideas for applications, and ways to solve problems, while medical technicians look for specific instructions for performing technical procedures, using medical equipment, and conducting tests.

You also need to know your readers' position in the organization. Are they middle-level executives or junior accountants? Their position matters because you can quickly establish that executives are interested in long-range planning, personnel-related matters, and profit and loss. Junior accountants, in contrast, are interested in learning more about accounting processes and techniques and how they fit into the organization's financial picture. Knowing the types of positions your readers are likely to have helps you design examples that relate to their tasks.

How long have your readers been in their jobs or careers? Are they thoroughly familiar with their jobs, or just beginning? If they are in management, was their background technical or nontechnical before they became managers? Are they more interested in understanding rationale and philosophy, or do they need only the steps and procedures to perform a set of tasks?

Assessing Technical Background

How familiar is your audience with the program or system you are documenting? How familiar are they with similar systems? For example, if 80% of your audience has written and maintained programs similar to the one you are documenting, your book needs to be very different in design and scope than if only 10% of your audience has ever worked on this or a similar system.

There are several ways to classify readers based on their technical background and expertise. We use the simple categories of *novice, technician,* and *expert,* as well as the audience reading level and any relevant psychological factors, to assess technical background.

Novice

A novice is someone with little or no training or experience in a specific field. For example, an accountant who buys a home computer without having ever used a computer is a novice when it comes to using computers. An accountant with extensive experience using relational database software might be a novice when it comes to using word-processing programs.

Typically, a novice is heavily dependent on the documentation if he or she is to master the set of tasks for which a product was acquired. To enhance the novice's opportunities for learning, you should adjust the tone, content, level of detail, illustrations, and reading level to better meet the novice's needs. When writing for the novice, you should pay particular attention to the following elements:

- Define technical terms carefully.
- Present concepts in simple language, using everyday illustrations with which the novice is likely to be familiar.
- Use simple artwork, such as simple tables and charts.
- Structure content so that the novice clearly understands what is the most and least important information.
- Don't overload the novice with too much technical information.
- Strive for a proper tone; avoid talking down to the novice or conveying any hint of what might be considered condescension.
- Simplify content with lists, summaries, introductions, understandable artwork, definitions, glossaries, indexes, clear reference points, and page layouts with ample white space.

Be careful of the assumptions you make when writing for novices. If you assume, for example, that your novice readers should understand basic operating systems before they move on to manipulating files, setting up tables, and using databases, what about those novices who barely know how to turn on a computer? It takes careful planning on your part to provide enough basic information (or at least explain where they can learn it) while keeping the attention of your more sophisticated readers.

The mark of a good designer and writer is to plan to accommodate both audiences, and to do so effectively.

Technician

Readers at the technician level have a basic understanding of the subject matter. That is, they are proficient with some computers and computer programs, they are familiar with terminology, many concepts, and the rationale behind many actions and decisions. They might not have a thorough grasp of some finer points, but they usually can learn easily because they already have a foundation of learning.

Because readers at the technician level have at least some familiarity with the principles (if not details) found in your book, you can present things to them a little differently than if they were novices. For example, you might choose to do the following:

- Define only unique or specialized technical terms.

- Present concepts with less need to relate them to everyday situations in the technician's workday.

- Use more sophisticated artwork—the technician has some experience in reading schematic diagrams and in interpreting different kinds of information from tables and charts.

- Structure content with more complexity—the technician can probably follow another layer of thought, or can understand the process of analyzing several alternatives and then selecting the most workable one, based on differing sets of circumstances.

- Feel free to use more technical information, assuming the technician has the knowledge and experience skills to understand.

- Strive for a proper tone; show the technician respect for his or her skills, and include appropriate examples and illustrations.

Expert

Most experts in the computer industry thrive on information, so you will find experts to be voracious but critical readers. They look for new information or variations on standard fare.

Do you have to be an expert to write for experts? Perhaps. An expert in local area network services, for example, can probably tell whether or not your book on a subset of that topic is written by an expert. Typically, experts scan information for new ideas, new viewpoints, interesting applications, and intriguing twists on established procedures. If they find those things lacking in the first few pages they scan, they probably will not continue to read.

When writing for experts, you don't have to be too concerned about defining terms, carefully gearing your examples or applications to situations your readers can understand, or using visuals that are too sophisticated. By definition, an expert is one with enough experience and education to move beyond adequate familiarity with processes and techniques to a broad grasp of a technology. An expert knows the literature, knows the key people on the leading edge of the technology, and probably knows the direction the technology or industry is headed over the next several years.

Reading level

The reading level of your audience helps you determine the most effective organization and language for your book. Be careful not to over- or underestimate the intelligence of your audience, but remember that no one enjoys reading incredibly difficult technical material (although some people seem to enjoy writing it).

An eighth-grade reading level is usually a good choice for most programming or maintenance books. This doesn't mean most readers have only an eighth-grade education. Rather, it's a recognition that most people in this country read at the level we call eighth grade. If your audience consists mostly of college graduates with years of experience in the discipline in which you are writing, you can probably go beyond the eighth-grade level. On the other hand, if your audience consists of data-entry operators or clerical personnel, a sixth-grade reading level might be more appropriate.

Reading levels are usually identified based on a formula that involves average sentence length and the number of words with more than two syllables, with a factor that converts the result into a number synonymous with grade level. Many computer software programs are designed to compute reading grade level of text, either on stand-alone PCs or PCs tied to mainframes.

Remember that simple is usually better than complex when you are determining the reading grade level suitable to your audience. Remember, too, that one mark of a good writer is to be able to produce complex information when you need to, but also to be able to communicate complex information in simple terms.

Psychological factors

Studies show that the typical users of computer programs prefer to ask their coworkers—perhaps at the next desk—for information that enables them to use the computers or programs. Often, the last thing they want to do is study a book.

Such reluctance to go to a book shows that they simply expect, based on past experience, that the book is difficult to use. Like most of us, they want answers in the shortest time possible. We are conditioned to want food, news, car tune-ups, service of various kinds, and many other items almost instantly. We like lists, shortcuts, synopses, condensed books, previews, overviews, and reviews. And if we must use a computer book, we want to use it only long enough to learn what we need to do our jobs and then go on to something else. That's as it should be. Your job as a writer is to make sure that readers are able to find the information they need as quickly as possible.

Readers approach your book with predefined sets of attitudes. Some are excited and anxious to learn whatever the book is designed to teach. Others are hesitant, not having any particular commitment (perhaps not even a need) to use the book. Still others might be apprehensive and fearful of learning a new program or learning how to operate a computer. They might fear that they will be replaced by the very program or computer they are learning to use.

For readers with these differing expectations, you can make adjustments in your writing, depending also on your findings about your readers' level of expertise. You can reassure those who are hesitant or anxious by providing clear instructions and by helping them relate unfamiliar ideas and concepts to familiar ones they already know. Your tone should be friendly and reassuring.

How Do You Obtain Information?

You can gather information about your audience in several ways:

- Reading trade press articles and research studies about the makeup of the market—who buys and uses certain computers and software

- Talking with experts who keep up with trends and developments in the industry

- Talking with planners and developers in your organization to understand their definitions of the audience

- Drawing on your own experience—what you know about people who are likely to be your audience, their background, the work they need to accomplish, and how they like to see information presented

- Interviewing potential members of your audience to learn as much as you can

- Distributing questionnaires and then tabulating and analyzing data you receive

One of the best ways to get information for an audience analysis is to interview members of your audience. Then you can ask specific questions about technical background, related experience, job requirements, and particular needs your documentation must satisfy.

Surprisingly, some programmers and writers have never talked to a customer—or at least do so very infrequently. With the current corporate emphasis on quality and defect-free products and services, many now are going out to talk to their customers for the first time. For too long, many have assumed that they know what their customers want, but they have done so without consulting those customers. Similarly, you can write documentation without talking with customers, but you can write better documentation by asking them what they want in it.

As you interview your audience members, make notes about the attitudes you sense. Attitudes about the organization, the job, coworkers and supervisors, and other computers and programs influence the way the audience perceives and responds to your documentation.

If the system you are planning to document replaces another system or another method of doing a job, find out exactly how the job is done now, so that you can relate the new steps in the new system to the steps in the old system. Pay particular attention to the steps or procedures of the old system that are the most difficult or likely to produce error. These steps might well require extra detail in your book.

Before you interview any members of your prospective audience, write down the questions you want to ask and outline your particular concerns. Here are some brief guidelines to follow when interviewing:

- Prepare for the interview by deciding what questions to ask.
- Use your questions during the interview to keep things on track, but be flexible enough to take advantage of any new information that the interviewee might provide.
- Interview a variety of people (and as many as possible) to get as much information as you can.

Summary of Audience Analysis

Following is a series of lists containing relevant questions to consider as you define your audience. Work through the lists to determine how age, education, level of expertise, reading grade level, and other factors affect your use of background information (especially theory), the need for repetition of key points to reinforce understanding, the types of examples, and the complexity of artwork in your documentation.

The importance of audience analysis to the success of a computer publication can't be overestimated. You must know how to present the information in such a way that the customer is not only able to read your documentation, but also is satisfied with it.

Demographic data

- What age range are most readers likely to be?
- Are most readers likely to be male or female?

- What can I learn about my readers' education (degrees, fields, institutions attended, years studied)?
- Do my readers live only in America? In Europe? In Asia?
- What languages do my readers speak?

Occupational data

- What can I learn about my readers' position, role, and power in the organizations for which they work?
- How will my book affect my readers' positions, roles, or power in that organization?
- What attitude towards the organization and their position in the organization do the readers have?
- What past occupational experience is typical of my readers?
- What size are the organizations in which my readers work?
- Does my audience include nonprofit organizations as well as for-profit ones?

Technical background

- How many years of experience with this system or program do my readers have?
- How many years of experience with similar systems or programs do my readers have?
- How much technical expertise do they have?
- What is their technical vocabulary level (novice, technician, or expert)?
- What particular technical interests do they have?
- Have my readers used books similar to mine?

Wants and needs

- What do my readers want to learn from this book?
- Are they most interested in being able to perform steps to accomplish a task? In learning how to use a program to do their own applications? In finding answers to technical questions?
- What are their needs in terms of finding information easily? Will they use this book frequently, or only when they encounter a serious problem?
- What kinds of graphics and examples do my readers want?
- How many different colors would they like?

Personal characteristics

- At what reading grade level are my readers most comfortable?
- Can I identify any relevant personal experiences that might influence my readers' attitudes toward the book?
- What are my readers' attitudes toward previously used books similar to mine?
- Why do they have these attitudes?

3

Getting Organized

Getting organized involves handling the wealth of information that you need to read before starting to write. Managing the technical documentation for a product, frequently called *source information*, generally requires finding and identifying useful source information, understanding the technical content, and physically organizing the source information.

Finding the Source Information

Finding source information for a book requires research and investigation. At the beginning of a project, you might receive various documents, but throughout the development cycle you need to spend time locating additional sources you can use. Knowing what to look for can help, because source information can come in many forms.

Technical specifications

The technical or functional specification for a product (the *spec*) is usually written by computer architects or designers. This document usually describes functions of the product in high-level terms and shows how the various components are supposed to work together. Technical specs also include information that marketing people use and instructions to programmers on how to implement the design. For a relatively small software product, the technical spec might contain several hundred pages. Large products often require thousands of pages to document all the functions.

The spec might be your most readily available source material. It should be the document you initially rely on for the accuracy and completeness of your documentation. Even approved specs can contain technical inaccuracies and omissions, however, and specs are seldom updated as they should be.

In some companies, technical specifications are divided into two different types. The *functional spec* usually details the business requirements of the product and describes the functions that meet those requirements. The *design spec* usually shows in great detail how the programmers write code to create the functions of the product.

Design change documents

Design change documents describe problems in the design or code and explain how to fix the errors. Ranging from fewer than five to over 50 pages in length, these documents might address problems with the internal workings of the code, or other topics not suitable in a book for customers. However, you need to look at all design change documents in case something affects your documentation. As you gain experience, you also gain speed in skipping over items that have no impact on your work. You also learn to spot things that you must include, such as changes to the screens the customers see, different names for components, additional error messages, and functions that are deleted because there isn't enough time to code and test them properly.

Interviews

Interviews with technical people are an important source after you have studied the spec thoroughly. The people who designed and wrote code for the product certainly know the tiny details, but you have to ask the right questions to get information you can use. Technical people might not always keep the customer's point of view in mind, so it's a good idea to plan a series of interviews during which you can ask increasingly complex questions as your knowledge grows.

Interviews are essential, even though they can be frustrating for both programmers and writers. In a typical situation, the technical people get a head start on the writers, sometimes by as much as a year, and might find it difficult or annoying to go back to the beginnings with you. Although many technical people are glad to talk about their work, they might be so busy that you need to negotiate for some of their time.

Working with technical people requires the same skills as working with nontechnical people:

- Tact and respect toward the person you're interviewing
- Courtesy and promptness during the interview
- Gratitude for help given

- Sensitivity to their schedules and other pressures
- Thorough preparation before an interview so that you can ask the right questions and understand the answers
- Establishing a common goal, namely documentation that enhances the product
- Sharing information, such as personnel and schedule changes
- Following up on work items and questions
- Showing an interest in their work and actively seeking to learn more about the product

In addition, you should develop a good working relationship with several technical people so that you don't overburden the same few every time you need information.

Interviewing lead programmers and designers. A fairly common problem in interviewing is that the one person who knows everything about a product might also be the busiest. Chief architects and lead programmers might also travel a great deal, give demonstrations, present at meetings, and have many other demands on their time. Following are some suggestions for gaining access to lead people:

- Avoid asking for elementary tutorials from the lead. Obtain your basic knowledge of the product from the spec and from other technical people.
- Ask a coworker of the lead to obtain an item of information for you. With a working relationship already in place, the coworker knows enough about the lead's schedule and work style to obtain the information you need.
- Ask that a backup to the lead be named and work with that person. If the backup lacks the details of a particular problem, he or she can go to the lead for help on your behalf.
- Instead of trying to interview a lead, write a few pages about the way you think something works and ask the lead to read them. Even the busiest of leads can usually find time to mark up a few pages.
- Ask if you can use a tape recorder so that you can cover a lot of ground in the shortest amount of time. If you still miss a few details, you can go back with a short list of specific items.

Prototypes

A prototype of the product that closely simulates the final result can be one of your best sources because you get an early look at what customers actually see when they buy the product. A prototype is most valuable if you're writing a user's guide or other introductory book, but it's also useful even for a highly technical programmer's guide.

For a user's guide, you have to describe the *interface*, that is, the screens that are displayed as the customer uses the product. It's sometimes easier to describe the possible pathways through the product after you've used a prototype than after you've read a spec. For a programmer's guide, you might not have to describe the interface, but the more you understand about how the product behaves, the better your documentation is.

Books from a previous release

Books from an earlier release of the same product and books on similar products can be among your best sources because, if they're well-written, they're already aimed at the intended audience and contain discussions at the right level of detail. If the product has an earlier release, your book is largely an update of the previous one. The only source information you need concerns the new functions being added or enhanced.

If a previous book had a number of flaws or failed to satisfy customer needs, you might want to rewrite the whole book. You should not start rewriting until you master the new material. Then, time permitting, improve the book as much as you can.

Miscellaneous sources

Miscellaneous sources that can shed some light on your topic might include programmers' notebooks and internal memos, marketing plans, test cases that the test groups write to verify the accuracy of the product before it's shipped to the public, papers and books that the technical people have written and published, and information available at other sites in your company.

These miscellaneous documents are hardest to find because they might not be circulated widely, technical people might forget about them, and they might be held by people you don't think of interviewing. It's a good idea to ask everyone you talk to for the names of other people who might be able to supply you with information.

Sources at other sites in your company can be valuable, especially if your product interacts with products produced at those other sites. If you don't know how to contact other sites, ask your own technical and writing people for some leads. Once you get a few names, you can start a very productive correspondence.

One way to proceed is to offer to review off-site books on topics even remotely similar to yours and then ask people at these sites to review your book. Whether your company is large or small, you can locate some experts at other sites who are willing to help you produce a high-quality book.

Published books and articles

Books and articles published outside your own company can sometimes provide background information for your general education. Whatever operating system or application program you need to learn about, you can usually find something in publicly available sources. For example, if the product you're writing about runs on the Unix operating system, but you know nothing about Unix, you can buy or borrow many books and articles that will give you the knowledge you need to understand the spec and talk with the technical people.

Understanding the Product

Learning the new product is a step that some writers try to skip, thinking that they can just rewrite the source material and produce an adequate book. However, to build quality into a book, you must thoroughly understand the functions of the product.

As a writer, you serve as the customer's teacher, but it's difficult to teach what you don't know. You might feel that the amount of knowledge you need depends on the audience and that you won't need to know as much to write a user's guide as you would to write a programmer's guide. Actually, you need just as firm an understanding for a user's guide, because you won't be able to use any of the language from the technical sources. You have to know the details so well that you can translate them from "computerese" into plain, simple English. For a programmer's guide, you might be able to lift passages from the spec, a perfectly acceptable practice and a widely used method of getting a book into print on a short schedule.

Why it's important to learn the product

For a new writer, learning the product can be a daunting task, but you must do so, for several reasons.

First, the person who is held accountable for the contents of a documentation is the writer. Not only do your manager and writing team leader expect you to know the material, but also the customers who use your book deserve a knowledgeable writer. Their complaints about inaccuracies and other problems won't arrive on a programmer's desk—they'll come to you, and you might have to respond, even if years have passed since the product was released.

Second, you must earn the respect of the technical people who review your book by demonstrating your mastery of the details. Chapter 10 of this book contains more information about the review process, but for now you should understand that you get better cooperation from technical people if you show a deep interest in their work and learn to speak their language.

Third, you can gain valuable training and experience by learning and thoroughly understanding the technical details. The knowledge you gain might qualify you for a better job or a different job if you want one.

Finally, a great deal of personal satisfaction can come from producing a high-quality book, which includes presenting the technical details well. You might feel very uncomfortable if you try to write about something you're not sure of. You might also feel powerless if you depend largely or entirely on technical people to correct your errors.

How to learn the product

Determined to learn all you can, you have a number of ways to go about it. Reading the spec is indispensable, even if you initially understand little of what you're reading. Keep going back over a section until enough of it makes sense for you to move on to the next section. Write questions in the margins and answer them as your knowledge increases.

Also, read technical books and magazines on the general topic of the product you're working on, even if you have to read them at home, after working hours. Read books on similar products to get an idea of how your fellow writers solved the same kinds of problems you face.

Taking classes, either within your company or externally, can give you good information. Classes don't have to be formal ones advertised and supported by the education department in your company. Some of the most useful can be informal tutorial sessions for newly hired designers, programmers, testers, and other technical people. Attending these classes gives you the same training and reference material that the new technical people get.

Listening to technical people talk about the product at meetings, in hallways, at the water fountain, and elsewhere can give you the right vocabulary for your own discussions as well as the latest developments with the code. Spending time with programmers is a particularly valuable way to learn about sudden changes, because the technical people might not think to call you right away when they encounter a problem in the design or the code. Since your success depends on the technical people, you should certainly keep up with what they're doing.

Writing a few pages of your book and having them reviewed early by just a few technical people can also be a good way to learn the product. If you have something on paper to show the programmers, they can focus their comments instead of discussing details you might not be ready to hear. Your first attempt might cause you some embarrassment if you misunderstood something important, but improving in subsequent attempts gives you confidence that your first complete draft of the book is good.

Once you have gathered your source information and understood the functions of the product well enough to start grouping things together in your mind, you're ready to begin organizing your information.

Organizing the Source Information

Organizing source information has two aspects: the *physical*, which many writers overlook, and the *rhetorical*, which many feel they don't need help with because they studied writing in school. Both areas have tripped up many a technical writer at first. Lack of initial attention in either area can cause problems that are easily preventable if you make a little effort at the beginning of the project.

Physical organization

Physical organization refers to arranging, storing, and retrieving all the source material you've gathered, as well as the pages, chapters, and complete drafts that you write. Despite talk of the paperless office, you'll find you have to manage great volumes of paper.

Storing and retrieving information.   How to arrange and store material in an easily retrievable way, what to save and what to throw away, and what to do with all the information when your project is finished are the major aspects of physical organization.

The way you store all the information you collect depends largely on personal preference and on the security rules your company enforces. Your method might also depend on the storage medium: diskettes, audio tapes, videotapes, hard drives, softcopy stored on a server or host computer, and various forms of hardcopy, such as printouts, handwritten notes, and formal documents. You need to devise or adopt a foolproof way of storing and retrieving information according to the media you use.

For diskettes, audio tapes, and videotapes, a careful system of labeling and dating is as important as the type of box or file used for physical storage. If your information is stored on a hard drive, you can take full advantage of the directory structure supported by your operating system to group similar items; you can also use various tools to search for a particular directory or subdirectory if you can't remember the name under which you filed something. For softcopy, the storage methods are usually determined by the library structure and naming conventions in effect on the server or host.

Hardcopy frequently presents the greatest problem, because you must devise your own storage and retrieval systems. In many writing shops, three storage methods for hardcopy seem to predominate: file folders, three-ring binders, and drawers or shelves. Most writers use a combination of methods. Writers who use file folders and a good filing system are among the best organized. They might alphabetize their folders, order the information by function in the product, or group the material according to the chapters they're planning to write once they do the rhetorical part of organizing.

A file system like this can be particularly useful if most of the source information comes in small units instead of, or in addition to, large documents. Such a file system might take a bit of time to set up, but it can save a great deal of time over the life of a project. For example, on many occasions you'll probably have to double-check details from your source late in your writing cycle. This is much easier to do if you can find what you need without having to search through months' worth of papers shoved into a drawer. The major disadvantage of file folders is that, in order to get any work done, you might have to get dozens of folders out on your desk, where pieces of paper can get mixed up and later misfiled.

Writers who use three-ring binders for storing their source information can be equally well-organized, and they also have the advantage of not getting their papers mixed up because everything stays in the binders most of the time. A technical spec usually fits into one or more of the largest binders, whereas even the smallest spec hardly ever fits into a file folder.

In each binder, the writer alphabetizes information or arranges it by function or chapter as in the file folder system. At the end of the day, instead of filing dozens of folders, the writer just closes a few binders and puts them away. The main disadvantage of this method is that it can take a considerable amount of time to punch holes if the paper doesn't already have the holes punched. Also, the binders can get heavy and bulky to use. However, this method is a good way to get, and stay, organized throughout the writing cycle.

Writers who stack papers in drawers or shelves more or less at random might save the time required for filing or binding, but they hardly ever save time in finding what they need. Occasionally, all writers probably resort to this way of clearing their desks at the end of the day. The next morning or within a few days, however, careful writers place source information into file folders or binders so they can find it months later.

Whichever method, or combination of methods, you choose to store your information, you'll be glad to be well-organized while you're doing revisions of your documentation. You can apply the file folder and binder methods to the important task of organizing comments returned by technical reviewers. Good organization ensures that you incorporate all the required changes to your work. It's a fatal mistake to lose or misplace something that you should revise or include in your book.

Saving and discarding information.   What to save and what to throw away can sometimes be a problem. How many iterations of a technical spec should you keep? If you don't think a particular design change or note applies to your book, should you save it just in case?

You probably should strike a compromise between saving everything and throwing away too much. In general, it's a good idea to save anything that you've written notes on, even if it's an out-of-date spec, until you have time to evaluate the relevance of these notes to your current work. You should save, and then return to the specific reviewer, all written comments on your book if that is your company's policy. Careful reviewers frequently want to compare their suggestions with the changes you actually make. If you're dealing with a disorganized or untrustworthy person, it's wise to make a copy of the comments before returning them, just in case the comments get lost or changed without your knowledge.

Saving a master copy. You should certainly save a master copy of each draft you distribute so that you can make last-minute copies for late reviewers, and so that you have your own record of the exact words you used in each draft. If possible, you should save both a softcopy and a hardcopy version. Once you start revising, your book will undergo many changes, and you might want to recover an old paragraph if a new one doesn't work as well, if a reviewer changes his or her mind, or if the design changes back to a former plan.

When your book is finally finished and you don't think you'll ever need the source material again, pause a moment before throwing it away and consider whether anyone else might need it. Also consider consolidating the source information into a history file for permanent storage somewhere other than in your own office. Some companies routinely save information of this type. Also, if you expect another release of the product, you should save your original source material so that you can compare the new material against it. If you're moving to a new job and someone else is taking yours, save the source material for the new writer to study and learn from.

If you have any doubts about throwing something away, ask your team leader, your manager, or the other writers in your shop what to do. When you have absolutely no reason to save source material, get rid of it before starting the next project. If your company recycles paper, you'll be contributing to future technical specs when you toss out papers you no longer need.

4

Dividing the
Information into Books

When you begin to work on a writing project, you might find that you have
to do a lot of tasks at the same time, such as analyzing your audience, locating technical source information, getting organized, and dividing the information into books. This chapter bridges the gap between analyzing your
audience and using the results in a single book or a library of books. If the
"library" for the product you're working on consists of only one book, you
can still use the information in this chapter to divide the information into
the sections of your book.

What Do You Do with Your Audience Analysis?

After you have found and studied the technical information your book will
present and have completed your audience analysis, you are ready to design your library or your book. As you do the planning and designing, answer the following questions:

■ Does the plan provide the right amount and level of background information for the intended audience?

■ Does the plan provide supplemental information in areas where the
background of the audience is weak?

■ Does the plan provide unnecessary background material? Although insufficient background information makes it difficult for users to do their
jobs, too much background information interferes with their ability to do
their jobs quickly.

- Does the plan identify the special technical terms that the audience already knows?

- Does the plan also identify the terms that you must define for this audience? Your audience must immediately be able to understand all the technical terms you use.

- Does the plan include suggestions about the types of metaphors and analogies that the audience would most easily understand? For example, analogies most useful for an audience consisting primarily of young men with high school educations might not be the best ones for middle-aged middle-management executives. Make a special note of the areas in which your own experience is significantly different from the background of your audience. Double-check your design to be sure you haven't made any unwarranted assumptions based on your own background.

Many writers find it helpful at this stage to construct an *idealized audience*. This idealized audience is an imaginary reader or sometimes a very small group of readers who match the characteristics of the defined audience. It's often easier to write if you imagine you are explaining the subject to an idealized audience, especially if you are able to give realistic "personalities" to the audience. Keep in mind that you're writing for real people who need to understand the information you're presenting. For the readers who might turn to your book in a panic over a dire error message, you need to be particularly considerate.

As a writer, you should genuinely like and respect your audience, whoever they are. A positive attitude will be apparent, however subtly, in your writing, and your readers will sense it and respond to it. Your tone and style show how you feel, whether you want to or not. To some extent you can control tone, but there's no substitute for being considerate of your audience.

Organizing Your Book

Rhetorical organization is something everyone is supposed to study in high school or college English and writing classes. You might remember something about the various rhetorical patterns, such as definition, comparison and contrast, cause and effect, and classification.

Unless you had a very good course in technical writing or took courses in instructional theory and practical course development, however, you probably didn't learn anything about the most useful pattern for computer books: instructional process. Also, you might not have studied task analysis and the effect of organizational strategies on your audience.

Beginning to organize your book

Organizing information to meet the needs of your intended audience is important, even if you don't expect your customers to read the whole book or to read it sequentially. For example, if your audience is application programmers and your book is mainly a list of commands to be used with the functions of a new product, you need to decide whether to organize the commands into one long alphabetical list or whether to break them up by function and alphabetize them within the discussion of each function. Knowing what your audience prefers makes your decision easy.

For any book or for any section of a book, keep in mind some general organizational strategies. First, the purpose of the book or section should determine the organization that you choose. Even though most books have the same general purpose—to explain a product to the intended audience—it's important to understand exactly what kind of explanation you should present for each type of information you're writing. Introductory material, for example, usually requires a general-to-specific organization in which you start with an overview and then move to more detailed information. As part of the introduction, you might also want to describe each function of the new product in a *classification pattern* that outlines the capabilities of the functions but does not explain how to use them.

In the body of the book, you can frequently use standard rhetorical patterns to good effect in various sections. You should define new terms as the reader encounters them throughout the book and also provide a glossary for those who prefer to look in one place for definitions. Steps or procedures for actually performing the tasks in the various sections must usually follow a chronological pattern, interrupted only for warnings or cautions.

Finally, remember that outlining a book, either formally or informally, is one of the most useful strategies for developing a good organization.

Types of books

Following are some common types of books for computer users. Each type is followed by a list of suggested topics that you might want to include when you're organizing such a book. A topic in the list might comprise just a few paragraphs or several chapters, depending on the specific product. Also, a particular product might not require all the topics listed—or it might require additional topics.

Since some topics are suitable for several types of books, you need to be careful, when working with a library of books, not to scatter redundant information through the library.

A user's guide

- Prerequisites (hardware, software, publications, knowledge)
- Brief description of the product and its functions
- Overview of the product and what you can accomplish with it
- Introduction to using the functions of the product

- Starting and stopping the product
- Using functions to accomplish the most common tasks
- Using functions to accomplish less common tasks
- Using functions to accomplish advanced tasks
- Customizing a function (if applicable)
- Understanding error messages and making corrections
- Getting help with problems
- Glossary
- Index

A programmer's guide

- Prerequisites (hardware, software, publications, knowledge)
- Notational conventions
- A brief introduction to the product
- Introduction to writing programs for use with the product
- Analyzing the syntax of a sample program in a supported language
- Designing a program for a particular result
- Coding a simple program in a supported language
- Compiling the program and debugging syntax errors
- Linking and binding the program (if applicable)
- Running the program and debugging runtime errors
- Tuning the program for better performance
- Modifying the program for more complex function
- Porting the program to a different environment (if applicable)
- List of supported commands and functions (if applicable)
- Glossary
- Index

A language reference for a product

- Prerequisites (hardware, software, publications, knowledge)
- Notational conventions of the language
- Introduction to using the programming language with the product
- Elements of the language

- Data types and data structures
- Storage characteristics
- Loops and branches
- Other decision statements
- Input and output handling
- Strings, arrays, pointers
- Functions and calls
- Library routines
- Files and directories
- Error messages
- List of commands or statements
- Glossary
- Index

An administrator's guide

- Prerequisites (hardware, software, publications, knowledge)
- Introduction to administrative tasks for the product
- Tools provided for administrative tasks
- Starting and stopping the system
- Configuring the product (if necessary)
- Authorizing and adding users
- Monitoring the system
- Managing users of the system
- Tuning the system for better performance
- Diagnosing problems and making corrections
- Collecting error information with traces and dumps
- Getting help with problems
- Glossary
- Index

An installation guide

- Prerequisites (hardware, software, publications, knowledge)
- Upgrading from a previous version

- Preparing the hard file
- Installing product files
- Complete or partial install (if applicable)
- Interrupting and resuming the installation (if applicable)
- Error messages and recovery procedures
- Testing the installation
- Glossary
- Index

A commands reference

- Prerequisites (hardware, software, publications, knowledge)
- Brief introduction to the types of commands provided by the product
- Invoking a command from the command line, from a user interface panel, and from an application program
- Name, purpose, authorization needed, syntax, parameters, options, examples, return codes, and notes for each command
- Glossary
- Index

A configuration or customization guide

- Prerequisites (hardware, software, publications, knowledge)
- Brief introduction to the product and the purpose of configuration or customization tasks
- Relationship between installation tasks and configuration or customization tasks
- Advantages and disadvantages of configuring or customizing the product
- Restrictions
- Tools provided for configuration or customization tasks
- Making a backup of the original settings
- Changing the defaults
- Modifying common functions
- Modifying advanced functions
- Writing macros or routines so that end users can modify small elements of the product (if applicable)
- Restoring the original settings

- Recovering from errors
- Glossary
- Index

An error recovery or problem determination guide

- Prerequisites (hardware, software, publications, knowledge)
- Notational conventions in error messages or return codes
- Brief introduction to diagnosing problems and recovering from errors
- Tools provided for problem determination and error recovery
- Obtaining information from dumps, traces, messages, logs, and other sources
- Identifying the location, source, or environment of the problem
- Classifying the problem by type
- List of error messages and recovery actions by type
- Getting additional help
- Glossary
- Index

A networking or connectivity guide

- Prerequisites (hardware, software, publications, knowledge)
- Brief introduction to the product and supported connectivities
- Planning for connectivities in like and unlike environments
- Planning for security on a network
- Supported protocols
- Tools provided for setting up the network
- Host connectivity tasks
- Controller and server connectivity tasks
- Workstation connectivity tasks
- Adding users to the network
- Managing the resources of the network
- Diagnosing and correcting problems in the network
- Monitoring and tuning the network for performance
- Glossary
- Index

Outlining a Book

Many writing shops require that you prepare, distribute, review, and get approval for an outline before you begin writing your book. Those that don't probably should, because the much-maligned outline can be one of the best ways to start getting your book organized. Writers who don't like outlining usually voice three main objections: They feel they don't know enough about the product to make a good outline early in the writing cycle, an outline sometimes changes drastically, and outlining has too many petty little rules.

Writers who have mastered outlining and have learned its advantages, however, can answer these objections fairly easily. First, if you don't know enough to outline, you also don't know enough to write. Second, outlines are supposed to change as you get into the writing and see holes, duplications, or poorly arranged material. An outline isn't a straight jacket. Instead, it's more like a poncho that can change to cover many different shapes. Finally, the rules for outlining are really few and simple.

Another objection to outlining that writers voice less often is that some technical reviewers don't take an outline seriously. These reviewers want to see long passages of text and might give an outline only a cursory examination. Solutions to this problem include the following:

- Have an inspection meeting for the outline.

- Require written comments to be submitted in advance of the meeting.

- Get management involved to ensure that technical people give the outline enough time.

- Present such a detailed outline that technical reviewers can see the topics the book covers as well as the organization and depth of detail.

These and other objections shouldn't stand in the way of your producing a good, clear, useful outline once you appreciate its advantages and review a few techniques for building a good one.

Advantages of outlining

The advantages of developing an outline and writing from it are many. One of the most important is that an outline helps you plan your work—not only the organization of the book, but also your schedule for researching, writing, and revising the information. You can spot problem areas early and allot extra time to them, and you can tell which sections will probably take you the least amount of time: those for which you have plenty of source information and a good understanding of the material.

Another advantage of an outline is that it gives you an overall view of your book. You can answer questions from technical, writing, and management people much better by looking at your outline than you can by racking your brain for stray thoughts. A major advantage of writing from a well-constructed outline is that you are never at a loss about how much you've done, where you are, and what comes next. The hierarchical structure of an outline helps you remember what you should stress and what you can safely downplay. Usually, the greater the level of detail in your outline, the easier your book will be to write. If the product undergoes major changes, just revise the outline to accommodate the changes.

Rules for outlining

The rules for constructing an outline are fairly simple. In fact, they're actually more like conventions you might choose to adopt than rules you must follow. One of the first to consider is the use of mechanics, such as Roman numerals or military-style numbers, to show the relationship between major and minor sections of the book. The numbering and indenting scheme shows in a visual way how important a particular section is to the whole. For most computer books, a three- or four-level outline provides enough detail.

The Roman style of outlining is familiar to most people, but the military style, also called the *legal style*, might take some getting used to.

As Figs. 4.1 and 4.2 show, outlining usually observes some conventions about capitalization. In the Roman type of outline, the first two levels (*I, II, III,...n* and *A, B, C,...n*) use capitalization appropriate for a title, while the other two levels (*1, 2, 3,...n* and *a, b, c,...n*) use initial capitals on the first words. In the military style, all the levels use capitalization appropriate for a title.

```
 I.  Configuring for the XYZ Program
     A.  Preparing for Configuration
         1.  Saving files
             a.  To diskette
             b.  To another drive
         2.  Setting up the directory
         3.  Updating the configuration file
             a.  Setting the path
             b.  Including the device drivers
     B.  Using the Configuration Utility
         1.  From the previous release
         2.  From the current release
 II. Installing the XYZ Program
     A.  The Installation Command
     B.  Additional Features of the Installation Program
```

Figure 4.1 Roman style outline.

```
1.  Configuring for the XYZ Program
1.1.  Preparing for Configuration
1.1.1.  Saving Files
1.1.1.1.  To Diskette
1.1.1.2.  To Another Drive
1.1.2.  Setting up the Directory
1.1.3.  Updating the Configuration File
1.1.3.1.  Setting the Path
1.1.3.2.  Including the Device Drivers
1.2.  Using the Configuration Utility
1.2.1.  From the Previous Release
1.2.2.  From the Current Release
2.  Installing the XYZ Program
2.1.  The Installation Command
2.2.  Additional Features of the Installation Program
```

Figure 4.2 Military or legal style outline.

Parallelism in outlining

An important convention of outlining is that the entries at the first two levels of the outline must be parallel in grammatical structure. For example, the entries for both Roman numerals in Fig. 4.1 are gerunds (*configuring* and *installing*), and the entries for 2.1 and 2.2 in Fig. 4.2 are nouns (*Command* and *Features*). For the other two levels, you should use parallel construction within a particular level. Parallelism makes it easier for you to show the relationships among the entries and enables you to use them as headings in your book and entries in your table of contents. Also, it's just a good practice to demonstrate a careful writing style, even in an outline.

In your outline, you can include sections on classification, comparison and contrast, cause and effect, chronological order for instructional process, and any other principle of arranging topics that you need, as discussed in this chapter in the section on using rhetorical patterns.

Topic vs. sentence outline

As you're working with the sections of your book, you should decide whether you want to use topics, as in the examples in Figs. 4-1 and 4-2, or complete sentences in your outline. Topics are easier to use, but complete sentences force you to do more thinking and, therefore, can be much more useful to you as you start the actual writing. In a topic outline, you might forget exactly what point you were going to make about a certain topic, but if you write a complete sentence with subject, verb, and object, you have the point you were going to make already built into the outline.

For example, a topic outline might include the entry *Installing the Device Drivers*. This topic entry contains no information on how to list drivers in the configuration file. A complete sentence makes it much easier for you to remember what you intended to say about the topic, such as "Installing the device drivers requires using an editor to set the DEVICE= statement to DEVICE=XYZDEV1, XYZDEV2 in the configuration file."

A sentence outline takes much more effort than a topic outline does, but it's effort well spent. The only disadvantage to making a sentence outline is that you can't use the entries as headings in the book or as elements in your table of contents.

Using Rhetorical Patterns

After you've compiled a list of topics around which to organize the book, select one topic to develop further by means of subtopics and rhetorical patterns. A rhetorical pattern is nothing more than a ready-made structure for a piece of writing. From ancient Greece to the present, writers have used models to ease the task of organizing their writing. A rhetorical pattern provides a logical, easily recognizable, useful arrangement for information.

Using the rhetorical patterns taught in writing courses can provide enormous assistance to you as you try to impose order on the chaos of source material. As you're reading and learning about the new product, or the new functions in a product that's being updated, you should be alert to the possibilities of using these patterns.

It's never a good idea to force information into a pattern that's not suited to the situation, but it's equally inefficient to ignore the very real help that using the patterns can give you. For example, if you need to show the differences between two functions, you'll do a much better job if you let the comparison and contrast pattern provide the underlying structure for your writing.

On the tight schedules that prevail in most writing shops today, you don't have time to write spontaneously or to invent new patterns. The patterns that follow don't provide an exhaustive survey of rhetorical methods, but they are some of the most useful in everyday technical writing.

General-to-specific pattern

Perhaps the most difficult pattern you'll have occasion to use is the progression from general to specific in an introductory section. This pattern tends to be difficult because you won't find source material for this section in most technical specs. You have to understand the product so well that you can write this part from your own knowledge.

You also have to write it in such a way that the technical people reviewing your book agree with it.

As a mental exercise for this pattern, you should think of the most general, all-encompassing statements you can possibly make about the product and then gradually get more specific so that you can go into the various functions. For example, you might think, "This product is a program that provides methods for manipulating information stored in databases on a personal computer." You could then expand the meaning of *manipulating* to include updating existing information, adding new information, deleting unneeded information, combining information from two different tables in a database, and so on. You could go on to think of the various *methods* a customer could use for these manipulations, such as entering commands, selecting items from a menu, or writing an application program to perform the actions.

By the time you finish this mental exercise, you should be ready to start. Many professional writers save the introductory sections of their books for last to give themselves every chance to understand the details of the product so thoroughly that they won't have to spend inordinate amounts of time on the first couple of pages. Others write the introduction first to ensure that they understand the overall product thoroughly before they go into the details.

Classification pattern

Describing functions of the product in a classification pattern is an organizational device that can fit into almost any section of almost any book. Usually, a spec provides plenty of material classifying the various functions, but you might not be able to lift sections from the spec because of the technical language or the excessive detail.

As you work, you can follow the same order in which the spec presents the functions if you think there's justification for it, or you can impose an arrangement that better meets customers' needs. For example, the spec might organize the functions alphabetically for ease of reference (*add, change, create, delete, edit, recover, save, verify*), but you might want to structure them chronologically or in a progression from beginning to complex tasks (*create, verify, save; add, change, edit, delete; recover*).

Once you decide on an overall organization for the functions, try to include the same types of information about each one. Some possible types of information are

- The purpose of the function
- Prerequisites for its use
- The customer's means of access to it
- The results of the function
- Any error messages it might generate
- Any alternative ways to use the function

Editor X provides two methods of naming and saving files.

The first method names and saves a file in a single action, while the second names and saves a file in separate actions.

In both methods, select Create from the File Action Menu.

In the first method, you must ignore the first prompt that asks you to name the file. In the second method, type a name at the first prompt.

In both methods, enter the information in the typing area and press the F5 (Save) key when you are finished.

In the first method, you are prompted for the name of the file. In the second method you are not prompted.

The file is saved in both methods. In both methods, you can exit the file by pressing F2 and Selecting EXIT from the menu that is displayed.

Figure 4.3 Point-by-point comparison pattern.

- The situations in which customers probably shouldn't use the function
- How the function interacts with others in the product

The types of information you include, of course, depends entirely on the functions. If something you need is not in the spec, you can do some more research and perhaps even get it added to the next issue of the spec.

Comparison-contrast pattern

Comparison-contrast comes in two versions. The *point-by-point* pattern, also called *part-to-part*, contrasts certain aspects of two things in nearly every sentence, somewhat like a ping-pong ball moving back and forth across a net. Figure 4.3 illustrates this pattern.

The other version, usually called the *whole-to-whole* pattern, compares and contrasts two things by developing the first idea fully and then going on to the second. The two things don't usually get mixed in together. This pattern, shown in Fig. 4.4, is widely used in every type of writing except highly technical information, where the point-to-point pattern usually works better.

In general, use the whole-to-whole pattern when there are few technical details, such as statistics, measurements, and other numbers, and use the point-by-point pattern when there are many technical details. The reason for preferring the point-by-point pattern for highly technical information is that it places two statistics, such as number of files in the first alternative and number of files in the second, close together where customers can compare them easily. Important numbers tend to get lost in the whole-to-whole pattern.

> Editor X provides two methods of naming and saving files.
>
> The first method is to name and save the file in a single action. Take the following steps:
>
> 1. Create a file by selecting Create from the File Actions Menu.
> 2. When you are prompted for the name of the file, press the Enter key. The screen that is displayed next gives you a typing area where you can enter information into the file.
> 3. When you have finished, press the F5 (Save) key. Since you have not yet named your file, you will be prompted for a name.
> 4. Type the name of the file and press F5 again. The file is saved.
> 5. Exit the file by pressing F2 and selecting EXIT from the menu that is displayed.
>
> The second method is to name and save the file in separate actions. Take the following steps:
>
> 1. Select Create from the File Actions Menu.
> 2. When prompted for the name of the file, type a name for the file.
> 3. Enter information when the typing area is displayed.
> 4. When you have finished, press the F5 (Save) key. Since the file already has a name, you are not prompted to enter a file name. The file is saved.
> 5. Exit the file by pressing F2 and selecting EXIT from the menu that is displayed.

Figure 4.4 Whole-to-whole comparison pattern.

Definition pattern

Definition is one of the shortest and most useful patterns. In one or two sentences, you make a formal definition of any term the customer might not be familiar with.

The traditional way of making a formal definition is to place the term in a class of similar terms, and then distinguish it from the other members of the class. For example, you can place the term *recover* into a class of functions, and then distinguish it from other functions that create a file, edit a file, and so on: "Recover is a function that restores a damaged file to a condition in which it can be opened and used."

Less formal definitions are also useful, such as providing a familiar synonym for an unfamiliar or highly technical term. If you provide a glossary for your book, you might have an opportunity to write an extensive list of definitions. Although some specs supply definitions and glossaries of technical terms, you shouldn't copy them without satisfying yourself that they're exactly right for your customers.

Chronological pattern for task-oriented instructions

Chronological organization is a reasonable way to arrange tasks and the instructions for carrying out the tasks. However, you might have difficulty in several areas of the task-oriented instructional pattern.

Understanding. One difficulty might be that the technical source does not help you fully understand what a customer has to do to use the function. Specs are typically written as functional descriptions, with little or no regard for where the customer should start, continue, and finish with a particular function. If you have a prototype or if you can get an early version of the code, you can figure out for yourself what the steps or procedures should be. Without a prototype, your best bet is to ask a programmer to demonstrate the function and then watch exactly what he or she does. You might get expert tips that frequent users develop but that don't get into the spec.

Numbering. Another difficulty is that most tasks are presented in numbered steps, but you might have some trouble breaking a task down into a reasonable number of steps. If you come up with only two steps, you might need to dig deeper for subtasks that help the customer see exactly what to do. For example, instead of just telling the customer to insert a diskette and turn on the machine, you can expand the steps for the novice user by telling where the drive is, how to hold the diskette for correct insertion, how to use the write-protect device on the diskette, and where the on-off switch is.

On the other hand, if you have 10 or more steps, you should analyze whether the task needs to be divided into subtasks, each with its own list of steps. You don't want to intimidate customers with a formidably long set of procedures. In each step, try to describe a single action and the information needed to accomplish that action.

Notes and warnings. Digressions might tempt you away from the main flow of the procedure, especially if the information is important. Usually, you can work vital information into a procedure by placing it in a short note or a warning that you embed between two steps.

Place a note just after the step containing the information that the note relates to, as in Fig. 4.5. A warning should have more attention called to it than a note, and should be placed before the step to which it applies. Use boldface for the word *warning*, blank lines before and after the warning, greater indentation so that it stands out from the surrounding text, and a box around it, as in Fig. 4.6.

Level of detail. Sometimes you might be puzzled about where to begin the list of steps. Should you assume that customers have any prior knowledge about the procedure, or should you give them everything? A careful audience analysis at the beginning of the project and some customer validation by means of test cases near the end of the project can help you answer the question.

In general, you should provide just enough information for your typical customer to perform the task with ease and confidence. Nothing is gained by including too much elementary information.

1. Select File Name from the Create Main Menu.
2. Type the name of the file you are creating.

   Note: The name can contain 1 to 8 characters
   including a – z, A – Z, 0 – 9, and the
   special characters ampersand (&) and number sign (#).

3. Press the Enter key to continue.

Figure 4.5 A note containing important information.

Advantages. An advantage of the task-oriented procedure over the function-oriented description is that you include customers directly by giving
them actions to perform. Figures 4.7 and 4.8 illustrate the differences between the two types.

Some books have a place for function-oriented description, but the task-
oriented procedure does a better job of instructing the customer on the actual use of the function.

Cause-effect pattern

The cause-effect pattern of organizing information is useful in some situations. Probably the most common use for cause-effect organization in com-
puter-related writing is for error messages. Some products, in fact, begin
each error message with the word *cause* and describe what happened to
create the error condition. The next section of the error message contains
the action for the customer to take in order to recover from the situation.

If the error has more than one cause, you should arrange the causes in an
order ranging from most likely to least likely. If the user needs to take a sep-

1. Select Erase File from the File Main Menu.
2. Type the name of the file to erase.

   Warning

   **Do not complete the following step
   unless you are sure that you want to
   erase the file permanently.**

3. Press the F7 (Erase) key to erase the file.

Figure 4.6 A warning.

To use the UNIX grep command for a string search, do the following:
1. Type grep (the search command) and leave a blank space.
2. On the same line, type the string you are searching for and leave a blank space.
3. On the same line, type a single file or a list of files to be searched.

Figure 4.7 Task-oriented procedure.

arate action for each cause, place each action directly after the cause to which it relates. If the user can take only one action for all the causes, place the action at the end of all the causes.

The purpose of the section on actions is to describe in precise terms what the customer should do to recover from the error. This type of information is usually hard for a writer to find because error recovery is difficult to predict in advance. The spec might list all the errors returned by the product and suggest ways of recovering, but unless someone tests every situation and every environment, you can't provide complete information. Often, it takes personal experience with errors to understand their causes and the actions to take for recovery.

Another common use of the cause-effect pattern is for cautions and warnings. The cause is generally that a customer does something, and the effect is what happens. As a general rule, you should caution customers that a certain action will destroy their data, damage their files, or make unavailable to them something you're sure they want to keep. You should warn customers in the clearest possible terms about anything that might cause pain or injury to them. Software writers seldom need to issue such warnings, but hardware writers might need to on occasion.

The grep command in UNIX facilitates locating strings in files without the need for an editor. Grep has several options, can search more than one file, and can send the results to the standard output or to a file.

Figure 4.8 Function-oriented procedure.

5

Writing Information Components

As a writer, your contribution to the product is to translate the designers' and programmers' highly technical language and illustrations into information that the intended audience can use. Doing so is no small task, and your value to the product is no small service.

Writing information components gets to the heart of producing a quality book. On the simplest level, a *component* is any unit of a book that contains related information. Also called *sections* or *modules*, components are the building blocks of a book. They can range in size and complexity from a half-page description of a simple command, such as the CD (change directory) command in DOS, to a 40-page discussion of configuring a personal computer for connections and communications with a mainframe or host computer.

A good way to think of a component is to define it as any section of a book that has its own topic heading. A chapter is a large component, consisting of smaller components (major topics), each of which can consist of even smaller components (subtopics). Every sentence in the book should belong to a component.

The task of writing a whole book might seem so intimidating or time-consuming that you might feel you can never complete it. For most writers, it's much easier to break the book down into manageable sections and worry about writing just one of those and then another and another until you have something that's long enough to be a section, a chapter, or a book. Then you can work on joining the sections together properly.

Another desirable feature of creating components is that this way of writing is characteristic of developing online documentation. If online documentation supplants printed books over the next several years, writers who know how to think and write in small, stand-alone units have an advantage over those who don't.

Writing Components and Nodes

Initially, you can think of each element of your outline as a component. Then you need to go in two opposite directions.

You'll need to break the elements of your outline down into smaller units, preferably into the smallest units that can stand alone and still make sense by relating to a central topic. A short paragraph with its topic sentence is probably the smallest unit you can write, although many are longer.

In online information, as explained in Chapter 19, these smallest units are often called *nodes*, and this chapter borrows that term for books. As you decide on the size and contents of the nodes, write something about what should go into each one. If you record only the topic without some information or at least some instructions to yourself on what you think should support the topic, you'll forget what you intended to do by the time you work through a hundred or a thousand small units. What you're really making is a road map, or schedule of milestones, for the book you're going to write.

After you've sketched out the nodes, you'll need to master the techniques of combining these smallest units into chapters or other large sections of your book. Going in this direction is much easier because you'll have the nodes written so that you can see what you've got. Then you can plan how everything should flow and hang together.

Advantages of developing a road map, or schedule of milestones

Developing node and chapter road maps has many advantages. One of the most obvious is that the book, or at least a good section of it, is completely thought-out before you begin writing. You won't have to rely on inspiration or creativity to get you through the writing. Also, if more than one writer is working on the book, following the road map does a great deal more to ensure a seamless book than does working from an outline, even with extensive discussions among the writers.

Other advantages of developing a road map include the following:

- It allows you or your planner to schedule the right amount of time for you to complete the book, based not on industry standards, hunches, or proposed product schedules, but on the number and complexity of nodes.

- It takes the panic out of the writing process. You'll always know where you are and what you need to do next.

- It makes the writing process into an ordinary, step-by-step procedure instead of something difficult or magical.
- It opens the writing process to the scrutiny of technical people and managers.
- It can give you a sense of accomplishment to check off the nodes in your road map as you finish them.
- It reveals omissions, redundancies, and other design flaws much more thoroughly than reviewing an outline can.

While the outline represents the last stage in getting organized and the first step in writing, the road map helps you get into the writing process because you jot down a little information about each node. If you don't have enough information about the node, you can at least write something about what kind of information should go in it.

Typical nodes in the road map

Some nodes, of course, will be similar to each other, such as those describing the commands available in the product. You'll want to cover the same information for each one, such as the purpose, the syntax, the parameters, the method of invoking the command, the potential error messages or return codes, the computer languages that support the command, the people who might want, or are authorized, to use the command, and similar information (see "A commands reference" in Chapter 4, page 44). This level of detail is inappropriate for all but the longest outlines, but it's just right for a road map.

Other nodes will be unique, such as those detailing the introductory material. Even these nodes, however, will closely resemble those similarly situated in other books. The nodes that you should consider for the introduction include clear, simple, high-level statements of the following:

- Prerequisites for using the product
- What the product does, which might not necessarily be what it was first designed to do
- How each function of the product works, described so that anyone not familiar with the product can understand
- What tasks customers can perform with the product and, if necessary, when and why they would want to perform the tasks
- How the product differs from previous releases, if applicable

Going from outline to road map

You'll probably have variations of some or all of the following major topics in your outline:

- Introductory information for a new or enhanced product
- Conceptual information to promote understanding of new or enhanced function
- Installing the product
- Configuring the product
- Instructions for the customer to use the features of the product
- Descriptions of procedures for various types of administrators to follow, including system, network, and database administrators
- Explanations of programming commands and routines
- Diagnostic and error recovery information

To start breaking the outline down to nodes, pick a topic, such as installing, and start thinking about preparing to install the product on your own machine. What would you need to do to get ready? What are your customers likely to need to do? The following list provides a detailed task analysis for an installation node. You might not need all the nodes listed, but it's certainly a good idea to think about them because the designers and programmers probably haven't had time and don't think in terms of a detailed task analysis.

Detailed task analysis for an installation node

- If installing erases files on the hard disk, what files should I save, and how should I save them?
- Do I need to reformat my hard file for the new product? If so, do I need to know any special tips, such as references to other books that can help me?
- Do I need to repartition my hard drive before installing? If so, do I need instructions on how to do the task?
- If I'm installing a new release over a previous release of the product, can I take any shortcuts?
- How long and complicated is the install procedure? Do I need help with it? If so, where can I turn for help?
- Does it matter which drive I install on? If so, why?
- Do I need to create a new directory to install in? If so, do I need a reminder on how to create a directory?
- What can go wrong during install? How do I know something's not right?
- If error messages appear, what do they mean and how can I recover from something that went wrong?
- Are any online installation aids, such as help panels, available? If so, how do I access them?

- Can I stop before installation is complete and resume at the same place I left off, or must I start over from the beginning?
- If I can resume from where I left off, how do I do it?
- How do I know that everything completed successfully? Does the product provide a completion message?
- What, if anything, should I do between installing and using the product? What comes next?
- What part of the documentation should I turn to first for common tasks?

If you think these questions are unnecessary, you might be right for small, simple products. However, for large, complex products, you need to think of these and many additional questions before you can do a quality job of writing about installation.

Many of these types of questions aren't considered by those who design and code the product, and they don't get into the technical spec. Yet, thinking of them and getting the answers can be a very important benefit to customers who need to perform these tasks.

Brainstorming new questions for the nodes might reveal that you haven't finished your learning and research after all. You might have to go back to the technical people, experiment on your own, or both as you're working on the nodes.

You might even be able to get some important usability improvements into the product if you're persistent enough. For example, if no completion message appears at the end of installation, but you feel one is needed, you might be able to convince the programmers who wrote the code to add it. If you can't, then set the node aside and go on to another one.

How to write a node

Two schools of thought exist on the kind of writing that should be in each node. One advocates writing a complete draft of the information that's so good you could show it to other people. The other advocates just jotting down the important points any old way and revising later.

For the node topic on installing over a previous release, for example, the first method would result in your writing something like the following:

```
If you are installing over a previous release of PRODUCT NAME,
two files, FILEONE.XXX and FILETWO.XXX, are not changed in the
current release. The install program checks to see if these
files are present and undamaged. If so, these files are not re-
installed, saving you about five minutes.
```

All the sentences in the node are grammatically correct, the spelling is accurate, the flow is logical, and so on. The writing might not be as elegant as it could be, but it gets the job done, and you won't have to return to it, unless you have the time, until you're revising the whole book.

The other method would have you writing something like this:

```
Inst. over old ver.—2 fls not changed (fileone.xxx +
filetwo.xxx)—code checks—skips—saves 5 min.
```

Obviously, this passage couldn't go into the book without extensive revision. By the time you get around to revising the node, you might forget or overlook several things that you'll have to fix, such as

- Your editors want you to use the term *release*, not *version*.

- Your style guide requires that you type filenames in all capital letters.

- The *code checks—skips* note might be too cryptic for you to remember later that the time savings of five minutes disappears if the two files are missing or damaged and have to be reinstalled.

- The time savings of five minutes is only an approximate figure. Some customer somewhere might complain to your company if he or she saves only four minutes and 52 seconds.

- You might even forget that *fls* is your abbreviation for files.

In the long run, using the first method of producing complete, usable nodes saves time. It's also a good way to build quality into the book from the beginning. For a long time, programmers have known that the best time to find and fix coding errors is as early as possible. The same applies to writing.

The best time to be concerned about quality is at the very beginning of the writing cycle. If you make your writing as good as you possibly can from the start, you have far less rework to do later. Just as most programmers enjoy writing code more than debugging it, so writers usually enjoy writing more than revising.

How not to write a node

One of the worst ways to write a node is to copy something from the product screens or from the technical spec without thinking about its effect on the customer. For example, in SuperDoc 1.0, a hypothetical new word processing product that you're documenting for end users, suppose a selectable menu item on the screen with the jaw-breaking name of *Keystroke Print Queue Facilitator* has the subitems *Enable Buffer* and *Disable Buffer*. Suppose further that you tried and failed to get the names changed to something more intuitively obvious.

For the node on enabling this function, do not write something like the following, because it explains nothing:

```
This selection item enables the buffer of the Keystroke Print
Queue Facilitator (KPQF) for use.
```

A small point is that some customers might not be quite sure what *enables* means in the context of a word processing program, and many more won't know what a buffer is. A more important point is that your node doesn't explain a thing about the KPQF, other than implying that it's important enough to warrant an acronym in the SuperDoc program.

Suppose you turn to the technical spec for help in understanding the function and read the following:

```
A larger print queue buffer for the OMNIEXCELLENT 345.6 printer
can be enabled by KPQF such that keystroke loss is minimized.
```

This sentence undoubtedly makes perfect sense to the programmers who designed and coded this function. But it takes a few phone calls or visits with them, as well as some reading about the marketplace, for you to understand it.

Suppose you discover that the OMNIEXCELLENT 345.6 is a printing device produced by another company that's selling very well right now. For understandable reasons, the designers of SuperDoc want to be compatible with this printer. They've had to add a function at the last minute that increases the size of the buffer, which is a temporary storage place where SuperDoc saves files until you print them. They had to do so because the print queue on the OMNI, another temporary storage place, accepts only blocks of text of an exact size—and not the size that SuperDoc uses for its buffer.

What happens without KPQF, let's suppose further, is that when you send a large file to the OMNI, SuperDoc can't transfer the whole file at once but can send only one buffer at a time, say 1024 bytes. The print queue on the OMNI, however, holds 2048 bytes. You'd expect the OMNI printer queue to accept two blocks of 1024 bytes, print them, accept two more, print them, and so on until the whole file was printed. But the OMNI hangs and prints nothing.

In your research, you find that the OMNI actually accepts one SuperDoc block plus 1020 bytes of the second block. The reason is that, in order to send blocks of text to the OMNI, SuperDoc must add two bytes of control information to the beginning and end of each block it sends. The two bytes at the beginning of the block contain a start-of-block indicator, an identifier for the SuperDoc file, an identifier for this particular block, the address of the printer, and the location of the SuperDoc file. The two bytes at the end of the block contain an end-of-block indicator and the other information in the first two bytes.

Thus, the first block becomes 1028 bytes long (1024 plus two at the start plus two at the end), leaving only 1020 bytes for the second block. When the second block can't fit into the OMNI queue, the last two bytes of text and the two bytes of control information at the end get lost. Since it hasn't received the end-of-block bytes, the OMNI waits forever for the two bytes that tell it that the transmission is complete.

Now you know what to put in the Enable Buffer node. It should read something like this:

```
Select Enable Buffer if you want to print files on the OMNIEX-
CELLENT 345.6 printer. If you do not enable the buffer, the
printer might discard some of the text and might stall indef-
initely.
```

You might be tempted to include everything you learned in the node, but most of the highly technical information is inappropriate for the audience of novices. They don't need to know about the size of the buffer and the control bytes, but it is important to tell them about the lost data and the stalling. If your audience were programmers, you would keep this node and add another paragraph containing the technical details.

How to keep on writing nodes, even when you're stuck

Writing isn't the easiest thing in the world. If it were, everyone would produce million-dollar bestsellers. Writing computer information might require a different type of creativity and inspiration than writing novels, but technical writers can fall prey to the same writer's block and can benefit from some of the same techniques novelists and other creative writers use to break out of a slump, stay productive, and enjoy their work. Following are 25 time-tested techniques to try:

1. If you don't know where to start, start anywhere. Pick any node and write it. You don't have to start at the beginning.

2. If you have plenty of information for a node but too little motivation, use the seat-to-seat method of writing. Apply the seat of the pants to the seat of the chair and write anything—even laundry lists, though preferably something about the subject of the node—until something clicks your brain into gear.

3. If you can't write a node because you don't fully understand it, call or visit a technical person, or do some reading on the topic. The instant you understand the subject, write it.

4. Remind yourself that you get to go home at five o'clock, or your usual quitting time, and that you don't have to think about these nodes until the next workday.

5. Reward yourself with a walk around the building or a trip to the coffee machine when you finish an especially troublesome node.

6. Think how wonderful everything will be when you're finished.

7. Consider that you're making more money now than you would if you were fired for not completing the book.

8. Copy as many words as you can from a similar node or from the technical spec. (There's no such thing as plagiarism when you write computer information for your company. If you find something usable in an internal document, use it!)

9. Talk about the subject of the node to someone who doesn't know much, if anything, about it. Then immediately write down what you said.

10. If one node just won't come, go on to another one.

11. Sit at your desk as many hours as it takes to get a node written, even if it's midnight before you go home.

12. If you just can't write any nodes, revise your outline. Move the elements around. You might discover a better organization. Sooner or later, you will be able to get back to the nodes, although with the tight schedules in most organizations, sooner is much better than later.

13. Read some nodes you've already written and realize that you got through them successfully. You might not have turned out brilliant prose, but you don't need to. You just need to get the job done for a first draft.

14. Switch your method of writing. If you always use a computer, try writing a troublesome node in longhand.

15. Leave your office and go to the lab, a conference room, someone else's office, your car, a bench in a nearby park—anywhere—and try writing a few nodes there.

16. Read an awful passage in the spec and recognize that you're the only thing that stands between the customer and the bad writing.

17. Turn on a tape recorder and talk about everything you know about the topic at hand. Play the tape back and listen for information you can put into the node.

18. Go back to a node you left in a less-than-satisfactory condition and rewrite it to make it better. Rewrite as many times as it takes to prove to yourself that you can still write. Then go on to a new node.

19. Review the status of troublesome nodes with the project manager or an equally knowledgeable person. Someone with the big picture in mind can often be surprisingly helpful and responsive to things that are real roadblocks to you.

20. Draw a rough sketch, or a carefully detailed picture if you can, that ex-

plains the contents of the node. One of the best ways to think about technical details is visually. (Frequently, a visual presentation works best for customers too.)

21. Put yourself on an impossible schedule. Try to create a little of the last-minute panic that you might have experienced as a student writing term papers. A deadline usually motivates writers very well.

22. Talk to other writers and ask how they kept going or how they solved a particular writing problem.

23. If you are truly burned out, exhausted from a lot of overtime, and completely unable to put subject before verb, take a three-day weekend, or longer if you can, and do whatever you need to do to take care of yourself and recharge your batteries.

24. Whatever happens, keep on writing. Just do it.

25. If these techniques don't work to keep you going, invent your own techniques.

Putting the Nodes Together

You don't have to wait until you've written all the nodes to start putting them together into larger components. As soon as you have a group of nodes written on the same topic, you can begin arranging them in the order that matches the outline and road map you developed earlier, or in an order that seems logical now.

At first, just place them together. If you created them as separate files in your host editor or personal computer word processor, first combine related nodes into one file. Then read through the file and see where you need a transition from one node to another.

Sometimes the best transition is a topic heading that groups several nodes together. Headings can come from the elements of your outline, or you can think up additional ones if the outline doesn't go into enough detail. Other kinds of transitions include the following words and phrases:

- Those that let the reader know how much material in the sequence has been covered and how much more is coming, such as *first, second, third* (and so on), or *to begin, next, then, last,* and *finally*

- Those that let the reader know that something different is coming, such as *but, however, yet, in contrast,* and *otherwise*

- Those that give a pointer to time, such as *now, then, soon, immediately, after, before,* and *later*

- Those that show a result is coming, such as *therefore, as a result,* and *in consequence*

- Those that point to a location, such as *above, below, left, right, inside, outside, opposite, on top, at the bottom,* and *near*

- Those that introduce an example, such as *for example, such as,* and *that is*

- Those that tell the reader to expect more on the same topic, such as *in addition, and, also, moreover, similarly, likewise, too, further,* and *as well as* (be careful not to overuse these)

- Those that show a conclusion or summary is coming, such as *finally, last, in conclusion, to sum up, in sum* (be careful not to overuse these)

Headings and transitions

Headings and transitions can do a great deal to improve the flow from one section to another. They also make the sections hang together in a way that's unobtrusive to the reader. Not every node needs a heading, and not every sentence needs a transitional word or phrase. If you don't use any of these devices, however, your readers will have a hard time making their way through your writing and won't quite know what's wrong.

Another consideration in putting nodes together is checking for the completeness and usability of the information. The best way to do this is to have someone else read the section. If someone is willing to read a very rough draft, and if you have time to print it out, this method can work well. Someone not familiar with the book but knowledgeable about the product can give you the best help, but anyone who reads with care can spot incomplete and unusable information.

Another method of checking your writing is to put the section away for a few days and work on something entirely different. Then read the section yourself, looking at it as if you were a customer. Ask yourself some questions:

- Do the heads prepare the reader for the contents of the section?

- Are there enough transitions to enable the reader to move through the section comfortably?

- Have I provided all the information the customer needs to understand the concept, perform the task, diagnose the error?

- Is the information written so clearly that the customer can use it easily and immediately?

Adding missing information might take you back to the researching and learning stages, but the task is easier than it was at first, because now you know enough to realize what is incomplete. You know the type of information you need and the people who can give it to you.

Combining groups of nodes into chapters

In a technical document, you might not be able to follow such rhetorical concerns as making each chapter the same size or structuring each chapter exactly the same way. These techniques are fine if you can accomplish them. However, the length and contents of your chapters should make sense in relation to the code, more than to an arbitrary, external standard. Similarly, the major divisions of chapters don't have to be balanced in length or structure. If three pages is the maximum amount you can write about installing the product, for example, then let the installation chapter be three pages long, at least for the first draft. It might be possible to combine installation with a related topic later on.

In organizing a chapter, be guided by the thinking you did earlier for the outline and road map, but also be open to different arrangements of the information, especially if you have added or deleted blocks of text since the time you developed the outline.

The most effective way to structure a chapter is to put yourself in the place of the customer and decide what needs to come first in a particular topic. Then continue with a chronological organization. During the review and test process (described in Chapter 10), you'll find out if your chapters are well organized and whether customers can find the information they need.

Revising Your Writing

Some writers love to rewrite just as some programmers love to debug, but the majority in both groups don't like to go over what they've already created. Yet revising is an absolute necessity if you want to produce quality information. Fortunately, writers have a lot of help with revising.

Take full advantage of online spelling checkers, grammar checkers, grade-level checkers, tag counters, and other such tools. Even the tools that aren't very good can be helpful because they help you look at your writing from an objective point of view. For example, if a grammar checker informs you that you've used 49 infinitives in an eight-page chapter, you might decide to vary your style a little if you have time. You have to correct the real mistakes in spelling and grammar, of course, but you can ignore errors of style and grade level, at least on the first draft. If your book is supposed to be written at the eighth-grade level, a common requirement in the computer industry, you might have to revise and simplify a great deal if your book comes out above the tenth-grade level. You might be able to get away with distributing a first draft that's at too high a level, but you certainly need to get to the right level before distributing the final draft.

Tag counters and similar tools for mark-up languages are useful for correcting formatting errors if you're using anything more complicated than a simple word processor. These tools can show where you've neglected to end a list with the correct tag, where your table tags have gone astray, and so on. You can then revise the formatting problems in your book more easily.

When you've done all you can with automated tools, you need to resort to the eyeball method—read your book many times, looking for different kinds of improvements each time. You probably won't have many actual errors if you've used automated tools, but you would be surprised at the number of other things you will find unsatisfactory about your writing.

The following section provides a set of items that often require careful revising for consistency and clarity.

Inconsistent point of view

If you sometimes write in the third person and other times write in the second person, you have inconsistencies in the point of view. The way to correct these inconsistencies is to decide on a point of view and stick to it. Any time you use the imperative mood of the verb, you're writing in second person with *you* understood as the subject. For this reason alone, it's a good idea to choose second person. The following example shows an inconsistent point of view and a correction:

Inconsistent point of view

```
Ensure that all users have user IDs. The administrator can en-
ter the user IDs into the logon table.
```

Correction

```
Ensure that all users have user IDs. Enter the user IDs into
the logon table.
```

Shifts of attention

Many computer manuals contain this error. They shift the reader's attention from the book to the machine and then try to get back to the book. Once a customer starts pressing keys or using the mouse or pointing device, you can't get him or her back to the book very easily.

The way to correct this error is to group all introductory, explanatory, and conceptual information together at the beginning and then go into the step-by-step, button-pushing information afterwards. Figures 5.1 and 5.2 show a shift and a correction. In Fig. 5.1, the reader must switch between understanding the conceptual information and performing the steps. In Fig. 5.2, the conceptual information and the steps are clearly separated. The reader doesn't start making selections until the reasons are explained. Using the same material, you can rearrange the steps so that the user finishes reading the instructions before beginning the steps.

The Main Menu contains three selection items:

1. Starting the XYZ Program
2. Transferring Files with the XYZ Program
3. Stopping the XYZ Program

Select Starting the XYZ Program. A pop-up panel is displayed. Type the Logon ID and User Password that the host administrator assigned to you.

When the host menu is displayed, the logon procedure is complete.

Return to the Main Menu by pressing the Return to Main Menu (F8) key. Then select Transferring Files with the XYZ Program.

Figure 5.1 Reader's attention shifts.

Passive voice

Some passive voice is acceptable in computer publications, but excessive use makes your writing hard to read. Since active voice is normal for English, it's important to understand it. Active voice also sounds more knowledgeable than passive voice.

Passive voice has four characteristics:

- The subject is not doing the action that the verb indicates.
- The subject is receiving the action of the verb.
- The verb always consists of at least two words: a form of *to be* (such as *was, has been,* or *are*), and the third principal part of the verb (such as

The Main Menu contains three selection items:

1. Starting the XYZ Program
2. Transferring Files with the XYZ Program
3. Stopping the XYZ Program

When you start the XYZ Program, you must supply the Logon ID and User Password that your host administrator assigned to you. After you are logged on to the host, you can transfer files.

Steps:

1. Select Starting the XYZ Program.
2. Type your Logon ID and User Password in the pop-up panel that is displayed.
3. When the host screen is displayed, press the Return to Main Menu (F8) key.
4. Select Transferring Files.

Figure 5.2 Reader's attention is clearly focused.

gone, *done*, and *been* for irregular verbs; and the *-ed* form of regular verbs.

■ Whoever or whatever is performing the action of the verb is either missing from the sentence or buried after the verb in a prepositional phrase starting with *by*.

A sentence written in passive voice, such as

```
The error message was issued by the host.
```

is easy to rewrite in active voice:

```
The host issued the error message.
```

When the prepositional phrase starting with *by* is missing from the sentence, the language can sound irresponsible or lack authority. In the following example, the passive voice doesn't tell who or what caused the disconnect:

```
Error code 1234 means that the communications link was discon-
nected because the allotted time for the program ran out.
```

The rewrite states who disconnected the link so that the reader knows whom to contact for a reconnection:

```
Error code 1234 means that the host disconnected the communica-
tions link because the allotted time for the program ran out.
```

Wordiness

Words cost money. It's cheaper to print a short book than a long one, and more concise online information takes less storage and memory. Therefore, eliminate all unnecessary words and phrases. For example, you can revise the Error code 1234 sentence in the last section to one that's not only 25% shorter but also more direct:

```
When the program times out, the host disconnects the communi-
cations link and issues error code 1234.
```

Also, avoid such redundancies as "4K in size" and "red in color."

Inconsistent terminology

A computer book is no place to get creative with terminology or the use of synonyms and ambiguities. Decide on the names of things and stick with them.

```
program / code / application / routine

host / mainframe / large computer

turn on / power up / boot / start / begin

menu / panel / screen / display / window / pop-up / pull-down

ensure / be sure / make sure / check / verify

item / option / selection / choice / element / member / entry
```

Figure 5.3 Inconsistent terminology.

For example, don't interchange terms, such as those listed in Fig. 5.3, as if they were synonyms. Inconsistent terminology can confuse, irritate, or alienate your readers. They'll wonder if you mean the same thing when you discuss a program on the host in one sentence, a routine on the mainframe in another, and an application on a large computer in yet another. You could really confuse readers by using all possible combinations of these words in 12 different places.

Another reason customers complain about different terms being used for the same thing is that the practice is completely unnecessary. A style guide or terminology guide can tell you what words to use.

Faulty parallelism

Faulty parallelism is the use of two or more different grammatical constructions in a list. Items connected by *and* in a sentence or listed in a table of contents or other list should be the same part of speech (for single words) or should use the same grammatical construction (for phrases).

The main place to check for parallelism is in the table of contents that is automatically generated by many word processing and publishing systems. As you write text, you seldom fall into parallelism errors if you write short, simple sentences, but it's easy to switch from gerunds to infinitives, for example, in the headings that go into the table of contents. Make sure that all the headings in a particular section of your book are parallel in grammatical structure. Although few customers might consciously be concerned about parallelism, correcting this type of error contributes to the quality of your book.

The following example shows faulty parallelism:

```
1. To prepare for installing

2. Installation of the ABC program

3. How to configure for ABC
```

4. Do you want to save the earlier version?

5. Using the ABC program

The grammatical constructions used in this list consist of an infinitive, a noun, an adverbial phrase, a question, and a gerund. Many editors recommend using gerunds in such lists, partly because you can make a gerund from any verb and partly because gerunds convey the force of verbs without implying that you must take the action immediately. The revision that follows uses gerunds:

1. Preparing for installation

2. Installing the ABC program

3. Configuring for the ABC program

4. Saving the earlier version

5. Using the ABC program

Dangling modifiers

The use of dangling modifiers is a very easy error to make and sometimes hard to catch. A dangling modifier is a verbal phrase (a gerund, infinitive, or participial phrase) that does not have a word in the sentence to connect to and modify. In the example below, the sentence contains no word for *communicating* to relate to:

The message arrived while communicating with the domain controller.

The message isn't doing the communicating, and the sentence has no other noun that could be doing it. Revising the dangling modifier requires that you include the entity that was performing the communication:

The message arrived while the program was communicating with the domain controller.

This revision adds a word to the sentence to show what the modifier relates to.

In the next example, the sentence contains a dangling modifier that implies that the application types the command:

After typing the command, the application begins opening files.

Revising the dangling modifier requires that you think about who or what was actually typing the command:

After you type the command, the application begins opening files.

Like faulty parallelism, dangling modifiers might not offend many customers, but they can cause misunderstandings and can diminish the quality of your publication.

Ending a sentence with a preposition

If you're writing in a formal style, you probably won't end sentences with prepositions. Your style guide might also require that you avoid ending sentences with particles that are grammatically part of the verb, because they resemble prepositions. For example, to avoid ending a sentence with a preposition, write

```
Drag the icon next to the folder to which it relates.
```

rather than

```
Drag the icon next to the folder it relates to.
```

To avoid ending a sentence with a part of the verb, write

```
Before you can use it, you must set up the computer.
```

rather than

```
Before you can use the computer, you must set it up.
```

No longer does a grammar rule require that sentences not end with a preposition or a particle that resembles a preposition, but obeying this rule is still a characteristic of the formal writing style. However, if you're writing in the middle or informal style, you can end sentences with prepositions if you want to.

Provincial and sexist language

Never use culturally specific and one-sex examples. Whether or not your book is translated and sold in other countries, you should be sensitive to customers of many cultures and both genders in this country. For example, a list of surnames in a sample database table should include Arabic, Hispanic, German, Jewish, and others in addition to English names. For first names, use both male and female names or those that can apply to both, such as *Pat*, *Terry*, *Robin*, and *Chris*.

Using an appropriate style

Style involves such elements of writing as the manner or way in which information is presented, the level of diction, the degree of formality, and the

> If you do not want to save the file, type the letter Q to quit using the file. Before you type Q, however, make sure that you will not need the file in the future because it will be erased. If you think you may need it later, type S to save it.
>
> To quit without saving, type Q. To save the file before quitting, type S.

Figure 5.4 Verbose and terse styles.

conventions used. Nearly every writing shop consisting of more than one writer depends on some kind of style guide that details conventions of highlighting, capitalization, punctuation, unacceptable words, and so on.

Many writing shops issue formal guidelines on manner, diction, formality, and other elements that are difficult to pin down. Others don't, requiring new writers to learn about these things by having their work reviewed and corrected by experienced writers and by reading what their peers produce. All writers on the same project should write in a similar way for the sake of producing a consistent library.

To understand how different ways of writing can affect customers, compare a verbose and a terse style, as in Fig. 5.4. The style of the first example in Fig. 5.4 is verbose and inappropriate even for the most nervous and inexperienced of customers. The style of the second is terse, but clear and easy to follow.

All readers are entitled to their personal preferences, but the terse, clear style conveys information more efficiently and costs less to produce because it's shorter.

Diction

Levels of diction are word choices that range from simple to complex. Nothing is wrong with using simple words; in fact, they communicate more efficiently than difficult words. However, the computer industry, like gov-

Complex	Simple
quiescent	at rest
system unit	box
select	pick
problem determination	finding errors
display	show
catalog	list
connectivity	link
referential integrity	data protection

Figure 5.5 Complex and simple word pairs.

ernmental agencies, often uses a very complex level of diction, as the word pairs in Fig. 5.5 show.

In some cases, you might have to use the level of diction that is entrenched in the industry so that customers get the vocabulary they expect. Where you have a choice, however, use simple words.

Formality

The degree of formality in writing can range from the highly formal, like a report addressed to public authority figures, to the very colloquial, like ordinary speech between friends. The range of styles is evident in the three examples that follow:

Very formal style:

```
If you do not wish to terminate the process, then
specify Continue.
```

Middle style:

```
If you don't want to end your process, select Continue.
```

Very informal style:

```
If you don't want to kill your job, hit Continue.
```

Many computer books use a formal style characterized by the following:

- No contractions
- No slang
- No figurative language
- No liveliness
- No human warmth

This style of writing might satisfy customers who don't spend much time with a book. They want only the facts they need in order to complete a task, and they want to read the information as fast as possible. The major drawback to the very formal style for these readers is that this type of language usually takes a little longer to read and digest because it's somewhat stilted and might use less familiar words.

Following are some types of books that are suited to a style ranging between formal and middle, and some reasons why this more-formal style works better than an informal style.

Error recovery books. An error recovery book is consulted when a problem occurs and the customer wants to correct the error. A style that's middle-to-formal fits better than an informal style, which might offend a harried, frustrated customer.

Reference books. A reference book is never read from beginning to end; thus, the reader and writer never have a chance to establish the social context in which an informal style would be appropriate. Since the reader dips into the book at various places, at different times, and under unpredictable circumstances, the style should be consistently formal or middle throughout.

Programming guides. A programming guide might or might not be read straight through, depending on the customer's level of expertise, but its content is purely technical and its purpose is to inform. A little informality sometimes appears in the introductory material of commercially published programming books, but the instructional material is still formal to middle in style.

The informal, colloquial style does have a place in computer publications. Following are some types of books suited to a less formal style, and some reasons why this style works better than the formal.

Short, introductory books. An introductory book for the complete novice needs to be as friendly and encouraging as possible in order to ease the novice into the unfamiliar technical material. Since the informal style sounds as if a friend is talking to you, the informal or middle style can appeal to this type of customer.

Planning books. A planning book usually contains more conceptual and somewhat less technical information than other types of computer publications. It's also intended to be read all the way through, usually in one sitting. Since the reader is typically a decision-maker who seeks advice on planning for hardware and software purchases, a somewhat informal style works well.

Marketing information. Information such as brochures, leaflets promoting classes on a new product, internal documents used to train salespeople, and similar information often employ an informal style as part of the sales pitch.

When deciding on the level of formality for your book, find out whether it will be translated into other languages. Books that will be translated should avoid the very informal style with its use of slang, highly idiomatic expressions, and cultural references. These characteristics make translation difficult or impossible.

Using an appropriate tone

Tone in computer information means the same thing as in literature: the
writer's implied attitude toward the topic, the reader, or the world in general. Tone usually implies emotional content, such as anger, sadness, or sar-
casm, but in computer publications, a better way to examine tone is to see
the range from a very distanced tone to an excessively intrusive tone, as the
following examples show:

Distanced, serious tone

```
To exit from the database program without loss of updates, the
Safe Quit button must be selected.
```

Warmer, friendlier tone

```
To leave the database program without losing your updates, se-
lect the Safe Quit button.
```

Nosy, intrusive tone

```
If you're worried about losing the updates you worked so hard
to make, just relax and select the Safe Quit button.
```

Many computer books are needlessly distanced and serious. They read as
if they were generated by a computer instead of a human writer. Nothing is
wrong with a little warmth and friendliness as long as it doesn't intrude into

---

Locate the small rectangular switch on the upper right of your system unit. The switch is
about ½″ wide and ¾″ long.

To the right of the switch are two embossed symbols, a circle about ½″ in diameter and, directly above it, a vertical line about ¼″ long. The circle represents the Off position, while
the vertical line represents the On position.

Now, note that the end of the switch is even with the circle. With your thumb or finger,
firmly press the switch upwards so that the end of the switch is even with the straight line.

When you see a small amber rectangle to the left of the switch light up and when you hear
a humming sound, you will realize that your system unit is receiving power.

Remember, the embossed circle means Off and the straight line means On.

Now let's try turning on the system unit.

Figure 5.6 One-up error in tone.

Unlock and remove the cover from your system unit. Remove any installed adapters from the expansion slots, saving them for reinstallation later.

When the ZM1 socket on the system board becomes visible, insert the math coprocessor card into the socket with the notch toward the rear, being careful about static electricity.

In addition, take care not to damage either the system board or the math coprocessor card.

Reinstall the adapters you removed earlier and simply replace the cover.

You are now ready to use the Starter Diskette to configure the system for your new math coprocessor.

Figure 5.7 One-down error in tone.

the reader's feelings. You can achieve this touch almost automatically if you write in second person and in the middle style.

As a writer, you should feel confident and knowledgeable about the product, and should convey that confidence and knowledge to the customer. However, two common errors in tone can make computer information less effective than it should be. Inexperienced writers can fall into either of them, the *one-up* or the *one-down* errors, as illustrated in Figs. 5.6 and 5.7.

One-up writing reveals that the writer feels superior to the reader. In Fig. 5.6, the writer shows a condescending attitude toward the reader, revealed by the use of *now, remember*, and the first-person plural. In fact, the use of so many words for such a simple action shows the writer's lack of respect for the reader's intelligence. Writers of such material are guilty not only of the one-up error in tone but also of wordiness. You can replace this entire passage with a simple drawing containing labels for the various parts of the system unit.

One-down writing reveals that the writer both feels inferior and assumes that the reader has great technical knowledge. Instead of questioning the logic and completeness of his or her writing, the writer takes the easy way out and hopes that the reader can figure everything out. In Fig. 5.7, the writer shows too little knowledge of the product and too much reverence for the reader's technical ability. How do you unlock and remove the cover? How do you remove the adapters? How does the ZM1 socket become visible? How do you insert the math coprocessor? What are the dangers of static electricity and how should you be careful? This passage needs a lot more explanation and a couple of good illustrations to convey its point. Writers of such material are guilty of both the one-down error in tone and of writing in a telegraphic style that needs to be fleshed out with more detailed information.

Diagnosing usability problems

Spotting missing information might be easier for you than spotting usability problems. Unusable information can have a variety of characteristics and causes, such as the following:

- It might be written inconsistently, sometimes getting too technical, sometimes too elementary. Even in a book with several audiences to satisfy, you should keep the writing at the same level of complexity throughout.

- It might match the technical spec but not match the code. Sometimes designs change but the spec is not updated. Also, programmers might find a different way to code the program than the one outlined in the spec. You must stay abreast of problems like these by keeping in constant contact with the designers and programmers.

- It might contain sentences or paragraphs that are too long and complicated for most customers to read and understand quickly. Provide the clearest possible language so that customers don't have to spend any time deciphering it.

- It might contain passages of text that would be more usable as tables, lists, or pictures. Occasionally, the reverse might be the problem.

- It might not contain enough breaks and divisions in the text. Everyone tires of reading page after page of unrelieved text. Your book is much more usable if you include headings of various levels.

- It might not contain enough examples for the customer to move from theory to action. Nothing makes a book more usable than clear, real-life examples that customers can either copy directly or use with a few modifications.

- It might contain such phrases as "The user must take the following steps . . ." or "The programmer uses this command to . . .". The reader might feel that you're addressing someone else and might not realize that you're writing directly to him or her. These readers might wonder who that user or programmer is. Write in second person, wherever possible, to make the book more immediate, direct, and usable. Don't overuse the word *you*, since some readers don't like it, but do write in the imperative mood with *you* understood as the subject, as in "Select Shutdown from the menu before you turn off the computer."

Editing Your Writing

All writing needs to be edited, even the wisdom of a genius. A good, objective edit can improve a piece of writing dramatically.

Two strategies for editing are having someone else do it or doing it yourself. The first is certainly preferable, but the second can also accomplish a lot.

Having your writing edited

Many errors not covered in this chapter can detract from your book, but you can only do so much alone. Once you're satisfied that the book is about as correct as you can make it, you should send it to the editor for the final touches.

Many writers are dismayed at the number of corrections the editor makes. However, you should take a positive attitude toward editing comments. An error the editor finds, and the writer corrects, is an error the customer won't find. Editors catch many mistakes you writers don't see not only because they look at the writing objectively, but also because they read a book five or six times, looking for different kinds of mistakes each time. Also, an editor might read all the books in a product library and be in a position to see things you haven't thought of because you were concentrating on your own book.

A good edit catches such things as the following:

- Trademarks that need to be acknowledged
- Ineffectively organized paragraphs
- Misuse of acronyms and abbreviations
- Incorrect references to other books in the library
- Inconsistent style and terminology in comparison with the rest of the library
- Front matter or back matter that doesn't fit in with other books in the library
- Indexing errors of various kinds
- Mistakes in highlighting and emphasis, such as using boldface where italics are required
- Incorrect layout for the title page, table of contents, or chapter headings
- Information that should go into a different book in the library
- Gaps in your book that could be filled by including information from other books in the library
- Redundant information contained in several books in the library
- Bad page breaks that leave a heading at the bottom of one page and the information it introduces on the top of the next page
- Places where artwork can replace or enhance the text
- Sections of text that need additional heads to break them into more manageable units
- Lapses into technical jargon that customers won't be familiar with
- Use of disallowed terms, such as *fatal error*

Having your book edited with the kind of care and attention it deserves can cost a lot, but it's money well spent. If your editing is done in house, these costs might be hidden as part of the normal cost of producing books. If you contract editing out to a vendor, you might be surprised at the size of the bill, which might run to several dollars per page. But there's no substitute for a good technical edit. If you're ever in doubt about the value of editing, just remember that the next person to see the book after the editor is a customer, at least an internal customer who reviews or tests the book for technical accuracy and completeness. Any customer should have the best possible book to work with.

Doing your own editing

If you're acting as your own editor, you want to take a systematic approach to catching problems and making appropriate corrections. While most edits fall into one of three basic categories (organization, content, copy), few writers are able to edit for all three categories in one pass. It is to your advantage to make several editing passes through your book, looking each time for a different set of items.

Organization edit.   As you check for organization, look at the table of contents to make sure the topic arrangement is logical. Check to see that topics of equal importance have headings of equal weight and that you can see, from the table of contents and the headings in the text, the relationships among topics. Check also to see that all appropriate parts, such as copyright notice, table of illustrations, preface, and so on, are present.

Content edit.   When you check your book's content, read to verify whether it accomplishes the purpose you've stated in the preface. The text should flow logically from one topic to the next, and each paragraph and sentence should support a topic or subtopic that contributes to the reader's understanding. Focus on logical divisions, transitions, development of examples, completeness of information, and coherence.

Copy edit.   When you do a copy edit, you examine the writing quality throughout the book; you also examine tables and figures to make certain that they are appropriate and executed properly. During the copy edit, check for grammatical correctness, conciseness, appropriate diction, and point of view. The following listings provide details about some of the items to watch for.

Editing points to verify

One way of systematically examining your book is to follow a detailed list of questions or checkpoints such as this:

- Verify that all appropriate components are in place.
  - ~ Title page
  - ~ Legal/warranty statements
  - ~ Copyright notice
  - ~ Preface
  - ~ Table of contents
  - ~ Table of illustrations
  - ~ Body/chapters
  - ~ Appendices
  - ~ Bibliography
  - ~ Glossary
  - ~ Index
- Make sure that headings are appropriate and parallel.
  - ~ Chapter titles and titles of other components such as the preface, table of contents, and appendices should all be of the same level.
  - ~ The table of contents should list only enough headings to show general organization of the book. That is, list only first-, second-, and perhaps third-level headings. A chapter table of contents, if you have one, should list every heading in the chapter.
- Check all graphics in the book.
  - ~ All graphics should support or enhance surrounding content, with the purpose of helping readers understand the discussion.
  - ~ All figures and tables should be constructed properly, numbered correctly, and positioned appropriately in relation to the text.
  - ~ All figures and tables should be introduced before they appear.
  - ~ Graphics should be appropriate in degree of difficulty for the target audience of your book.
- Examine the text throughout the book.
  - ~ Content should be appropriate for your targeted reading audience.
  - ~ Content should relate to performing tasks and should provide enough information to enable readers to do those tasks.
  - ~ Each chapter and each section within a chapter should logically develop from previous ones.
  - ~ No contradictory statements should appear within the text.
  - ~ Terms that might be unfamiliar to readers should be defined when they first appear in the book and also included in a glossary.

~ Tone should be appropriate for the readers and for the content you are presenting.

- Problems such as those identified earlier in this chapter should be identified and resolved.
  - ~ Inconsistent point of view
  - ~ Shifts of attention
  - ~ Passive voice
  - ~ Wordiness
  - ~ Inconsistent terminology
  - ~ Faulty parallelism
  - ~ Dangling modifiers
  - ~ Ending a sentence with a preposition (if you're using the formal style)
  - ~ Provincial and sexist language
  - ~ Others such as subject-verb agreement, proper pronoun-antecedent agreement, spelling, punctuation, and transitions
- Page breaks should be appropriate.
- Highlighting (such as boldface and italics) should be appropriate and used only when necessary.

6

Presenting the Information

After you find, understand, organize, and write information for your book, the next step is to plan which components a particular book will include.

A typical book consists of information divided into front matter, the body, and back matter. Each of the three major sections might have several components. The front matter might include the following:

- Title page
- Legal/warranty statements
- Copyright information
- Preface
- Table of contents
- Table of illustrations

Each of the chapters or parts that make up the body of the book might include the following:

- Introduction
- Explanations
- Steps and procedures
- Artwork and examples
- Conclusion

The back matter might include the following:

- Appendix(ces)
- Glossary
- Bibliography
- Index

While not every book contains all of these elements, many contain most of them. Some of the elements are optional, depending upon your needs.

Front Matter

Every book must have *front matter*—those items preceding the body of the text or the main part of the book—although the mix of components varies from one book to another. Most publications contain at least a title page, legal or warranty statements, copyright information, and a table of contents.

You'll want to follow standard publishing conventions by using those items found in most books, but you need not feel restricted only to those items. You might also include as part of the front matter one or more of these items:

- Glossary of key terms
- List of abbreviations and symbols
- Table of illustrations, figures, or tables

This section shows examples of typical front matter components. As you inspect various publications, you'll find different formats and methods of presentation for these items. Feel free to devise whatever formats you find attractive, but you should be certain that they are compatible with the overall design and layout of your book.

Title page

The title page is different from the cover that goes on the outside of the book, although the two often look very similar and might contain virtually the same information.

A good title page contains the name of the publication, the name of the software or hardware the book is about, and the name of the publisher (you or your organization). Before your book goes out to customers, it needs additional information on the title page. While it's still an internal book in the development and review stages, it should include the items mentioned above, plus some or all of the following:

- Internal reference numbers
- Security classification

- Date of publication

- Name, telephone number, and electronic address of the individual responsible for the book

Legal/warranty statements

Because of the intricacies of licensing agreements and warranty statements, you should use current statements available from your legal department or consult an attorney for the appropriate information. These statements must be carefully worded to identify clearly the rights and obligations of the organization and the buyer of the product and book.

Licensing agreements often appear on the outside of the slipcase or notebook containing software and books, but they can sometimes appear inside the front cover of a book. Warranty information usually appears on the inside front cover.

Copyright information

Standard copyright notices usually appear on the back of the title page and might also include edition or revision notices, warranties, if any, and a legal disclaimer, protecting you or your organization from being held liable in case of loss of data, damage to other software, and so on.

You should consult an attorney for the proper wording for this section. In many large companies, the copyright and legal/warranty information for each product library is written by staff attorneys and provided to writers in a file they can embed in their books.

Some copyright pages include acknowledgments and information about trademarked products to which you refer in your book. Other books with too many trademarked products to list on the copyright pages put complete trademark listings immediately after the preface.

You'll want to make sure that attorneys review these trademarks; improper handling of the trademarks might have legal ramifications. Remember that trademarks are the legal property of their owner; as a result, legal restrictions govern the use, placement, and presentation of those trademarks. See Fig. 6.1 for an example of copyright information.

Preface

A preface (sometimes called *About This Book* or something similar) orients the reader to the organization, contents, treatment, approach and purpose of a publication, and might advise the reader on how to read and use it. Since many topics are possible, the preface can become too long. Unfortunately, surveys show that few people really read the preface, so it should be short and easy to read.

APPLE COMPUTER, INC.

This manual and the software described in it are copyrighted, with all rights reserved. Under the copyright laws, this manual or the software may not be copied, in whole or part, without written consent of Apple, except in the normal use of the software or to make a backup copy of the software. The same proprietary and copyright notices must be affixed to any permitted copies as were affixed to the original. This exception does not allow copies to be made for others, whether or not sold, but all of the material purchased (with all backup copies) may be sold, given, or loaned to another person. Under the law, copying includes translating into another language or format.

You may use the software on any computer owned by you, but extra copies cannot be made for this purpose.

© Apple Computer, Inc., 1987
20525 Mariani Ave.
Cupertino, California 95014
(408) 996-1010

Apple, the Apple logo, ImageWriter, LaserWriter, and MacPaint are registered trademarks of Apple Computer, Inc.

HyperCard, HyperTalk, Macintosh, MultiFinder, and Stackware are trademarks of Apple Computer, Inc.

Adobe Illustrator and POSTSCRIPT are trademarks of Adobe Systems Incorporated.

CompuServe is a registered trademark of CompuServe, Inc.

GEnie is a trademark of General Electric Information Services Company, USA.

Microsoft is a registered trademark of Microsoft Corporation.

ITC Avant Garde Gothic, ITC Garamond, and ITC Zapf Dingbats are registered trademarks of International Typeface Corporation.

Simultaneously published in the United States and Canada.

Figure 6.1 Example of copyright information. Reproduced with permission of Apple Computer, Inc.

Many prefaces cover some or all of these points:

- The book's purpose
- The audience's identity
- The book's main subject
- The level of knowledge the reader is expected to have
- An indication of how the book is to be used
- Tasks the reader needs to perform before going further
- A list of prerequisite publications or recommended and required reading
- Safety concerns or warnings

For easy reference, these topics should be identified by headings. The preface usually appears on the page following the copyright information. See Fig. 6.2 for representative topics covered in prefaces.

Table of contents

Tables of contents come in several forms. Most usually show at least the major headings in a publication. Some authors show every single heading, thus providing a long, very detailed table of contents. Still others provide a brief master contents page, with a detailed chapter outline, sometimes called a partial table of contents, preceding each chapter.

No single formula works for every situation. The best table of contents is one that provides a level of detail good enough to help the reader locate specific chapters and headings within those chapters as quickly as possible.

Many electronic publishing systems and word processing programs generate tables of contents automatically. You'll need to decide how many headings to show and whether to include leader dots between the headings and the page numbers. See Fig. 6.3 for an example of a table of contents with leader dots.

Without the leader dots, the page numbers might be a little harder to locate in a long table of contents. See Fig. 6.4 for an example of a table of contents without leader dots.

Table of illustrations

Many books have a table (similar to a table of contents) that lists illustrations for easy reference. Illustrations usually are divided into two categories: figures and tables. A table is a columnar listing of numbers or similar information. All other types of art are considered to be figures.

PREFACE (or) ABOUT THIS BOOK

Who Should Read This Book
    Part 1. Site Planning and Preparation (description)
    Part 2. Software Planning
    Part 3. Communications Planning

How This Guide Is Organized

Some Conventions Used in This Guide

What You Need to Use This Product

Prerequisite Publications

On-Line Help and User Groups

Figure 6.2 Representative topics covered in prefaces. Reprinted by permission from *IBM Operating System / 2 Version 1.2 Information and Planning Guide* ©1989 by International Business Machines Corporation.

Figure 6.3 Table of contents with leader dots .

Depending on the types of illustrations in your book, you might include only a table of figures, only a table of tables, or a table of illustrations divided into figures and tables.

Figures and tables are identified by separate captions, and each usually is numbered within its own subset, as in Figure 1, Figure 2 and Table I, Table II. Traditional numbering conventions dictate that figures are numbered with Arabic numerals, while tables are numbered with either Roman or Arabic numerals; many publishers today use Arabic numerals for both. You can number illustrations consecutively as they appear in your book, as in *Figure 1, Figure 2* or you can number them consecutively within chapters, *Figure 1-1* and *Figure 1-2* in the first chapter, *Figure 2-1* and *Figure 2-2* in the second. See Fig. 6.5 for an example.

Glossary of key terms

If the book contains key terms with which most of your readers are probably unfamiliar, you might want to include them in the front matter. Try to keep the list as short as possible to facilitate understanding and retention.

An alternative to including a glossary in the front matter is to identify terms in the text that might be unfamiliar to your audience. You can put the terms in boldface or identify them with an asterisk. Readers can then turn to a glossary in the back matter to learn more about those terms.

List of abbreviations and symbols

Front matter sometimes contains lists of abbreviations and acronyms used throughout the text. Such listings, like the glossary of key terms, are designed to help readers understand important information from the beginning.

Listings of symbols, icons, terms, and expressions used by the product might be defined here, especially when those items are critical to the reader's success in using the book or program. For a book with few abbreviations and acronyms, you don't need a separate list, but you should spell them out the first time you use them in a chapter, as in *Systems Network Architecture (SNA)* or *10 megabytes (Mb)*.

Body

As you saw in Chapter 4, different organizational plans enhance the readers' abilities to learn from your book and to extract useful information from it. To a great extent, the body of your book is governed by the overall organizational plan you develop for the type of information you're presenting—a tutorial, a user's guide, a reference book, on-line information, or others.

The first chapter in most books serves as an overview chapter, providing readers with a solid introduction. A general information book, for instance, typically contains in the first chapter a discussion of the product, its capabilities and functions, its abilities to connect to and function with other products, and other useful information.

In a typical first chapter of many other books, the overview and introduction are much shorter. In a programmer's reference, for instance, the introduction might consist of one or two sentences. In a user's guide, one or two paragraphs might serve as the introduction to the first chapter.

Many (but not all) introductions provide information about the purpose

Figure 6.4 Table of contents without leader dots .

Figure 6.5 Partial listing of figures and tables.

of the chapter or book and some background so readers can find reference points and understand where the book is directing them. However, some of this information might appear in the preface, and you don't need to repeat the same information.

Parts or chapters?

Some books are neatly focused on one uncomplicated theme, but others are more complicated. While you might be able to present six or eight chapters without providing a larger organizational framework, sometimes you need to help orient the reader further.

To better organize your book and help the reader understand the book's framework, you might consider dividing the book into two or more parts or large units. Each part might contain several chapters focusing on related aspects such as installing and customizing, troubleshooting, connecting to peripherals, and other topics.

Parts containing chapters are identified in the table of contents (Part One, Part Two), with chapter divisions and titles listed underneath. See Fig. 6.6 for an example of parts and chapters in a table of contents.

Chapter structures

To bring uniformity and cohesion to your book, structure all the chapters the same way. That is, make sure that readers encounter similar types of information, examples, and tutorial exercises in the same general sequence, regardless of which chapters they read.

For example, in a user's guide, you might structure the chapters as follows:

- Objectives (what readers can expect to learn)
- Overview of specific tasks
- Detailed instructions for performing tasks
- Tutorial exercise for readers to perform
- Summary of functions and steps

In addition to structural similarities, book chapters should have similar layouts and overall appearances. Again, readers should find no real surprises in terms of the way most pages look or in the sequence in which common chapter elements are presented.

Examples and illustrations

Concrete examples and illustrations often help readers understand concepts and ideas, especially in software publications. All examples should be as simple as possible, and be logically developed.

Always use realistic examples that might occur in likely situations. The example can be a description of what happens when you enter a command, or it can be presented as a detailed analogy, such as *A database is similar to a gigantic series of mailboxes in a post office, where anyone with the right authority can add entries by using the address on the mailbox.*

Some examples are only one or two lines long, while others might run for several pages. Weigh the complexity of the concept and the options you have for explaining that concept to a variety of readers.

```
Part One.   Installing the XYZ Program
      Chapter  1.   Preparing to Install
      Chapter  2.   Deciding which Features to Install
      Chapter  3.   Installing the Features

Part Two.   Configuring the XYZ Program
      Chapter  4.   Preparing for Host Connections
      Chapter  5.   Configuring for Host A
      Chapter  6.   Configuring for Host B
      Chapter  7.   Configuring for Host C

Part Three.   Using the XYZ Program
      Chapter  8.   Accessing the Host
      Chapter  9.   Using Electronic Mail
      Chapter 10.   Transferring Files

Part Four.   Using Error Recovery Information
      Chapter 11.   Problems with the Host
      Chapter 12.   Problems with the Personal Computer
```

Figure 6.6 Parts and chapters in a table of contents.

> Appendix A. Using the Tutorial Program for Best Results
> Appendix B. Troubleshooting Problems

Figure 6.7 Examples of appendix titles.

A useful piece of artwork can greatly simplify and explain a concept by showing relationships, processes, alternative procedures, and so on.

Back Matter

The most common elements considered to be back matter are appendixes, a glossary, a bibliography (or list of references), and an index.

These items usually serve as references—sources for locating useful information if the reader needs to turn here. Readers in a hurry, for example, might look up a term in the index before reading anything else.

Certainly some readers will use your book and never turn to the back matter. Nevertheless, this information must be included if your book is to meet the needs of those readers requiring the back matter information.

Appendixes

Use appendixes (or *appendices*) sparingly. Sometimes you'll find a book with as many as 15 appendixes. A good guideline to follow is to make chapters contain the information that is essential to readers, and make appendixes contain information that is peripheral to the chapters but beneficial to readers.

Give each appendix an alphabetic designation and a clear title, as the example in Fig. 6.7 shows.

Begin each appendix on a right-hand page, and number appendix pages consecutively as in the rest of the book (for example, *A-1, A-2, B-1, B-2* if pages are numbered according to chapters).

Glossary

Your readers appreciate a glossary defining terms with which they are unfamiliar. You should remember to define those terms when they are first used in the text, but a good glossary is a genuine help to most readers. One of your tasks during the writing of the book is to select terms and definitions on which you, the engineers, and the programmers can all agree. Here are some guidelines for framing your definitions:

■ Make sure that your terms are defined at a level appropriate for your target audience. That is, if your audience is not very technically oriented, you should define terms in simple, understandable language.

- Do not use the term being defined in the language you provide to define that term. For example, avoid something like "**reproduction** The process by which publications are reproduced by photographic and printing processes."

- If you produce several books within a product family, make sure that terms are used consistently from book to book and within each book; also, make sure that they are defined the same in the glossaries.

- Include in your index references to terms defined in the text or the glossary. For terms defined in both places, refer only to the one in the text.

See Fig. 6.8 for examples of glossary entries in a typical format. Terms are highlighted in boldface.

A bibliography is important especially when other books are available to readers that might help them increase their understanding of your information. Often, these are books in an extended product library or books for similar or related products.

Use traditional formats for entries in the bibliography—listing author or publisher first, the book title, and publishing data, including date of publication. Usually, you want the items listed in a bibliography to be the latest editions available. See Fig. 6.9 for an example of typical entries in a bibliography.

A bibliography is different from the list of prerequisite publications that some writers place in the preface. Prerequisite publications are usually other books in the same product library—related publications that readers are expected to have on hand and might need to consult. A bibliography, on the other hand, lists books that readers might have to make an effort to find in a bookstore or a public library.

---

serial transmission. Transmitting each bit of a data character separately over the same electrical path.

server. On a network, the computer that contains the data to be accessed.

session. A logical connection that enables two network addressable units to communicate with each other.

session-level pacing. A flow control technique that permits a receiving half-session to control the data transfer rate (the rate at which it receives request units). It is used to prevent overloading a receiver with unprocessed requests when the sender can generate requests faster than the receiver can process them.

Figure 6.8 Sample glossary entries. Reprinted by permission from *IBM RT Personal Computer Planning Guide* © 1987 by International Business Machines Corporation.

Books

A significant number of books have been written about OS/2 to help both developer and user to better understand and utilize the powerful features of the system. Thanks to Robert Shook, IBM, Austin, Texas for his help in creating this list. The following is a selected list of those books:

Aaron, Bud. *OS/2 Presentation Manager Developer's Guide*. TAB Books, 1989. 480p.

Aaron, Bud. *OS/2 Presentation Manager User's Guide*. TAB Books, 1989. 380p.

Alonso, Robert. *OS/2 Reference Guide*. Scott, Foresman, forthcoming.

Baker, David C.; Banning, William I.; Myre, William W. *Creating Applications with the IBM OS/2 Database Manager*. Addison-Wesley, 1989. 320p.

Beam, J. Emmett. *Illustrated OS/2*. Illustrated series. Wordware Publications, 1988. 264p.

Borland, Russell. *Running OS/2*. Microsoft Press, forthcoming.

Busch, David. *Supercharging OS/2 Batch Files & Utilities*. Addison-Wesley, 1988. 304p.

Figure 6.9 Typical bibliographical entries.

Index

The most common and most useful retrieval tool is the index. A well-constructed index leads your readers directly to the information they need.

Many readers, searching for a specific bit of information, consult only the indexes of various books until they find the desired topic (or give up in frustration). Thus, it is essential that your index be as complete as possible. Every topic must be indexed, usually in several ways. Preparing an index involves the following steps.

Decide what should be indexed. Every topic—every separate idea or fact—in your book should be indexed. Figures and tables also illustrate topics, so they should be indexed. Remember that a topic can be a narrow, specific piece of information such as *data transfer rate* or *STRING parameter*, or a broad piece of information, such as *file management*.

Spelling, capitalization, and use of highlighting (boldface, italics, underlining) in the index should reflect exactly the usage in the text.

The same principles of audience analysis used to design your book apply when you select topics for indexing. Try to anticipate the different ways readers might approach each topic, and provide an index path for each approach. Remember that some readers are expert in some topics; others are novices in some or all topics. Experts tend to use more technical and specific language, while novices might remember only more general terms.

Determine the structure of each index entry. Index entries usually appear in two-column layouts, often in a type size two points smaller than the text type (to save space). Often index entries have one or two (rarely three) subentries. Subentries are also alphabetized by level. In alphabetizing subentries, skip articles, prepositions, and other unimportant words.

A *primary* entry consists of a topic heading and at least one page reference. A primary entry should always contain a noun, and can contain modifiers of the noun, for example:

```
Edit Release subroutine, 223
```

A *secondary* entry consists of a subject and a subheading. The subheading usually contains modifiers (or subsets) of the subject heading. In relating a subheading to a subject heading, always be careful to maintain a logical relationship between the two. The subheading must have at least one page reference; the subject heading might or might not have page references. The following examples show secondary index entries:

```
Edit Relate subroutine, 223-226, 245, 289
   data areas used by, 228, 236
Symbol
   coding of, for printer, 88, 92
   use of, in SELECT command, 171
   for wild card, 56-58
```

A *tertiary* entry consists of a subject and two levels of subheadings. The greater number of subheadings requires greater care to assure that logical relationships are maintained among the levels. The following examples show primary, secondary, and tertiary index levels:

```
Edit Release subroutine, 223-226 (primary entry)
Entry-sequenced data set (ESDS)
   alternate index on, 24, 26 (secondary entry)
   record length formulas
     nonunique key, 342 (tertiary entry)
     unique key, 343 (tertiary entry)
   SELECT statement syntax, 330 (secondary entry)
Error handling, 203-206 (primary entry)
```

Your word or text processing system might have an indexing facility, so check your instructions for the precise methods for identifying primary, secondary, and tertiary entries. Your system might use somewhat different terminology, but the overall structure of the final index is probably very similar.

Keep track of each topic and its associated page number. An automatic indexing system keeps track of entries and their page numbers automatically, usually based on tags that you enter throughout the text. If you must prepare your index manually, you cannot really begin until you have the page proofs of your book (so you'll have final page numbers). The traditional way to prepare an index is to use an index card for each topic. As you record each topic and subtopic, along with the appropriate page number, you construct a database which you can alphabetize. You can also consolidate entries and eliminate duplications. And you'll find that some topics logically become primary, secondary, or tertiary entries.

Many potential problem areas in indexes can be taken care of with *see* and *see also* cross-references, which efficiently show alternate pathways to information in your index. Cross-references enable readers to find information even if they do not remember specific terminology. *See* references direct readers to other terms of similar or identical meaning. The example below directs readers more familiar with end-of-file terminology to the entry, *end-of-data*, that applies to the system described by the book. Note that a period separates the index entry from the *see* reference:

```
end of file. See end of data
```

Also list acronyms in the index with a *see* cross-reference to the spelled-out term:

```
CA. See control area
```

The *see also* cross-reference directs readers from a general subject to specific subjects in the index. For example, a reader looking up the word *restart* might find the following:

```
restart. See also checkpoint routine, 17, 26, 99
```

When using *see* and *see also* references, be extremely careful to avoid circular or nonexistent cross-references. Perhaps the most maddening error an indexer can make is to have a circular cross-reference in an index. For example, during preparation and consolidation of index entries, it is possible to emerge with the following loop:

```
control area. See control block.
control block. See control interval.
control interval. See control area.
```

During the final edit, make sure every *see* and *see also* reference has a genuine target and is not circular.

When constructing indexes, you must decide how to handle numbers. Some readers look for "80-byte line length" as a numerical entry, and others might look for "eighty-byte line length." Many systems let you decide how you want to handle numbers. In most cases, you'll want to use a *see* reference to include the other entry.

Most automatic indexing systems list symbols and special characters before or after the alphabetic listing. You can structure such entries in several ways. They can be entered in a separate listing of special characters:

```
#START, 34, 40-43, 203
```

They can be listed as if the special character does not exist:

```
standard file, 78
#START, 34, 40-43, 203
Starting point, 56
```

They can be entered in a separate listing, with a *see* reference to the main body of the index:

```
#END (See #END listed as END)
#START (See #START listed as START)
#TERM (See #TERM listed as TERM)
```

Put synonyms in parentheses, but also include a cross-reference to the term appearing first:

```
virtual disk (minidisk), 5, 11-16, 99
minidisk, see virtual disk
```

Ⓐ

adapters, communications 12-1
    Advanced IBM Personal Computer 3278/79
      Emulation Adapter 12-16
    IBM PC Network Adapter 12-17
    IBM Personal Computer AT Serial/Parallel
      Adapter 12-7
    IBM RT PC Baseband Adapter for use with
      Ethernet 12-18
    IBM RT PC Multiprotocol Adapter 12-13
    IBM RT PC 4-Port Asynchronous RS-422A
      Adapter 12-11
    IBM RT PC 5080 Attachment Adapter 12-22
    IBM S/370 Host Interface Adapter 12-21
    IBM Token-Ring Network RT PC
      Adapter 12-19
    6150 Native Serial Ports 12-6
Advanced IBM Personal Computer 3278/79
  Emulation Adapter 12-16
airflow 6-4
AIX Operating System 11-4
    Asynchronous Terminal Emulation 11-4
    Base PC Network Services 11-6

Figure 6.10 Sample index entries.

Edit and revise the index.   The only way to be sure that your index is complete and accurate is by thorough editing after the entries are identified and alphabetized. This task is time-consuming, but essential.

Some indexing programs have a facility that prints the index entries beside the topic to which they refer, enabling you to check that the entry matches the topic, and that every topic has at least one index entry. See Fig. 6.10 for sample index entries.

The checklist in Table 6.1 can help you thoroughly check your index, whether you generate it manually or automatically.

TABLE 6.1. Checklist for Generating Indexes

Did you	No	Yes
Check the overall length of your index? As a rule, you should have one column of index entries for each 10 pages of text. Adjust this guideline if your book has many sample programs, large tables, charts, or illustrations, which usually require only a few index entries. Check to see that your index is neither too general (much too short) nor too specific (much too long).		
Make sure that every *see* and *see also* reference has a genuine target?		
Make sure that every *see* reference results in a synonym after the target term?		
Review the punctuation of each entry?		
Make sure that all topics, samples programs, figures, tables, charts, and illustrations are indexed?		
Verify that page references are accurate? Check a sample of items from each column.		

7

Planning Layout

Layout is the physical design of the book, including the arrangement of the text on the page, the page number, headers and footers, the style and size of the typeface, the cover of the book, and the quality of the paper and cover stock.

Who Does the Design Work?

If you work in a large organization, you might not need to be concerned with design work and layout; whoever sets up the library design for the books in your product library also does the packaging design work, or arranges to have it done. Or your employer might have a standard library and book format and a set of generally accepted practices that you plan to follow. If the design is already in place, you probably have a design guide to follow, and perhaps special book profiles on your computer system that conform to the specifications in the design guide.

If you are responsible for some or all of the design work, however, then you have two basic options:

- Do the design work yourself.
- Employ a professional designer.

If you must do the work yourself, the advantage is that you have greater control over the final product. The disadvantage, of course, is that doing the design work requires time you might otherwise spend writing. In addition, you might not have much knowledge about design and those questions that must be considered in preparing effective book packaging.

Doing the design work yourself

A rushed schedule, a limited number of prospective readers, or a limited budget might mean that you must act as the designer for your book. If you have no prescribed format to follow, where do you begin?

With no specifications to study, begin by surveying the documentation published by other organizations to see what you find useful and attractive. While you don't want to copy the work of others, certainly you can pick up tips and techniques used successfully by other writers and designers. Make decisions about the elements listed in the section "Principles of design" on page 104.

The advantages that accrue from working with others as a team (see Chapter 1) also apply to the design effort. By dividing responsibilities for design work into categories such as desktop publishing, graphics, packaging, and printing, you can share the workload and often produce a more effective design. You might find that you can produce some or all of the design elements internally. In any case, you must identify the design elements you or members of your team can produce and those for which you must seek help.

Finding and choosing a designer

If you decide to hire a designer, the following are recommended procedures for finding someone with appropriate expertise:

Locate the best individual or firm for your needs. You can locate designers through reference books in your local library (such as *Graphics Design USA*, *American Showcase*, *Art Directors' Index to Illustration*, and *Graphics and Design*). Reputable printers often can refer you to expert designers who have done projects similar to yours. Check your telephone directory or talk with book publishers in your area for suggestions.

You should choose a designer who has handled projects similar to yours—someone who can understand technical information, who has ideas for solving presentation or packaging problems, and who demonstrates a knowledge of color, form, typography, and visuals. And finally, it should be someone who is cost-conscious and will produce the best possible design for the amount of money you can spend.

Review design portfolios. A designer's portfolio is the way he or she secures new clients, and is also a good indication of the designer's best work. Check the portfolio for examples similar to the type of product you want to produce.

Be conscious of the various images you see represented in the portfolio. A designer who has worked mostly on advertising might not be what you need: one who has never produced anything longer than a brochure almost certainly is not what you want.

Investigate the designer's skills.   You want a designer with the expertise to produce top-quality illustrations and integrate those into the text. You can tell from a brief conversation whether the designer seems able to understand the rudiments of your particular subject matter enough to produce an effective design.

Solicit bids or estimates from designers.   It's only prudent to solicit estimates from at least two or three designers, as fees and production costs vary considerably. To receive those bids or estimates, you'll need to convey some detailed information to the designer:

- A precise description of the scope of work you want the designer to do, being as specific as possible—do you want just a logo and cover design? Or do you want page layouts, retrievability aids, and some "instructional" design as well?
- Appropriate information as needed on estimated number of pages, page size and measurements, use of color, components such as front matter and back matter, estimated number and type of illustrations, and types of binding
- Schedules for design, production, and printing
- Quantities wanted and other requirements such as shrink-wrapping and packing in cartons
- A copy of the manuscript, including rough art, if it exists at the time of the discussion
- Budget restrictions

Review bids and select a designer.   As with any other type of project, you'll want to weigh a variety of factors when reviewing bids or estimates. These include the designer's past performance (from wherever you can get that information) and your perceptions of work quality. You also have to assess how confident you are of schedules being met, how the designer's creativity and problem-solving skills strike you, and how easily you think you can work with the designer.

After you have talked with designers, reviewed portfolios, evaluated their skills, and reviewed bids, you should be able to decide which designer you will use. You probably want to draw up a contract for work to be performed, with strict specifications about the designer being able to meet deadlines.

The importance of good design

Effective design of page layout, which includes selecting appropriate typography and integrating useful graphics, is very important in at least two

ways: as an aid in marketing the product, and to increase the usefulness of
the information you've written.

Marketing specialists sometimes use good documentation as a marketing
tool. In today's competitive environment, when hardware and software of-
ferings from different manufacturers are often quite similar, effective documentation might be the added bonus that clinches a sale. Therefore,
physical design and appearance are important.

Effective physical design also is important to the reader. Readers gain the
most from information that is:

- Easy to use
- Attractive and easy to read
- Well-organized and consistently presented
- Complete and accurate

If you provide a book that meets their expectations, readers appreciate
your good planning, and you make their jobs easier and more productive.

With attention to the effective presentation of even very complicated and
highly technical information, you should be able to make readers feel more
comfortable as they use the information you have provided. The more you
understand about presenting that information through good page design
and graphics, the better.

Principles of Design

Remember that good design is transparent to the reader. If good design is in
place, the reader can focus on the content and on the task at hand—learning, using, understanding, or retrieving information—basically unaware of
the design elements.

Depending on the design elements required in your organization, here
are several items to consider as you think about design:

- Library design
- Paper stock
- Page size
- Size and length of books
- Binding
- Slipcases, dust jackets, covers
- Page layout
  - ~ Grids
  - ~ Thumbnail layouts
  - ~ Line spacing and length

- ~ Column width and number
- ~ White space
- ~ Tracking devices
- ~ Text justification
- ~ Type styles and sizes
- ■ Use of color
- ■ Art and graphics
  - ~ Conceptual art
  - ~ Line art
  - ~ Tables and charts
  - ~ Display screens
  - ~ Keys and keyboards
  - ~ Menus
  - ~ Photographs
  - ~ Prompts and messages

These items are discussed in detail in this chapter.

Planning Page Layout

Page layout, which is the organization of various elements on the page to present a unified and attractive whole, immediately affects your readers' ability to understand the information you present. Good layout helps them recognize major points through useful headings and good organization. It also helps them visually isolate sections of information through the use of paragraphs, lists, pictures and diagrams, and white space.

The aesthetic balance that readers see on a page also affects how comfortable they are with the book. If the information is crowded together on the page, they'll find the layout is neither attractive nor conducive to easy understanding. Inconsistencies in page layout as they turn through a book are confusing and inhibit easy understanding. Some layouts ,however, also enhance usability through appropriate page size, running headers or footers, tabs, foldouts, rules, graphics, color, and good bindings.

The publishing system you use might already have page formats in place, or you might follow one commonly used in your organization. However, if you do have liberty to create your own page layouts or employ a designer to do so, take the time to look at hardware and software books you (or others) consider to be good. Look at the different page formats, and see if you can determine how those formats contribute to the readers' understanding of content and their ability to identify pieces of information and instructions.

Look for consistency in page layouts within chapters in the same book. You might find four basic layouts, for example, used to display certain types of information or for specific purposes.

Components of good page layout include the following:

- Grids
- Thumbnail sketches
- Rules
- Headers and footers
- Line length and spacing
- Justified margins
- White space

System-generated page layouts

Some word-processing programs and most desktop publishing systems have several page layouts available from which you can select. Your organization might specify which layouts you should use for your book. In such cases, you might find the existing layouts to be completely satisfactory. If they do not meet your needs, usually you are able to modify them until they do.

Layout based on grids

Grids are tools for designing effective page layouts by organizing content blocks in relation to the space they occupy on a page. They contribute significantly to the perception of quality in your reader's mind by enabling you to present an orderly, structured series of page formats. Most publications you see today, ranging from brochures and flyers to magazines and computer books, use page layouts based on a series of grids.

A grid consists of horizontal and vertical lines positioned in various patterns. Those patterns usually are based on combinations of one or more vertical columns and on one or more horizontal blocks.

The grid arrangements help you decide column width, number of columns, position of visuals, and position of headings.

By adhering to the layouts permitted by the grids you establish for your book, you can produce aesthetically pleasing layouts that enhance the overall design of individual pages as well as your entire book—and even a series of books in a library or product family.

Figure 7.1 shows several possible basic grid layouts, with plenty of white space to emphasize headings for quick reference and understanding. These grids are flexible enough to help you build many different page layouts; Fig. 7.2 provides an example of two pages produced from two different grids.

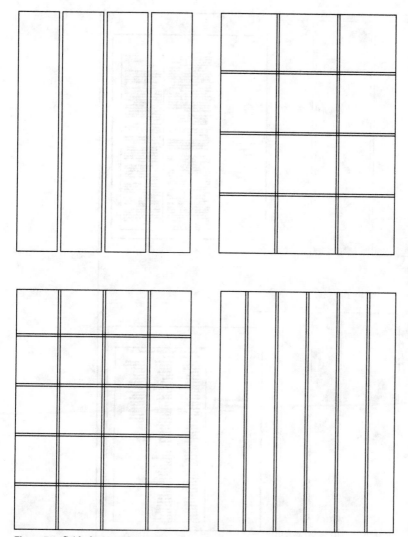

Figure 7.1 Grids for page layout.

Thumbnail sketches or layouts

Thumbnail layouts are useful because they help you separate yourself from concerns about text and graphics to focus on attractively organizing visual and typographical elements on the page. They can be produced on some desktop publishing systems and word-processing programs, or you can produce rough thumbnail sketches with a pencil and paper. Figure 7.3 is an example of a thumbnail sketch produced by a computer.

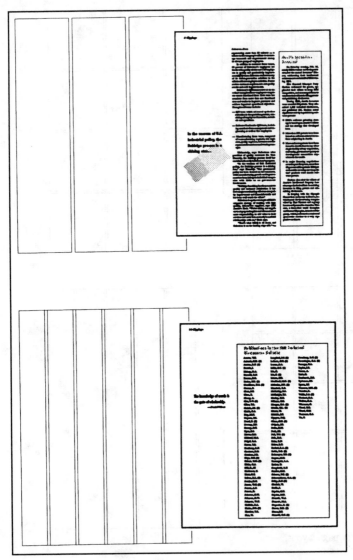

Figure 7.2 Two pages produced from grids.

Vertical and horizontal rules

A very common element on many page layouts is the use of *vertical* and *horizontal rules*—lines used to separate sections of the page from one another. For example, a very popular use of a rule is to identify a new heading or section by placing a rule immediately before the heading and extending it partially across the page.

Too many rules or rules that are too heavy impede, rather than enhance, the reader's comprehension. Typically, lightweight rules are better than medium and heavy ones for most purposes. The weight of the rules you select depends on the function you want those rules to play; the heavier the rule, the "louder" its impact. A heavy, dark rule tells the reader that what follows it or what is contained within a box drawn with it is very significant.

Running heads and running feet

Another component of page layout is deciding whether to include running heads and running feet. *Running heads* appear at the tops of most or all pages, and *running feet* at the bottom. Some books have both, and some have only a running head or a running foot.

What do you include in a running head or foot? While you might want to include the chapter number and title and page number, you have other options. Some books show the book title on the left-hand (even-numbered) page; some show the topic under discussion on a given page. Still others show identification data, such as document numbers, filenames, and dates.

Many authors set off heads and feet from the text by putting them in a slightly smaller or darker type; some separate headers and footers from the rest of the page with horizontal rules, usually running completely across the page.

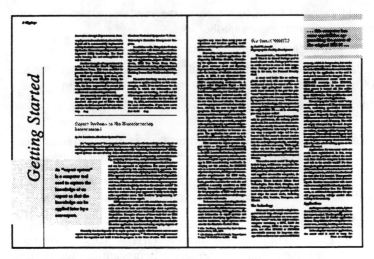

Figure 7.3 Example of thumbnail sketch.

Deciding on line spacing and length

Most authorities recommend an average line length of about 65 to 70 characters in printed materials in single-column format; they suggest 35 to 45 characters for two-column formats. These column widths are fairly standard in the publishing industry for easy reading and comprehension. That's not to say that you can't use either shorter or longer line lengths, but you should do so only for a good reason.

While most people might not be conscious of variations in line spacing, they subconsciously prefer double-spaced lines in typewritten manuscripts, but single-spacing on the printed page. Typically, spacing between lines is governed by *leading*. Leading is the distance from the baseline of one line of type to the baseline of the next.

Standard leading is 120% of the point size of the type. For example, 10-point type usually has 12-point leading to leave enough space between lines for easy reading. Leading can vary, depending on characteristics of certain type families and line length.

Some desktop publishing systems provide automatic leading, which automatically compensates for variations in type and line length.

Justified vs. unjustified margins

Authorities disagree on whether text that is *fully justified* (justified at both the left and right margins) or *ragged right* (unjustified at the right margin) is easier to read and to understand. As a result, you can select the form you prefer.

Some general practices, however, are related to justified or unjustified text:

- Ragged right margins seem to enable some readers, especially young ones, to read somewhat more rapidly.
- Most online information has ragged right margins.
- Full justification often is used in formal, glossy, and expensive publications in which neatness, formality, and symmetry are important.
- Full justification often (but not always) is used for three- or four-column layouts.
- Using ragged right margins is a cost-savings factor, since corrections can be made without having to reset a full paragraph (or more) of type.

The argument about which type of justification is better will continue. Examine both styles and make your decision during the design process.

Fully justified margins are attractive and tidy, as you can see by comparing Fig. 7.4 with Fig. 7.5, but since text with ragged right margins is thought to be easier to read, most online information is presented ragged right. Also, full justification can look strange if the particular word-processing

For successful capacity planning, it is necessar to anticipate the memory and fixed-disk requirements of a complete set of system and application components. The end-user scenarios supplied on the following pages have been designed to reflect typical working environments. They can be used as models for a specific case analysis. These scenarios are provided to demonstrate memory and fixed-disk estimates and are not intended to suggest that you use these exact environments.

Capacity estimates for spreadsheet and wordprocessing applications used in the ace-narios are based on an imformal survey. The low requirement for data files is based on the assumption that many users store document and spreadsheet files on the off-line media, such as disks or file servers.

Figure 7.4 Fully justified text.

system you use does not produce true proportional spacing. Noticeable spacing gaps between words can produce very awkward-looking lines—worst of all is the line containing only three or four words awkwardly spaced on a 60-space line.

Using white space

Increasingly, white space is being recognized as a separate design component that is just as important as the typographical and graphic components. A considerable amount of white space on a page (as much as 50 percent) creates a visual balance that many readers find attractive. Effective use of white space can also do the following:

- Focus the reader's attention on a typographical or visual point, such as a heading, paragraph, or piece of line art, by visually separating it from the text.
- Make reading and concentration easier by eliminating large, heavy blocks of text (or *gray pages*).
- Open pages up visually to remove subtle negative feelings sometimes created by dense blocks of information.

An effective use of white space combines text and graphics into a harmonious relationship. You might, for instance, use a three-column layout—two

Chapters 7 through 12 are of particular value to those planning to install or develop programs. Topics include prerequisites, installing planning, migration and coexistence, program development, performance considerations, support personnel, and education requirements.

The appendixes address additional topics, such as national language and application program support, host communication requirements and prerequistes, supported hardware, system limitations, program upgrade information, related publications, and installation planning checklists.

Figure 7.5 Text with ragged right margin.

columns of text and graphics, and one column of white space. In that blank column, you might put headings, key words or review questions.

Planning for Retrievability

Ensuring that customers can find what they need in your book is easier to do if you design retrievability into the book from the beginning.

While it's certainly possible to go back and add in retrievability aids, it's better if you think about making information easily accessible from the beginning.

Following is a list of activities that can help you control your information for retrievability:

- Use consistent terminology so that you won't be discussing the same concept under different names in different sections of your book. You can include index entries for common synonyms, but use the same terms throughout your book.

- Avoid excessive cross-references within your book. If you find yourself frequently pointing to other sections of the book, you should consider reorganizing the book so that all the information on a particular subject is located in the same place.

- Hold conceptual material down to the bare minimum because it doesn't lend itself to the use of retrievability aids, and also because customers seldom need it after their first acquaintance with the book.

- Anticipate customers' needs for error recovery, and make diagnostic and problem determination information very easy to locate. Not all computer users panic when the system goes down, but many do. Don't upset them further by making them hunt for the answers to their problems.

- Make the illustrations, tables, and examples accessible with a figure list and with entries in the index.

- Put yourself in the customer's place and provide the retrieval aids you'd like to see in every book.

If you design each book so that its information is easy to locate, then you help your readers make fullest use of that information. The techniques that you choose depend to some extent on the money and the time you have available. Color and graphics are expensive, but even with limited money and time, you can incorporate several useful techniques to enhance retrievability.

In a product library consisting of a number of individual books, all relating to the same product, retrievability is critical. While it's certainly frustrating to be unable to locate information you need in a single book, it's even more so not to find what you're looking for in a library of 15 books.

So the first place to begin is with the organization of the library. After doing a task analysis and planning the library, make certain that your design for retrievability is consistent throughout all of its books. The books should look as much alike as possible. For example, if you have an index, decision trees, and tabs in four of nine user's books, you should think carefully about including them in all user's books in the library. Your readers are more comfortable with consistency.

Most of the retrievability aids described in the following sections should be familiar to you; some less common ones are illustrated with examples from existing product books. Study each of the aids to decide on those that seem most appropriate to incorporate into your design.

Tabs

The function of *tabs* (dividers designed to separate chapters or sections of the book) is to help you more easily locate information. Tabs take various forms, but the most common are die-cut to allow the tabbed portion of stock to extend beyond the page for easy handling. Tabs are of heavier stock than the pages, and might be colored or laminated. They're useful, but they're often very expensive.

Die-cut tabs containing general information won't help readers searching for specifics. For example, labels like *Chapter 5* and *Appendix B* probably aren't worth the money. Better examples of effective wording for tabs could use chapter names or section titles like *Getting Started* or *Entering Data*. See Fig. 7.6 for an illustration of die-cut tabs.

A second type of tabs, *bleeding tabs*, requires that a half-circle or rectangle about one-half inch in diameter be located at the same position on each page within a chapter. The position of the tab on the page changes from chapter to chapter. The tabs are either black or some other color, with the color extending beyond the margin to the edge of each page. By looking at the outside edge of the book, you can see where individual chapters are located. Of course, you gain no information about the chapter except where (more or less) it is in the book. Commonly, dictionaries, Bibles, and encyclopedias offer bleeding tabs as retrieval aids.

Table of contents

A table of contents is a comprehensive listing of headings from the various chapters, usually down to a second or third level. Most tables of contents contain only two to three pages, so you probably won't be able to list every single heading in your book. Make certain that the headings listed are identical in wording to those found in the text. (See Chapter 6 for examples of tables of contents.)

Many word-processing programs and electronic publishing systems generate tables of contents automatically. You can tailor the system to pick up only those levels of headings that you specify.

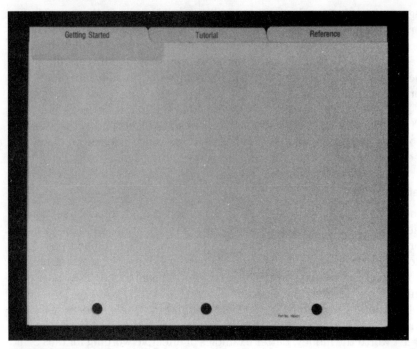

Figure 7.6 Die-cut tabs.

Chapter table of contents

In addition to a table of contents, some books have a detailed contents listing at the beginning of each chapter to show the reader the contents of that chapter.

In most books, the level of detail in the chapter table of contents is greater than that in the table of contents for the whole book. The chapter contents might also be on colored paper or on a die-cut tab to help readers easily locate the chapter.

Chapter organization

Structuring chapters similarly within each book makes it easier for a reader to locate information. If all or most of the chapters begin with an introduction to material, then present steps for performing tasks, examples, and illustrations, and conclude with a summary and a checklist, finding material in a certain chapter is easier. The reader learns where to look to locate specific types of information.

Chapter structure might vary from one book to another, depending on whether the book is a programmer's reference, a user's guide, a setup guide, and so on. But books in a product library that are similar in function should resemble each other as much as possible—especially in terms of organization.

Descriptive headings

Descriptive headings are one of the most useful devices in helping a reader locate information. Headings identify the topic about to be discussed.

To make good use of headings to break information into retrievable units, you should have one or more headings per page. The heading order or hierarchy should be obvious from the position of the heading or the typography. As a result, readers should be able to page through a book, looking at headings to locate needed information and to understand the hierarchical arrangement; that is, they should easily be able to identify major topics and subtopics.

You can choose one of several ways to position headings on a page to show hierarchy. Here is a common format:

- A major first-level heading is positioned in the center of the page in boldface and uppercase.

- A second-level heading is also in boldface and uppercase, but located at the left margin.

- A third-level heading is at the left margin in boldface with initial caps.

- A fourth-level heading is indented and in boldface, followed by a period or a dash, with the first sentence of the paragraph immediately following.

- A fifth-level heading is indented and in boldface, but actually part of the sentence; that is, it is used as the subject of the sentence.

See Fig. 7.7 for an illustration of this heading hierarchy.

Another common format is a combination of headings and descriptive captions, shown in Fig. 7.8. While captions help readers associate the caption with the content of the associated paragraphs or examples, they don't communicate hierarchical relationships.

If you're using an electronic publishing system, you can specify where you want a first-level head, a second-level head, and so on. The system takes care of generating the heads in the position, size, and typeface defined for each heading level.

Consistency in handling headings is critical. You must set a pattern of identification so that the reader understands not only the heading hierarchy but also the rationale for grouping information under the various headings.

Headings should be short and topical, accurately describing the information that follows. You can test the logic and completeness of your topics by reading only the headings in a chapter. If you get the gist of the organization and the information contained in the chapter from scanning the headings, you probably have good headings. Another strategy is to compare the head-

---

HEAD LEVEL ONE

Xxxxxxxxxxxxxxxxxxxxxxxxxxxxxxxxxxxxxxxxxxxxxxxx.
Xxxxxxxxxxxxxxxxxxxxxxxxxxxxxxxxxxxx. Xxxxxxxxxxxxxxxx.

HEAD LEVEL TWO
  Xxxxxxxxxxxxxxxxxxxxxx. Xxxxxxxxxxxxxxxxxxxxxxxxxxx.
Xxxxxxxxxxxxxxxxxxxxxxxxxxxxxxxxxxxxxxxxxxxxxxxxxxxxx.

Head Level Three
  Xxxxxxxxxxxxxxxxxxxxxxxxxxxxxxxx. Xxxxxxxxxxxxxxx.
Xxxxxxxxxxxxxxxxxxxxxxxxxxxxxxxxxxxxx. Xxxxxxxxxxxxxxxx.

  Head Level Four. - - Xxxxxxxxxxxxxxxxxxxxxxxxxxxxxx.
Xxxxxxxxxxxxxxxxx Xxxxxxxxxxxxxxxxxxxxxxxxxxxx.

  Head Level Five xxxxxxxxxxxxxxxxxxxxxxxxx.
Xxxxxxxxxxxxxxxxxxxxxxxxxxxxxxxxxxxxxxxxxxxxxxxxxxx.

Figure 7.7 Heading hierarchy.

How This Book Is Structured

Overview   The first chapter provides a brief introduction to the compo
                various functions of both Standard Edition and Extended Ed
                participation of the OS/2 Editions in the IBM Systems Applic
                the advantages of using the OS/2 Editions on an IBM Person.
                covered. Individuals involved in the decision-making process
                environment will find this chapter of assistance.

Functional Descriptions
                Chapters 2 through 6 discuss OS/2 elements in some detail a
                scope of the various components. The base operating system
                communications support, database capabilities, and general
                covered. Individuals wishing to gain a broader perspective
                these chapters helpful.

Planning, Programming, and Administration
                Chapters 7 through 12 are of particular value to those planni
                programs for OS/2 Standard Edition or Extended Edition. To
                installation planning, migration and coexistence, program de
                considerations, support personnel, and education requireme

Appendixes The appendixes address additional topics, such as national l.
                program support, host communication requirements and pre
                system limitations, program upgrade information, related pu
                and installation planning checklists.

Figure 7.8 Headings and descriptive captions.

ings with the outline you were working from to make sure you've covered the topics you planned to include.

Typographical aids

Plan to use typography to help the reader locate information. If you use boldface in the text to identify all words found in the glossary, you help your reader locate useful information. Or if you put all prompts or messages in italics or in a special typeface, you help the reader form an identification pattern that always conveys certain types of information. You'll want to use a separate typeface throughout the book to show the reader how something appears on the screen. Figure 7.9 shows the use of a different typeface to identify items the reader must type to perform an action.

Other ways to distinguish among types of information include highlighting with italics or all capital letters. When used judiciously, these techniques serve a legitimate function. But when overused, they become both annoying to the reader and useless in terms of emphasis and retrieval.

Text signposts

If your book has text signposts throughout, the reader will find it easier to locate information. A *text signpost* is a label or sign by which readers can identify where they are in the book. For example, many books use footers to show chapter titles at the top or bottom of every odd-numbered page.

In addition, some books have content keywords at the tops of pages (Fig. 7.10) to help the reader locate information on that topic. These text signposts usually go on the upper right or left corner of each page.

Page numbers are also important signposts. Finding the page number in an obvious place on the page, large enough to see easily, is important to the reader.

Symbols and icons as signposts

Symbols and icons, or *tracking devices*, often are used to help the reader spot sections with information about major topics. The key, however, is to devise symbols and icons that are recognized easily, and to use them con-

---

To log on to the host, type your user ID in the space provided. For your first logon, before you have a unique ID assigned to you, type the default:

USERID

Next, as the selection menu appears, place the cursor on or next to the program you wish to use.

Figure 7.9 A different typeface for items the user must type.

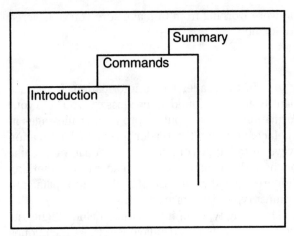

Figure 7.10 Text signposts.

sistently throughout the book. Tracking symbols are useful to show a relationship among books in a series, such as several related applications for a product, and a relationship among books that are part of an application package, such as training, planning, and reference books.

The most common tracking symbols are numerals, large letters, and graphic icons—usually in various colors. These symbols substitute for words and explanations, helping to streamline textual explanation, make pages look more attractive, and let the reader more easily and more quickly spot relevant information.

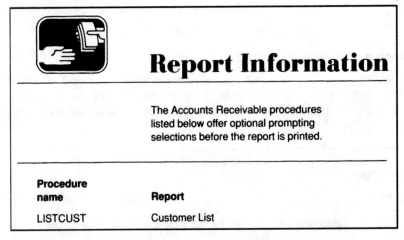

Figure 7.11 Symbols as signposts. Reprinted by permission from *IBM System / 34 Distributors Management Accounting System* Π *Reports and Displays* © 1981 by International Business Machines Corporation.

For example, you might use a symbol for a diskette to help the reader locate information on using diskettes. Or you might use a symbol for a data entry form at the top of every page containing sample data entry forms. As more software products make use of icons or symbols on the screen that the user can manipulate with a mouse, more readers expect to find graphic symbols identifying blocks of information in books. If you use several related graphic symbols, you can help tie together into a coherent package what might seem like unrelated components (such as diskettes, forms, messages on the display, and pieces of hardware). Figure 7.11 provides examples of symbols used as identifiers throughout a book.

Checklists

Devising a checklist or a worksheet is a good way to make sure that readers can both retrieve and use information. Checklists come in a variety of forms, but their main purpose always is to help the reader keep track of the items or actions needed to complete a procedure, such as installing a system. Some checklists require readers to write in their responses and then, based on the collected information, assess their needs or status.

Airplane pilots use checklists to do a safety check before takeoff; your customers should, too, because they provide an easy format for recording and reporting data. Table 7.1 is part of a checklist for users to fill out before configuring for ASCII terminal emulation.

Fast paths and slow paths

Many successful books provide two *tracks*, or paths, for completing procedures. As a result, they can serve two audiences—one learning the procedures for the first time, and one with substantial experience who might need only a brief checklist or summary of procedural steps to do the task at hand. Though a book might present detailed steps and explanations for

TABLE 7.1. Part of a Checklist for Configuring an ASCII Terminal Emulator

Element	1Mb RAM	2Mb RAM
Network A		
Network B		
Network C		
Network D		

completing a setup procedure or for customizing some software, it might also have a summary of steps at any of various points:

- At the beginning of a chapter
- At the end of a chapter
- In an appendix with summaries of all procedures
- On an easy-reference card

There are several ways to write and format fast and slow paths; Fig. 7-12 shows a fast path summary placed in a box for easy identification. The experienced user can read the summary, and the inexperienced user can read the detailed steps shown in Fig. 7.13. Figure 7.13 includes the same basic steps as those shown in Fig. 7.12, but with more detailed information for the user who needs additional help.

Charts, tables, and figures

Because graphic illustrations can convey much useful information and help readers understand sometimes difficult concepts, they are useful retrieval mechanisms. Readers often remember visual images better than detailed explanations of abstract concepts. (Graphics are discussed in detail later in this chapter.)

Make sure that each illustration is properly titled and numbered. Also consider including a list of figures and a list of tables immediately after the table of contents, as well as referring to them in your index (under the term that best describes the graphic aid—*sales, error rate, revision level,* rather than a generic reference to *Figure 12*, for example.

Retrievability worksheet

Table 7.2 is an example of a worksheet you can use to ensure that your book helps customers easily find the information they need.

Selecting Typefaces and Sizes

More than 2000 typefaces are currently available for you to choose from. They provide a tremendous variety, but most computer books use only a few typefaces. Selecting the appropriate one can be a confusing task—especially when

---

Summary
1. Note the error identifier in the message pop-up.
2. Locate the error text in the Message Log and display the help.
3. Take the actions specified in the help for the error.
4. Rerun your procedure. If you get the same error, phone 1-800-555-5555.

Figure 7.12 Fast-path format for experienced users.

---

1. Note the error identifier in the message pop-up.
   If the procedure you are running does not complete successfully, you will receive an error message identifier in a pop-up box on your display screen. This identifier is an 8-character name, such as **RGL30691.**
   li.Locate the error text in the Message Log and display the help.
   An error message matching that identifier is placed in the message log.

   - To display the text of the error message, go to the main menu of the XYZ program.
   - Select **Message Log** from the action bar. A panel displays the identifier and the text of the last three messages in the log.

2. Take the actions specified in the help for the error.

   - Press the function key for help (F4) to see the cause of the error as well as the steps to take for recovery.
   - Follow the steps to correct the error.

3. Run the procedure again. If you get the same error, phone 1-800-555-5555 for assistance with error recovery. Please have the serial number for your program package ready when you call.

Figure 7.13 Detailed (slow-path) format for inexperienced users.

you realize that most typefaces range in size from six to at least 72 points (12 points equals 1 pica; 6 picas equals 1 inch). And for each point size, a font is available (a complete range of characters available in that particular typeface). Figure 7.14 shows a few of the different sizes of type available.

Above all else, you should strive for legibility as you select typefaces and type sizes. Your audience's ability to read the typeface and size you select depends on whether the type is too large, too small, too exotic, too close between lines, or reversed against a distracting background.

Most typefaces are variations on either the *Roman* or *Gothic* type categories. Roman typefaces are characterized by *serifs*—small strokes at the ends of larger, heavier strokes in the letters. Gothic typefaces (also referred to as *sans serif*) have no serifs; thus all lines have straight strokes of equal weight. Most authorities believe that serif typefaces are easier to read; as a result, there are more Roman typefaces than Gothic. Figure 7.15 gives an example of several different typefaces.

Each typeface category contains *type families*, which are typefaces with very similar basic designs but with differences in the width of characters, degree of boldness, and weight of strokes. In addition to Roman and Gothic, there are three other categories of typefaces:

- Script (usually slanted and similar to handwriting)

- Ornamental (novelty typefaces usually used only for special purposes, such as headlines or advertisements)

- Text (the Old English or German typefaces that usually are difficult for us to read today)

TABLE 7.2. A Checklist to Ensure Easy Use of
Documentation

Retrieval Aid	How Many?	Where?
Tabs		
Table of contents		
Chapter table of contents		
Heads		
Typographical aids		
Text signposts		
Symbols as signposts		
Checklists		
Quick paths		
Index		
Glossary		
Charts		
Tables		
Figures		
Other aids		

Figure 7.16 gives an example of each of these categories.

Each type family includes a range of sizes, usually from six to 72 points. And each range of sizes includes several fonts. A *font* is a complete set of type (characters, numbers, symbols) within one type size in the range. Within the font is still more variety—italics, condensed type, boldface, and possibly other distinctions.

The technology available to you today includes printers that can produce any point size, desktop publishing software, and sophisticated electronic publishing systems. Having access to so many capabilities makes it tempting to use a wide variety of type styles, sizes, and fonts. However, careless use of too many available choices can be confusing and detrimental for your readers. Less really is better than more. Select only a few fonts, and make sure that they are compatible.

If you're unfamiliar with typography, be sure to talk with your designer and printer. In addition, you might want to consult various books on typog-

6 pt.	Different sizes of type
8 pt.	Different sizes of type
10 pt.	Different sizes of type
12 pt.	Different sizes of type
14 pt.	Different sizes of type
18 pt.	Different sizes of type
24 pt.	Different sizes of type
30 pt.	Different sizes of

Figure 7.14 Different sizes of type measured in points.

Century Expanded Italic	**Egyptian Bold Condensed**
Cheltenham Old Style	Elizabeth Roman
Cheltenham Bold	ENGRAVERS ROMAN
City Light	Fortuna Light
City Medium	Friz Quadrata
Clarendon Bold	**Friz Quadrata Bold**
Clearface Bold	Galliard
Clearface Extra Bold	*Galliard Italic*
Cloister Old Style	**Galliard Bold**
Cloister Bold Italic	Garamond Old Style
Cochin	*Garamond Old Style Italic*
Cochin Italic	Garamond Bold
Consort	Garamond Book (ITC)
Contact Bold Condensed	*Garamond Book Italic (ITC)*
Contact Bold Condensed Italic	**Garamond Bold (ITC)**
Cooper Black	**Garamond Ultra**
Cooper Black Italic	Goudy Old Style
Cooper Black Condensed	*Goudy Italic*
COPPERPLATE GOTHIC LIGHT	Goudy Bold
Corvinus Medium Italic	**Goudy Extra Bold**
Craw Clarendon Book	Goudy Handtooled
Craw Clarendon	**Goudy Heavyface**
Craw Modern	**Goudy Heavyface Condensed**
Deepdene	H-8 (Alphabet)
Deepdene Italic	H-15 (Alphabet)
Delphin No. 1	H-19 [Alphabet]
Delphin No. 2	**H-20 (Alphabet)**
E-5 (Alphabet)	HADRIANO STONECUT
	HIDALGO

Figure 7.15 Examples of typefaces.

Figure 7.16 Script, ornamental, and text typeface categories.

raphy and design. For your readers' welfare, it's probably better to select typefaces in common use, rather than something exotic.

Achieving readability

How readable are various typefaces, sizes, and fonts? The controversy that has raged for centuries on that question continues today. It centers around the advantages and disadvantages of serif type versus those of sans serif type.

Serif, remember, refers to the small horizontal lines at the base and often at the top of letters. These short lines help focus the eyes on the movement of the line toward the right. Sans serif type is type without those small horizontal lines.

For years, authorities have argued that serif type is more readable, but in today's environment, when both serif and sans serif type are common, there is actually little or no measurable difference in readability. In fact, other factors than the category of type used can actually have a greater influence on readability.

Initial caps and lowercase versus all-caps.   Most authorities agree that a mixture of initial capitals and lowercase letters enhances readability. Headings that are all capitals serve as attention getters, but the longer the item, the more difficult it is to read. All-caps paragraphs are extremely difficult to read.

Type size.   For easy reading, type should be no smaller than eight to ten points for most purposes. Certainly, there are exceptions, and a large type size can be used for emphasis; that is, you might use 18-point or 24-point type to attract attention.

Emphasis.   Some traditional means of providing typographical emphasis include using boldface, underlining, italics, and mixed typefaces.

Putting words and headings in a boldface type emphasizes those elements to the reader and also helps the reader better comprehend (through scanning) the contents. However, too much boldface provides unintended results: de-emphasizing the very points you wanted to emphasize.

Underscoring key words or phrases helps the reader identify those key elements. Like bold, though, too much underscoring makes passages difficult to read and creates a lack of emphasis.

Italics usually are thought to be emphasizers, but in reality they might not be. The lighter, slanted line of italicized characters actually might not stand out as much as unitalicized letters. Their main virtue is that they are different from unitalicized letters.

A common rule of thumb about mixing various typefaces suggests that you use only a few typefaces in a single publication. You have many fonts and sizes to select from within those typefaces, but you still should not use everything available. With desktop publishing and electronic publishing, you always have more typefaces available than you need, and you might find it tempting to use them liberally. But clean design involves making a minimum number of choices. Too many typefaces and fonts only confuse your readers.

Experiment with typography; used effectively, it adds much to your document and enhances your readers' comprehension. Remember to seek the advice of a designer and printer if you need to.

Graphics

Using art to illustrate and highlight information for your audience often is critical to their understanding or impressions. Most hardware and software books provide diagrams, line drawings, flowcharts, and other types of art to help readers understand the topics being discussed.

The most common types of art in computer books today include tables and charts, photographs, and line drawings. Many of these items are still prepared by graphics specialists or illustrators and pasted into the final manuscript before going to the printer. Increasingly, however, the artwork is computer-generated and automatically pulled into the computer file or scanned into place with one of the high-quality scanning devices now available.

Why use graphics?

Nearly every computer book uses graphics. Your readers are accustomed to seeing graphics that support textual discussions, and they might expect to find graphics in your book. Because today's readers live in a world of video and television communications, some might evaluate the worth of a book, at least in part, on the number and quality of the graphics they see as they turn through it.

Types of graphics

Which type, or types, of art should you use? You might be able to choose from photographs, tables, bar charts, line graphs, pie charts, flow charts, and line drawings. As you decide which type of art to include in your book, here are several questions to ask:

- Is this type of art the most suitable type for the readers I've identified as the audience for my book?
- Does this type lend itself to the particular function that I must address here, such as showing relationships over time, illustrating various pieces of equipment, or depicting a rather difficult process?
- Where can I get this artwork? From a computer file? A book that already exists? My graphics department? A vendor? Can I produce it on my computer?

Table 7.3 lists the characteristics and uses of the most common types of art.

Photographs

Photographs, also called *halftones*, convey a lot of information, especially when you want to show people using equipment.They provide detailed closeups of equipment, illustrate a sequence of steps being performed, or create strong visual appeal.

Although photographs are effective illustrations, they often are out-of-date soon after they are published. When books containing photographs are updated, usually the photographs must be retaken to match lighting differences. In addition, to be sure that your book represents the color and ethnic components of our society, you should consider having appropriate representatives in any photos of people.

Black-and-white halftones reproduce very clearly and inexpensively. As you might expect, four-color photographs are more expensive (but very eye-catching). Much depends upon your budget.

Line art

Line art (the use of simple lines) usually is the most inexpensive way to prepare renderings of equipment and even people. Often it can be used to supplement instructions or to enhance process descriptions. With the right software, you can produce effective line art and not have to rely on an artist. See Fig. 7.17 for an example of effective line art.

Tables

Tables often provide the best way to present complex data to your readers. If you've ever read the tables and charts provided in most annual reports, you know that translating such detailed information into text would require many pages. And, no doubt, somewhere you've read pages of information that you wish had been put into tabular form.

As you decide whether to use text or tables and charts, think about your readers and your subject matter. Determine how your readers are likely to

TABLE 7.3.   Usage and Characteristics of the Most Common Types of Art

Type	When to use?	Characteristics
Photograph	To depict close detail of equipment or to show people performing some task	High visual appeal, especially to show people performing tasks or to convey conceptual information. May be difficult to make revisions without updating of replacing all photos; may raise concerns about equal representation of minorities, men and women.
Table	To present accurate statistical or numerical data in compact, readable form	The most accurate visual for presenting detailed figures. Able to present much information in small space; can show contrasts and comparisons. But not the most visually attractive type.
Bar Chart	To draw attention to contrasts and to show trends over specific periods of time	Visually attractive, simple to understand, good for showing relationships and comparisons. Good for simplifying large amounts of detailed numerical data. Easy to construct. Not as accurate as tables.
Line graph	To show trends, forecasts, and comparisons over time	Ideal for showing trends and future projections. Easy to construct and understand. Visually attractive. Not always the most accurate way to show detailed information.
Pie chart	To indicate divisions of the whole	Attractive, especially for nontechnical readers. Good for showing distribution of revenue, expenses, time.
Flow chart	To illustrate sequential steps of a process	Often clarifies very complicated processes and illustrates sequential development of process stages. May sometimes be too simplistic, however.
Line drawing	To show details about equipment and the relationship of people and equipment	Enhances descriptions of processes and instructions on how to perform certain tasks, especially installing and maintaining.

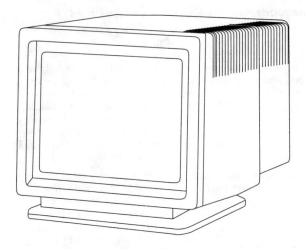

Figure 7.17 A typical piece of line art.

learn or understand the information best. Some types of tables and charts are more difficult to understand than others. Make sure that the type you choose is compatible with your readers' levels of comprehension.

Tables are the most accurate graphic that you can include in a report. They provide an excellent way to convey large amounts of data, while helping readers draw comparisons or see relationships among the data presented. Most tables, however, are rather dull; you might do well not to rely heavily on them.

Tables come in two forms: informal and formal. An informal, or *spot* table, has its information simply incorporated into the text, without formal titles, columnar headings, or rulings. Figure 7.18 shows how a spot table might appear in text.

Formal tables follow more rigidly specified conventions, as shown in the following guidelines. Of course, not every component included here is necessary for every table.

- Title and number each table properly. Place table titles (and subtitles, if appropriate) above the table, and number tables with Roman or Arabic numbers. The numerical designation and title might appear as *Table II. Floating-Point Performance Data.*

- Make certain that the table is complete, and identify all columns, units, quantities, and dates.

- Keep tables to one page or less if possible. If a table must be continued on another page, break the table at a convenient place. Write *continued* or *Cont.* at the break. Where the rest of the table starts on the next page, write *Table I. (continued).* Repeat the columnar headings on the second page.

- Document the table if you take it from another source. The documentation can appear in parentheses just after the title, or in a footnote under the table.

- To document information contained within the table, place footnotes at the end of the table. Key the notes to references (usually symbols) in the table columns. Use symbols to avoid confusion with numerical data in the table.

Figures

Graphics other than tables generally are classified as *figures*. Typical figures include bar charts, pie charts, line charts, diagrams, flow charts, and photographs. The following guidelines apply to figures used in most books, and to structuring the figures described in this chapter:

- Number and title each figure correctly, placing figure numbers and titles beneath the illustrations, numbered consecutively throughout the book or throughout each chapter.

- Include a legend, caption or explanatory material commenting on the figure.

- Position figures as closely as possible to the text to which they refer. Always introduce figures in the text, unless they appear in the appendix.

- Make certain that figures have complete information so readers can identify all the components. See if the figure can stand alone, independent of comments in the text.

- Place any documentation references after the figure number and title so they cannot be overlooked.

- Weigh each figure in view of its intended purpose, the purpose of the chapter and book, and the needs of your audience. Include figures only when they serve a genuine function, such as clarifying, summarizing, or emphasizing.

In conjunction with the product announcements, customers may take a number of training classes that offer hands-on use of the hardware and software products. Currently, these classes are available:

Manufacturing software	AS1006	May 4-6
Hardware installation	BT6003	May 8-10
Systems support	RQ4448	June 3-4

Classes are tailored to the needs of those attending and prepare customers to make full use of their new products as quickly as possible.

Figure 7.18 An informal, or "spot," table.

Bar chart

Sometimes called a *bar graph* or *column graph*, a bar chart is an effective way to present statistical information. It's also ideal for stressing comparative relationships. Because of the clearly defined columns, bar charts have more visual impact than do tables. For this reason, many writers convert tables into bar charts where possible.

One limitation of bar charts is that you cannot present exact figures. But if you want to compare figures over a period of months or years, bar charts really are effective, as the example in Fig. 7.19 shows.

Line chart

A single-line graph shows two values: an element to be measured, such as money or production, and time. Time ordinarily is plotted along the horizontal axis, while the variable measurement is plotted on the vertical axis. The zero point of the axes is identified where they meet.

The grid used in line charts should be of moderate to large size, since the focus should be on the line indicating trends rather than on the grid itself. Provide complete information about units of measurement and time spans.

Multiple-line charts allow comparisons among different (but similar) factors. The example in Fig. 7.20 shows variations in lines (usually colored, broken, dotted, and solid). It's extremely important to include a legend with your line chart so the reader can understand the information.

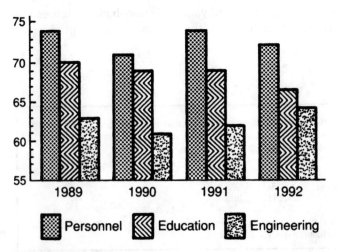

Figure 7.19 A bar chart.

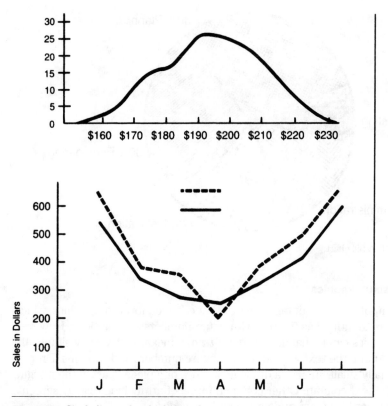

Figure 7.20 Single-line and multiple-line charts.

Pie chart

Pie charts are effective when you want to show a reader portions of a whole, or 100 percent. As shown in Fig. 7.21, a pie chart is a circle divided into pie-shaped wedges proportionate to the amount represented by each wedge. The wedge representing the most important element can be shifted slightly away from the circle for a clearer representation.

Make sure you identify the wedges in terms of the percentage and/or specific amount they represent. Place identifying labels on the wedges, or right next to them, to allow easy reading and comprehension.

Flow chart

A flow chart is a graphic representation of a process, usually showing the process (or a subprocess) sequentially from start to finish. While most flow charts represent the process as a series of labeled boxes, as in Fig. 7.22, some contain pictorial forms. If the flow chart makes use of symbols unfamiliar to some readers, provide a key for easier understanding.

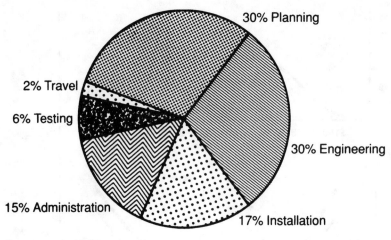

Figure 7.21 A pie chart.

Other useful graphics

Most computer books contain several other common forms of graphics, which usually are identified as figures, with figure numbers and captions. However, some graphics can be handled as *drop-in art*, meaning that they simply are integrated into the text without formal figure numbers and captions. Drop-in art is usually small, such as a drawing of a key, or a piece of art in the margin, out of the text column. Other common forms of art include display screens, keys, keyboards, menus, and partial and full pages.

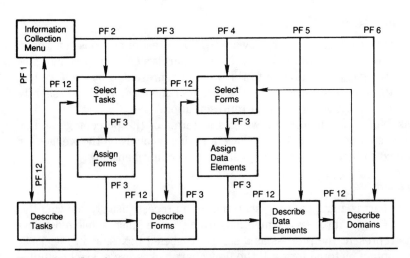

Figure 7.22 A flow chart. Reprinted by permission from *Information Systems Analysis and Design User's Guide*
© 1985 by International Business Machines Corporation.

Display screens

For your reader's benefit, you might want to depict display screens filled with information as it might appear on the reader's own display screen. You might choose to do one or more of the following:

- Highlight the screen with a color background
- Draw the edge of the screen with heavy black lines
- Isolate the screen from surrounding text with white space
- Show complete or partial screens

Full and partial screens should be of a uniform size throughout the book, with type large enough to be easily read. What readers see should be an accurate representation of what will appear on their screens as they follow your instructions; see Fig. 7.23.

Keys

To show individual keys or groupings of keys, you can use *callouts* (enlargements of specific keys shown next to a smaller keyboard), or you can simply show larger illustrations of individual keys, without showing the keyboard each time. Figure 7.24 shows one way to handle key callouts.

```
3280 MODIFY ISAD Tasks Descriptions

Collect all tasks of the information system

┌─────────────────────┬──────────────┬──────────┬──────────────┐
│ TASK NAME           │ FREQUENCY    │ MODE     │ TASK TITLE   │
├─────────────────────┼──────────────┼──────────┼──────────────┤
│                     │              │          │              │
│                     │              │          │              │
│                     │              │          │              │
│                     │              │          │              │
└─────────────────────┴──────────────┴──────────┴──────────────┘

    3=CONT  4=LIST  5=TABLE  6=QUIT  7=UP  8=DOWN  9=RET  10=LE  11=RI  12=END

──►
ENTER A COMMAND, 'END' OR 'QUIT' TO LEAVE
```

Figure 7.23 One way to show a screen full of information.

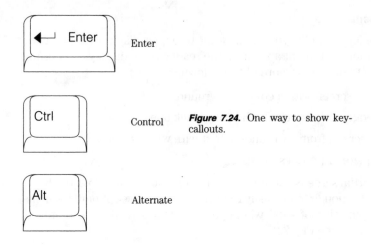

Enter

Control

Figure 7.24. One way to show key-callouts.

Alternate

Keyboards

It's often helpful to show an entire keyboard, with various key functions identified. Doing so helps your readers understand the relationships of certain key functions on the whole keyboard and helps them visualize those functions on their own keyboard as they use it. Figure 7.25 provides an example of a keyboard layout with key functions identified.

Menus

To provide ample detail for the reader, you'll want to reproduce menus exactly as they appear on the screen. You can show a complete or partial menu, depending on the information you want to communicate; see Fig. 7.26.

Partial and full pages

You might sometimes want to represent a letter, report, or memo as art in your documentation, especially if your product involves word processing or desktop publishing. You'll ensure consistency if you settle on dimensions for representing pages in all your examples. Typically, documentation shows representations of both partial and full pages, depending upon the amount of material to be shown in the example. Figure 7.27 shows one way to depict full and partial pages.

Color

Many computer books today are printed in either two or four colors. The effective use of color certainly makes such books more attractive, easier on the eye, and more marketable. But color serves other utilitarian functions, as well.

The world that surrounds us is filled with color, and your audience is very familiar with dazzling graphics from videos, movies, advertising, and so on. They read magazines filled with color, but must often read books that are black and white.

Look at two books side by side, one in black and white and the other filled with color. Which one are your eyes drawn to?

Various studies show that color enhances readers' understanding, often by emphasizing relationships or clarifying complicated graphics. Another quality is difficult to measure: color adds interest and enlivens otherwise dull pages of text. Like children, most of us prefer to reach for items with lots of color, just as we prefer color displays over monochrome displays.

If your budget permits and if your audience is large enough to justify it, by all means plan to use some color in your book. An experienced designer or printer can help you understand the effective use of color. When used deliberately and properly, it can do a number of things for the reader:

- Highlight or emphasize

- Add energy and vibrancy to a page

- Help the reader track related concepts or points of information

- Clarify or enhance the reader's understanding

- Delineate sections or divisions

You can use color for such items as diagrams, bullets, instructions, commands, displays, prompts, photos, line art, tracking symbols, chapter dividers, headings, and rules.

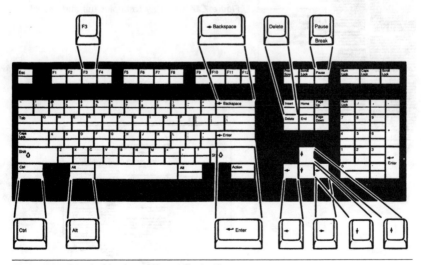

Figure 7.25 A typical keyboard layout illustration.

3180 DISPLAY ISAD Information Collection
To select an option, press the corresponding PF-key

Option	Description
1	Describe Tasks
2	Select a Task and Assign Its Forms
3	Describe Forms
4	Select a Form and Assign Its Data Elements
5	Describe Data Elements
6	Describe Domains

9=RETURN 12=END

———————▶

DISPLAY COMPLETED

Figure 7.26 One way to show a menu. International Business Machines Corporation.

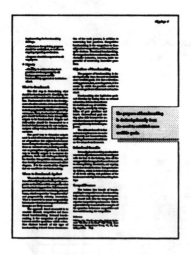

Figure 7.27 One way to depict full and partial pages.

Conclusions

The design phase of producing your book and getting it ready for your readers is very important; the image created in the minds of your readers as soon as they see the book and its page layout persists until they are through with it. The amount of attention you pay to producing the best book possible, therefore, is well worth the investment of time and money.

8

Packaging and Publishing the Book

While you are completing the steps required to get your writing project ready for publication (designing, writing, testing, revising), you should also be planning the packaging of your book and looking forward to the production phase. This phase includes preparing all the components that are part of the complete project. Depending on the size and complexity of your publication, the production phase can be quite simple or extremely complex.

Because publishing is so expensive, investigate various options carefully in order to get the best results for the best price as you package and publish your documentation. Work closely with the production people in your organization to produce the highest quality publication possible for the lowest cost.

If you have no in-house production resources, work closely with a good printer. Make sure that you are comfortable with your printer's recommendations and with the selections presented to you. A mistake at this stage can be very costly.

Recent surveys show that some major corporations spend as much as 10% of their budgets for publishing costs.

As you might expect, for a major developer of computer software or hardware, publishing costs can be a large item. For some corporations, publishing ranks as the second largest cost of doing business—second only to labor and personnel costs.

Packaging Your Book

How your book is packaged and what it looks like is important if it is to sell well and if it is to make readers feel comfortable as they begin to use it. Increasingly, a book's appearance plays a role in marketing computer programs and equipment.

Among packaging concerns to consider are the following:

- Choosing a paper stock
- Selecting a page size
- Estimating page count
- Selecting a binding
- Choosing slipcases, dust jackets, and covers

Choosing a paper stock

Paper stock makes a real impact on your readers, who form a subconscious impression of your book based on the *weight* (thickness), *grade* (quality), and *finish* of the paper used. Whether your book is for internal use only or for sale to external customers, you'll want to check with a designer or printer about selecting the most suitable paper stock.

Thousands of kinds of paper are available today, in various colors and finishes. White is almost always the best choice. Coated paper is best for reproducing high-quality graphics, especially when you want colored illustrations and designs.

Recently, much recycled and recyclable paper stock has become available. Your printer might even have coated stock that consists of at least 50 percent recycled paper. Using recycled and recyclable paper is good for the environment. You might even find it advantageous to print, somewhere on the book, the symbol that indicates you are using recycled paper.

Most paper used for books is 60- to 70-pound stock (standard typing bond, by contrast, usually is 20-pound stock). However, the difference between 60-pound stock and 20-pound stock might not be truly proportionate, because heavier weights often are determined from weighing sheets that are 25 by 38 inches, while bond is weighed using sheets of 17 by 22 inches. Generally, heavier paper gives a nice feel to the page and keeps ink and colored illustrations from bleeding through to the other side.

Cover stock is a stiffer, heavier stock for printing book covers. The heavi-er stock withstands more use and handling; it also provides clear reproduction of high-quality printing and graphics for a really attractive appearance. Some covers are laminated with plastic to make them more durable and attractive.

Selecting a page size

Your choices for selecting page size depend on the purpose of the document, the traditions and policies in your organization, the size of artwork and illustrations, your budget, and other constraints.

Books are printed in a variety of page sizes. Generally, if you select the standard large sheet that printers in the U.S. use (25×38 inches), you save on printing costs. Printers base paper cost in part on how many pages they can cut from a sheet. If you select an odd size, then the printer wastes more paper through trimming. Your costs are then higher.

Several standard page sizes (measured in inches) are available:

- $8\frac{1}{2} \times 11$
- 9×12
- 6×9
- 7×10
- $5\frac{1}{2} \times 9$
- $5\frac{1}{2} \times 8\frac{1}{2}$
- 5×8
- 5×7
- 4×9

The most common page sizes in the U.S. computer industry are $5\frac{1}{2} \times 9$, 6×9, and $8\frac{1}{2} \times 11$. But you'll also find that other sizes are used by some manufacturers and publishers.

Which size do you choose? Much depends on the nature of the document you want to publish. Usually quick reference folders or brochures are as small as $3\frac{3}{4} \times 6$ or $3\frac{3}{4} \times 8\frac{1}{2}$ inches, and can be carried in a shirt pocket if necessary or placed handily by a PC. Books consisting of schematic diagrams often are printed on 9-x-12 or even 12-x-17 paper. You might find that page size for your book is dictated by the size of a slipcase or even the size of a pocket in a computer into which the book must fit.

Estimating page count

How long should a book be? Abraham Lincoln reportedly was asked how long a man's legs should be, and he said, "Long enough to reach the ground." The same principle applies to most books—they should be long enough to do the job.

A book really can be too short, especially if it doesn't contain the information that readers want and need. On the other hand, a book can be so long that it's difficult to handle. A book containing 1200 pages, for example, might intimidate readers by its sheer size. Unfortunately, even though you might plan to produce a reasonably short book, by the time you get approvals from development and testing, you might have to incorporate more information than you expected. Sometimes the length of your book is beyond your control.

Task-oriented documentation broken into several relatively small books have two major advantages. First, they look smaller and seem more inviting and manageable than longer books. Many organizations have rejuvenated their sales by breaking two or three large books for a product into several smaller units that are more manageable. Second, they provide users with an additional psychological boost by enabling them to see that they are making progress as they move through a series of short, compact books.

Consider your audience as you decide how long your books should be. An internal audience of programmers probably won't be as concerned about length as an external audience of paying customers, but you still should plan for a usable size.

When determining page count, considerations other than the expertise of your intended audience also deserve your attention:

- Depending on its binding, a thick book might not stay open easily.

- A book that has grown too thick during reviews and rewrites might not fit into a slot in the machine as you planned. Or it might require a larger binder and a larger slipcase, both of which add expense. Mistakes such as these do happen.

- Thought should be given to where the book will be used. If the user is likely to lay the book next to the computer, it should be small enough to handle easily. Balancing a bulky book in one's lap while trying to read it and work at the keyboard obviously is difficult.

Remember, too, that while it might be okay for the documentation to weigh more than the disks containing the software, it's not good psychology for the documentation to weigh more than the machine itself!

Selecting a binding

You can select from a variety of sizes and types of bindings, some expensive and some inexpensive. Base your decision on the expected life of the product and on whether the binding is an important part of the marketing strategy for the product. A printer can imprint the company logo, title, and other items on the binders, or simply provide plain binders with printed labels that can be inserted into a clear plastic pocket on the front of the binder and the spine.

The most common types of binding are perfect, saddle-stitching, spiral, comb, and looseleaf. Each has its advantages and disadvantages. Figure 8.1

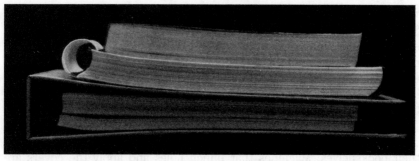

Figure 8.1 Commonly used bindings: perfect (top), spiral (middle), and looseleaf (bottom).

shows a perfect-bound book, a spiral-bound book, and looseleaf in a three-ring binder.

Perfect

Perfect binding involves gluing pages into a one-piece cover. The cover usually is heavy card stock printed with the book title, product name, company name, and release or version level. A perfect-bound book might also have punched holes that allow it to be placed in a three-ring binder with other materials.

Perfect-bound books look very professional and neat, and take much less room than three-ring binders. Pages usually are bound very securely and cannot easily be pulled out.

The major disadvantage of perfect binding is that you cannot easily update a perfect-bound book because the pages are not designed to be replaced. Perfect-bound books also might not lie completely flat when opened.

Saddle-stitching

Pages in a saddle-stitched book are usually bound inside a folded double-size sheet of heavy cover stock. For example, an 11-x-17-inch sheet is used for 8½-x-11-inch pages. All the pages in the book are 11 × 17, printed on both sides, and folded. The sheets are held together by staples from the outside center fold. Many such books are drilled so they can be included in three-ring binders.

Saddle-stitching provides a very neat, professional appearance, and can be done very economically. However, it can be used only for books with less than 200 pages, and, like perfect-bound books, saddle-stitched books are not designed to be updated. They also might not lie perfectly flat when opened, but the pages can be folded back to help the book lie flat.

Spiral and comb

Spiral and comb bindings are very common, primarily because they are inexpensive (for short print runs) and readily available. The bindings are plastic (comb) or wire (spiral), usually with heavy cover stock. Some covers are clear plastic, allowing the title page to become the cover design and layout. Others are opaque, but include plastic windows that reveal the book title from the title page.

Various sizes and colors are available for the covers. Some comb bindings can be imprinted with the book titles so users can easily locate them on their bookshelves. Machines that punch holes and apply the covers are readily available, and many print shops can do the job for you.

Spiral and comb bindings are perhaps the cheapest methods for producing a limited number of books. (Perfect binding and saddle-stitching are more economical for longer print runs.) These bindings are also the most convenient for the reader; when the book is opened, pages lie perfectly flat.

Plastic or wire bindings are not especially attractive, however, and are not designed for easy updating. To update a spiral- or comb-bound book, you must have pages prepunched with holes of the right shape in the right places; inserting pages is a time-consuming job. Also, few spiral-bound books have titles or other information on the spine for easy retrieval, and such books often do not stand up by themselves on shelves. Finally, keep in mind that perfect binding and saddle-stitching are more economical for long print runs.

Looseleaf

Looseleaf binders (usually three-ring binders) are probably the most common method for binding computer documentation. Binders come in a variety of sizes (usually, from ⅜ to 3 inches thick). The most common sizes for paper are 8½ × 11 and 5½ × 8½.

Using looseleaf binders, you can easily insert, remove, or replace pages when updating is necessary. Most binders are very durable and long-lasting. Several binders designed to contain books from a product library look nice together and help add design coherence to the individual books in that library.

When a binder is too small for the number of pages it holds, however, pages might be difficult to turn.

Or, if it's too large, it might look formidable and discouraging to the typical user. Also, the rings can open accidentally, and the pages fall out.

Choosing Slipcases, Dust Jackets, and Covers

Many manufacturers produce books that are enhanced by fitting into slipcases or that have dust jackets or covers. These items provide a very pro-

Figure 8.2 Slipcases.

fessional appearance and often are necessary to make books attractive and consistent with competitive books already on the shelves. Figure 8.2 shows two books in slipcases.

Slipcases

Slipcases are very popular and are particularly desirable from a marketing standpoint because they focus attention on the uniform appearance of books in a product library. They also are attractive and neat when placed on shelves. Slipcases are rather expensive, though, and require that book titles be imprinted on them, or that a dust jacket with appropriate information be used with the slipcase. Many slipcases contain a single ring binder; others also contain one or more comb-bound or perfect-bound books as well.

Slipcases provide a uniform, attractive appearance to a product library. They also provide very good protection for the book contents. However, when a book is encased in a ring binder and then a slipcase, it can be very bulky and thus inconvenient to handle. The use of ring binders, slipcases, and dust jackets, therefore, requires careful coordination to ensure good design and ease of use.

Dust jackets

A dust jacket is a paper cover that fits around the outside of a book or slipcase. The dust jacket on a hardback fiction book displays the title, name of the author, information about the publisher, and information about the book.

Dust jackets for documentation slipcases are very similar to those for books. They display the title and name of the publisher; often they list required software and hardware, and they might include information about a limited warranty and license agreement. Often you'll see an attractive photograph or some colorful artwork on the dust jacket, since it also serves as a useful marketing tool.

The principal advantage of dust jackets is that you can use the same generic slipcases for all your products but design an appropriate dust jacket to distinguish one offering from another. Dust jackets also can be quite attractive, offering strong visual appeal to your books.

Dust jackets are expensive to produce, especially with four-color art. Also, because they are paper, they're fragile and can tear.

Covers

First impressions are important; therefore, the physical design of the cover is important.

Color and design should capture the reader's interest, pique curiosity, and invite the reader to open the book.

Harsh colors or designs might leave negative impressions that affect whether your intended audience uses the book. The cover design should include a strong graphic element: a photograph or other graphic design to grab attention.

As you glance at the cover, you should immediately see the title. You should also be able to identify the purpose, subject, and audience of the book. If you have to work at understanding the title or identifying the content or type of book, then the cover is inadequate.

You form an immediate impression of the book (and sometimes the product and manufacturer) from looking at the cover. While you react subjectively to what you see, you carry that impression with you as you work your way through the book's contents. The use of color, graphics, and other design elements helps you decide whether you find the cover attractive and inviting. In addition, the print quality, the registration of colors, and the apparent quality of the binding affect your impressions of the book.

If you decide on a cover that has mostly text with little or no graphics, make sure that the type is bold enough to be seen from a few feet away. Study the covers of several books similar to the ones you are producing. See what you like about them—how bright or subdued the colors are, what your impressions of the books are from the covers, whether you feel inclined to look inside, whether they appear warm and friendly or cold and foreboding. Also look at the use of typography and of visual elements—from photographs to abstract designs.

Selecting a Printing Process

Your decision on which printing process to use for your documentation depends on several factors:

- Budget
- Number of copies to be printed
- Audience—external or internal
- Amount of color in the document
- Complexity of artwork
- Kind of bindings, covers, and dust jackets you want

Printing processes from which you can choose include desktop publishing, electronic publishing, offset printing, and photocopying.

Desktop publishing

The excitement of being able to create documents on your personal computer that once could be produced only by print shops is contagious, and it makes all of us think we are publishers. With a minimum of equipment (a personal computer, page layout software, and a laser printer), you can produce your own book, brochure, flyer, or sign.

Desktop publishing has brought production costs down for all kinds of documents—often by 50% or more. At the same time, it puts control of format and design into the hands of the desktop system user. Typesetting costs can also be reduced significantly, as can the labor-intensive layout process.

The cost savings with desktop publishing are evident when you have to make last-minute changes that would require a commercial printer to reset type or alter artwork—always an expensive proposition during the final stages of the printing phase. With desktop publishing, you can make the last-minute changes, do the layout, and generate high-quality type.

If you need higher-quality typeset copy than you can produce on a laser printer, you can take diskettes containing your document to a typesetter, who can print out fully composed pages for you—for only a few dollars per page.

The computers, software, and printers now available give you almost unlimited abilities to design formats, use various type fonts and print styles, incorporate sophisticated graphics, and print near-typeset quality pages. In addition, you can use scanners to convert drawings, photographs, and text into images to be pulled into your document wherever you wish.

The laser printers commonly used for desktop publishing produce high-quality work, but usually not equal to the quality of typesetting. When you want extremely sharp, high-quality work, and when expense is not an over-riding concern, you'll probably want to work with a designer and traditional typesetting and layout operations. But you should investigate desktop publishing; it might well meet many of your needs.

Software packages

Software packages useful in desktop publishing are both easily available and sophisticated enough to produce just about anything you might want for your publication. Today, several word-processing programs incorporate features that once were found only in desktop publishing or text systems. Several now provide WYSIWYG (what you see is what you get) on-screen displays of pages and fonts. Some have graphics features to incorporate art-work and halftones that can be integrated into a document.

The chief advantage of desktop publishing is that you can control details that only typesetters could control previously, including kerning (spacing) between letters and words, line lengths, rules, boxes, borders, type sizes and styles, hyphenation, column depths, justification, and so on.

Desktop publishing software falls into two basic categories: systems fea-turing the ability to manipulate many pages of text (these work especially well on long documents with repetitive page layout patterns), and systems built around the traditional cut-and-paste concept, which enables a user to build an attractive page layout with high visual impact. Cut-and-paste-type programs offer good graphics capabilities but do not manipulate text as eas-ily as might be desired.

Some programs now work with network servers to make files available to a number of writers who want or need to work on the same document. The ability to share files among several users offers great advantages to anyone who must produce documents under tight schedules.

Hardware requirements

Most desktop publishing programs require expanded memory require-ments, especially if you use scanners and graphics. The longer the publica-tion you're working on, the greater the space requirements. Some programs suggest at least 40 megabytes of storage, but in reality you probably need 100 or more if you really are serious about doing much desktop publishing. Because of the sizes of files for large documents and graphics, the faster your machine and the more memory it has, the more you're going to enjoy desktop publishing.

Monitors are important, and many large-size monitors are available to enable you to see a single page in actual size. On some monitors, with proper software, you can zoom in on specific parts of the page, or you can see a representation of the layout of 12 or 16 or 24 pages at once.

Laser printers are essential to satisfactory desktop publishing, and good desktop printers that produce five to 10 pages per minute are available from a number of manufacturers. Larger printers that several individuals can share also are available.

Desktop publishing puts you in control of your publishing. While it is possible to produce a limited number of copies of a document entirely within your own office, chances are you'll want to take diskettes containing your document to a printer to produce the final camera-ready copy on a linotype-quality printer.

Electronic publishing

Organizations that must produce large volumes of high-quality publications invest substantial amounts in electronic publishing systems. These are computer systems dedicated to the publishing process, with facilities for many writers to enter text and graphics, do page layout, produce camera-ready, and typeset copy. With most such systems, you can do virtually everything from your workstation:

- Enter text
- Construct and place graphics
- Automatically do page layout
- View a layout on the screen as it will look on the printed page
- Edit and revise
- Print either near-camera-ready copy or actual camera-ready copy

Electronic publishing differs from desktop publishing in the scope and amount of publishing to be done; electronic publishing is to desktop publishing what a professional football team is to a Sunday afternoon "flag-tag" game in the park. The hardware requirements for electronic publishing systems vary, ranging from sophisticated workstations to a large mainframe with literally hundreds of workstations connected to it. Laser printers and high-quality typesetting output devices usually are included.

Software requirements vary; many commercially available programs serve the needs of some firms, while others have developed specialized proprietary systems for their own use. Some systems require that the writer enter formatting codes to tell the system to begin a new paragraph, begin and end bulleted lists, print text in single or double space, and use underlining, boldface, and various type styles. Sophisticated tables also can be constructed through the use of predefined codes. These codes are part of a *markup language*, or *tagged language*, that writers must learn to use.

Predefined style sheets or macros can be written and used to produce books, even entire libraries of books, according to design specifications. The uniform production of quantities of information is the strong suit of electronic publishing systems.

Agreeing on the design and specifications before using electronic publishing is critical to the success of the operation. Designers and systems professionals should work with writers and editors to design the book or library and to construct the macros and commands necessary to do the production. Sample layouts should be produced and modifications made until everyone is satisfied with the design and layout. Then the production work can begin.

Offset printing

An economical printing technology for large print runs involves *offset lithography*, or photographing a camera-ready page and making a negative, which can be used (with drop-in photos) to make a plate from thin metal, plastic, or paper, and run on an offset printing press. During the printing process, ink is transferred from the plate to a rubber drum that transfers the image to paper.

Printing costs for offset printing are fairly high initially, but the more copies you print, the lower the per-unit cost. Several variations in offset printing are available to reproduce photographs, complex artwork and illustrations, and two- or four-color printing. Offset printing is the cheapest way to produce a large number of high-quality impressions.

Photocopying

Photocopier technology has reached such sophisticated levels that the smallest desktop copiers can produce better-quality copies than did even the very large machines a few years ago. Choices range from small personal copiers to those capable of automatically copying, collating, stapling, and stacking copies. Another tantalizing choice is the color copier, capable of producing four-color copies nearly equal in quality to color photographs.

Because such high-quality copies can be produced, if you need a small number of copies and if professional printing is not required, you might choose to use a copier to reproduce your book.

The chief advantage of simply copying pages for books is that there are no initial setup costs as there are for commercial printing. Each copy costs exactly the same to reproduce; you get no price break with large numbers of copies. Also, turn-around time is short because copies are quickly and easily produced.

Copies can be bound in three-ring notebooks or with comb bindings. They can also be perfect-bound, but the cover for a perfect binding must be produced in some other way; it usually cannot be copied on heavy cover stock.

Investigate the capabilities of copying firms, some of which have merged copying and printing technologies to enable them to produce copied documents that closely resemble professionally printed materials.

Reviewing and Proofing

A very important part of the publishing process is reviewing and proofing during the printing phase. You, your designer (if you have one), and your printer might all check proofs for accuracy, completeness, and layout during this phase.

Desktop publishing and electronic publishing cut certain steps out of the reviewing and proofing cycles. You can review page layout, headlines, text columns, and other elements before going to typesetting. While the procedures vary according to the situation, you might receive *galleys* from a typesetter—usually in the form of long columns of printed text. Check these carefully for consistency among headings, uniformity of type styles and sizes, complete information, and any special symbols or markings that you requested.

When the typesetter makes corrections, usually you can expect to see a second set of proofs for another review. At the same time, you might receive a set of galleys to paste up as a dummy of your publication. Or, if your designer or printer is handling the layout, they will see that you get a dummy layout to examine.

The *dummy* is a rough copy of what your publication will look like in finished form. Check for balanced page layout, headers, footers, and accurate placement of captions for figures, tables, and other graphics.

Page proofs and mechanicals

Depending upon the complexity of your project, you should next receive *page proofs*, which come to you either on layout boards or as *mechanicals*—camera-ready pages ready to go to the printer. You have another opportunity at this point to make sure that every component, every piece of text, every graphic is present, in place, and correct. Check for proper alignment of text, captions, and artwork. Make certain that page numbering, footers, headers, and chapter titles and numbers are correct.

Bluelines

You might see still another set of proofs known as *bluelines*. Bluelines are the final stage before printing actually begins. They represent the way the publication will look when printed. Every element is in place, and all corrections should have been made by this point.

You should avoid making editorial corrections and changes on the bluelines, because you pay a premium to make corrections at this point in the process. But do take the opportunity to look for proper shading of screens, proper alignment of graphics and artwork, and dirt that might have been present on the negative and shows up as dots or lines in inexplicable places on a page. Also look for broken type and misaligned letters or rules.

Printers request that you sign off on the bluelines, approving them as-is or with corrections as marked. When you sign, you are telling the printer to proceed with the printing, after making any requested changes. Of course, you can request to see another set of bluelines with the corrections in place.

Color keys

If you use color in your publication, you might want to see *color keys*, or color proofs. Check the density and the consistency of color, making sure that it falls precisely on the page where you want it. Check to see that shaded areas or screens are what you want. The printer can adjust the colors to meet your needs and preferences.

Conclusions

The production processes that your publication must go through are critical to the readers' perceptions about the quality of the publication. Be sure to seek the help of designers and printers in producing the best publications possible. With careful attention to the production process, you can produce high-quality publications that communicate effectively with your readers.

9

Producing Online Documentation

Online information includes anything seen on the computer screen. From a writer's point of view, however, online *documentation* excludes the interface itself and the messages to the user, since these are commonly written and designed by programmers or specialists in interface design. A typical interface consists of some or all of the elements shown in Fig. 9.1.

The interface includes product panels and menus that allow end users to install, configure, and use the product. These panels and menus might have items to select and fields into which to enter data. Many interfaces also have an action bar at the top of a panel from which users can select various actions that they can perform on the panel, as well as an area at the bottom that lists the function keys that are active on the panel. The interface might also display various pop-up or pull-down panels and windows that overlay part of the screen.

A message can be displayed in one of these panels, either on a line near the bottom of the screen or in a message log. Figure 9.2 shows messages displayed on a panel.

If a message contains critical information or an important warning, it should:

- Be displayed prominently
- Occupy the entire screen, if appropriate
- Use an attention-getting color
- Require a series of keystrokes to remove it

If a message contains only a notification, such as the information that files

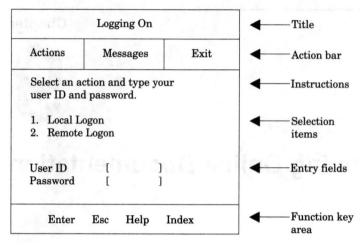

Figure 9.1 Typical elements of an interface.

are being copied, it is usually displayed inconspicuously and removed in a few seconds or at the next keystroke.

As a writer, you might have little or no influence on the interface and the messages because they're considered part of the code. At most, you might have "editorial rights." However, it's important to understand something about online design and about the differences between online and printed

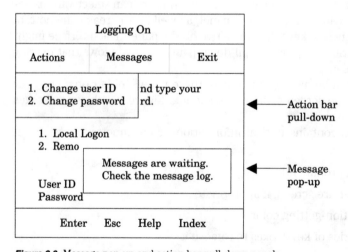

Figure 9.2 Message pop-up and action bar pull-down panels.

documentation both to review the interface and messages and to write other types of online documentation.

Differences between Online and Printed Documentation

Many of the differences between online documentation, sometimes called *softcopy*, and printed documentation, sometimes called *hardcopy*, are easy to see; others aren't. The following sections discuss, first, four differences that are readily apparent, and then six that are less apparent.

Ease of reading

Online documentation is harder to read than printed documentation. The ascend-ers and descenders on the alphabetic letters are often less clear than those on printed letters.

It's been proven that staring at a screen all day is much harder on the eyes than reading books all day. Therefore, you should make effective use of blank space, lists, and graphics in all online documentation. Never crowd a screen with so much information that the user can't absorb it in just a few moments. You might find that you have to leave as much as 50% of the screen blank to make the information readable.

Portability

Online documentation is less portable than printed documentation. You can take a laptop, notebook, or palmtop computer many places, but you probably can't take one to as many places as you can a book, nor can you carry it as conveniently. Information that the user must read and study at any length, such as programming information, should be presented in a printed book instead of, or in addition to, online.

Audience perception

Online documentation is almost as revolutionary a change from printed documentation as printing was from Medieval manuscripts. Some people find the change unsettling, even unnerving. Fear of technology sometimes manifests itself in dislike of online documentation.

As a writer, you should be sensitive to your audience's needs and provide a comfortable style for online documentation. Use plain English, maintain consistency, provide completely reliable information, and give appropriate feedback so that the user gains confidence with every successful use of the product.

Accessibility

Online documentation can't be used when the computer isn't working. If something serious is wrong and you can't get the computer to work, you also can't see the online documentation that might provide help for the problem. Error messages and other diagnostic aids should always be in printed books rather than online.

Organizational devices

Online documentation can seldom use the organizational devices of printed documentation in exactly the same way as in books. Devices such as introductions, careful development of an idea over several pages, transitions, and cross-references require special handling in online documentation. For example, online introductory and conceptual information should be presented in small units, or stand-alone chunks, so that the reader won't have to absorb screen after screen of abstract information.

Entry points

With online documentation, you should proceed on the assumption that you can never predict where the user will start reading. You can have as many entry points into the information as the code supports. The sections of information you write must not depend on any other sections. Instead, you should design online documentation as stand-alone units.

You might need additional training to write high-quality online documentation, because writing "chunks" is different from writing pages.

Development cycle

Online documentation can often continue to be developed later in the product cycle than printed documentation because you don't have to go to the considerable trouble of formatting a book perfectly, producing camera-ready copy, and giving a publishing company or printer several weeks or months to print the book. Since online documentation goes on diskettes or other storage devices, which are manufactured very rapidly, you can finish your writing at the same time that the programmers are finishing their code. Then test groups can verify the accuracy of the code and the information at the same time.

Cost

Online documentation is usually less expensive to manufacture than printed books are, sometimes by a factor of ten. One diskette can hold hundreds of pages of information but costs less to produce than the traditional book with its covers or binders, paper, and illustrations.

You might get some pressure from the financial people in your organization to put everything online in order to cut the costs of a product. However, it's important to know what your audience wants and to produce the right kind of information for each kind of user.

Features

Some online documentation provides such features as a *search facility* that lets users locate information almost instantaneously by means of a keyword search. Some online documentation also includes a cut-and-paste feature that lets users copy bits of information to other locations, such as copying a piece of code from a sample program to an application that a programmer is developing.

These and other features give some users the impression that online documentation is superior to books, and they have come to expect a lot from their online documentation. If the tool you are using to create online documentation has no such options, you might be better off producing books than producing online documentation that isn't technologically competitive in the marketplace. Plenty of customers still prefer printed books.

Translation

If the product you are working on will be marketed outside the United States, some of the books, such as a programming reference, might not be translated on the grounds that the users of that book will have the kind of education that includes the study of English.

However, if the interface panels will be translated, then the help panels accessible from the interface must also be translated, and you must write the kind of English that is easy to translate. Your writing must avoid the following:

- Cultural references
- Emotion, humor, and slang
- Abstract words
- Excessive nominalization, in which several nouns are used as adjectives in front of a final noun, such as "terminal emulation configuration tool;" instead, write "tool that helps you configure for terminal emulation"
- Long sentences and paragraphs
- Unexplained technical words and phrases
- Figures of speech
- Highly complicated grammar, such as subjunctive and absolute constructions
- Ambiguity of any kind

Apply everything you know about writing plain, clear, concise English to online documentation. Leave extra blank space to accommodate languages such as German and Japanese, which tend to need more room on the screen than English does.

Design Principles of Online Documentation

Three design principles help you produce effective online documentation (no matter what you're writing): maintain consistency, write stand-alone units, and determine the quantity of information to display.

Maintaining consistency

Probably the most important design principle concerns consistency. Consistency is also one of the hardest principles to achieve because writers, reviewers, and editors forget the details of the first panels in a help system by the time they get through several hundred or several thousand. Still, consistency is important in many areas.

Navigation devices. You can never predict where a user will enter the information, so you must provide exactly the same navigation techniques on each panel of the information. Use exactly the same name each time you refer to a navigation device. For example, don't tell the user to press the Esc key in one panel, the Escape key in another, the Esc (Escape) key in another, and the Escape (Esc) key in still another.

Also, don't refer to the names of selection items, entry fields, and panel titles in any way other than exactly as they are presented on the product panels, character-for-character and in the same case (uppercase or lowercase). If you see inconsistencies in the interface itself—a common occurrence—use your company's method of reporting and tracking coding errors to ensure that the inconsistencies are fixed.

Reference to interface names. Often you want to change the name of an item in an interface screen to make it more user-friendly. Unless you can get the interface designers or programmers to change the name in the interface, you have to use the name as it exists so that you don't risk puzzling or irritating the user. For example, a selection item listed as *Directory Services directory function* might sorely tempt you to omit one of the uses of directory. Before you assume that one of the words is redundant and leave it out, however, you should check with the programmers. If they think all four words are needed, then you have to use them all whenever you refer to the selection item. Users will wonder if the Directory Services directory function they see on the product panel is the same as the Directory Services Function they see in the online documentation.

Highlighting for emphasis. Consistency also requires conforming to certain rules for capitalization, highlighting, style, and tone. In the example just discussed, you would have to capitalize the selection item exactly as it is capitalized (or not capitalized) on the product panels. Inexperienced users might become confused if names don't match exactly.

To emphasize certain words and phrases, be consistent with your use of boldface, italics, color, and capitalization so that the user comes to trust your use of emphasis. For example, you might decide to italicize all the commands that the user can type in the product. Don't change to boldface in the middle of your writing, unless you change the previous italics to boldface.

Style and tone. Similarly, if you start out in a formal, serious style, don't change to a more colloquial one later on. It might be hard for you to analyze your own tone, but a general guideline is to write as if you were helping a peer or a superior perform the tasks of the program. Keep all emotion, including excessive cheerfulness, out of your writing.

Consistency is hard enough to maintain in one writer over a period of time. It's extremely difficult to manage in a team of writers, which is the writing environment for much online documentation. The lead writer or the editor might spend a great deal of time looking for inconsistencies and bringing errant writers into compliance. If you have a good style guide, you have a better chance of maintaining consistency.

Writing stand-alone units

Another general principle of online documentation is to write the information in small, discreet units, or *nodes* that can stand alone. Don't point back to a previous chapter or module, or ahead to the next, because you won't know what the users have already read or what they might read next. Cross-references or pointers don't work in any type of online documentation except hypertext, and even hypertext has some stringent limitations.

Depending on the online tool you're using, you might not be able to refer to information in "the previous screen" the way you can refer to "the previous page." The user might be able to minimize the screen size and display far less information than you assumed. Also, the user might be able to scroll through the online documentation either one line at the time, half a screen at a time, or a full screen at a time. These and other characteristics of the online environment make it impossible for you to point to the "next" or the "previous" information.

Another consideration for writing stand-alone nodes is to provide everything users need in each node of the online documentation. You can't assume that they've read anything else before they read a particular node. You can't predict where they'll start reading, how many nodes they'll read, what order they'll read in, or whether they'll use the online documentation at all.

No writer, of course, can control any reader. For writers of online documentation, however, this lack of control has more serious repercussions than for writers of books:

- You have to know the product so intimately that you understand exactly what makes the user invoke the online documentation, especially the help panels. The user's situation or context can have a profound effect on the documentation you provide.

- You have to repeat important information far more often than you do in books. For example, if the tool you're using doesn't provide a way to link to a glossary, you must define an unfamiliar word on its first use in each node.

- You have to spell out an abbreviation or acronym on its first use in each node if the tool provides no way to link to a list of abbreviations and acronyms.

- In error messages and the help panels that explain them, you have to include all the pertinent corrective and recovery information the user might need. You can't group error messages under a heading as you can in books, nor can you refer to information in another message because you can't predict whether the user will make the error that generates the message.

Determining the quantity of information

A final general consideration concerns the amount of information to place on the screen at one time. "The less, the better" is a good rule of thumb. You can expect the reader of a book to get through large amounts of text, but you can't make similar demands on users of online documentation.

Sometimes the decision about how much information you can provide is made by the online tool you have to use. For example, you might be told that you can have only the right half of the screen, say 36 characters wide plus borders, and only 12 of the 24 lines available on the average screen. You might be able to place about 50 words into such a small area, after allowing room for the title and function keys. Before you write 50 words, however, consider the layout of your words on the screen. Allow some blank space for possible translation into other languages by using short paragraphs with blank lines in between.

Use bulleted lists that are indented and have extra blank space between list items. Also make the margins larger than one character wide. After allowing for blank space, you might end up placing only 30 words on a screen that has room for 50, but your information will be easier to read and understand than on a crowded screen.

Types of Online Documentation

Online documentation is relatively new and is developing at such a rapid rate that any detailed classification of types is bound to become obsolete.

However, it is likely that some version of most of today's four main types of online documentation will remain popular for some time:

- Tutorials
- Softcopy books
- Help panels
- Hypertext nodes or modules

Each type has its own purpose, usefulness to customers, and design considerations.

Tutorials

A tutorial is a series of online panels that introduces the main functions of a computer product to the customer. Sometimes customers look at the tutorial before they install the product it describes and before they read the books that accompany the product.

The purpose of a tutorial is to lead the user gently into the product by providing a friendly, easy-to-use set of exercises or tasks that are performed at the keyboard. The tutorial doesn't usually replace the introductory manual, often called a *user's guide*; it supplements the reading material by asking the user to set the books aside and get into the product itself. Since users in the early days of personal computers sometimes felt so intimidated that they would never use a new computer or product, the tutorial was one of the earliest types of online documentation because it could make a product appear more inviting and easy to learn than a book could.

Although tutorials are not completely unknown on mainframes and minicomputers, their major association is with personal computers and the novice audience. For new users, a well-designed tutorial can be very helpful. It can introduce the major functions of the product, provide a safe way to explore some of those functions, give the user a comfortable feeling after each successful exercise, provide enough animation, sounds, colors, and icons to entertain the user, and encourage him or her to begin using the product in earnest. The tutorial can even help to sell a product if a potential customer is sufficiently impressed with it. Since the main purpose is educational, however, it is important for you as a writer to understand how to teach the use of the product in a tutorial.

Characteristics of tutorials

If you are accustomed to teaching by means of printed books, you might need to get accustomed to the differences in writing tutorials.

Cooperation requirements. While a book might be almost entirely under your control, a tutorial seldom is. The code that runs the tutorial permits only certain functions—never everything you want. Also, unless you write the code yourself or use an online authoring tool, you need to work closely with the programmers to get at least some of the functions that you want into the code. For example, suppose the best way you can think of to show the flow of data in a communications network is with arrows moving along links between pictures of computers. Animation like this is not particularly hard to code, but you might have to convince the programmers to do it for you. Some writers switching from books to tutorials don't enjoy the loss of autonomy in their work lives, but others enjoy the difference.

Disposability. Customers usually keep computer books, even after they have read them, because they might need to look up advanced functions, or they might have problems someday and need the book. An online tutorial, on the other hand, is seldom viewed more than once. It's usually written at such an elementary level that customers can absorb the information in one viewing.

In fact, after an initial look at a tutorial, many customers remove it from their hard files to save disk space or, if they didn't install the tutorial, they tend to lose the diskette that contains it. Some writers have to adjust to producing throw-away products. Occasionally they have trouble convincing themselves to maintain high quality in a product that won't be used much.

Space constraints. Because of the space constraints of online documentation, you won't have many panels in which to explain functions to the customer. Also, depending on the authoring tool you're using, you might not have high-quality illustrations, a table of contents, an index, and other features of books to help you present information. Some tools have these features, and some don't. And, if the product you're writing for contains highly technical features, you might not be able to explain them at all in a tutorial. Some writers find it frustrating to write such simplified material, but others enjoy it.

Diminishing usefulness. Since tutorials are so elementary, their usefulness might diminish as customers become increasingly sophisticated. In general, there might be less need for tutorials in the future than there was in the past. In a particular product, there is probably less need for a tutorial in later releases than in the first release. Today, a writer probably shouldn't specialize in writing tutorials, because the job opportunities in this area will decrease over the next 20 years or so.

However, writing tutorials can be rewarding. Since a tutorial is the most simplified unit of documentation supplied with a product, it is also often the most challenging to write. It's much easier to write about technical details in highly technical language. Translating these details into simple, user-friendly words can be interesting. Also, the tutorial is often the jazziest unit of documentation, and you might enjoy all the color, sound, and animation that some tutorials use.

Tutorial design problems

From a design perspective, the biggest problems for the writer of tutorials are how much information to include and how best to simulate the product you're writing about.

Using time and space well. How much information to include in a tutorial depends upon two factors: the amount of time you want the customer to spend learning the product before actually starting to use it, and the complexity of the functions.

In general, you can't expect users to spend more than 30 to 60 minutes on a tutorial. A tutorial that runs over an hour is seldom completed. You should aim to introduce each section or function of the product, but only hit the highlights. Refer the customer to the books for further details.

Simulating product screens. Deciding how much information to include is easier than deciding how to represent the screens of the product. Unless you are using the same code the product uses or an authoring tool that provides excellent screen simulation, you might not be able to make your example panels exactly the same as the actual panels in the product. You might have to caution the customer that the actual product looks somewhat different from the tutorial.

Even with close approximations of the product panels, you might be frustrated to find that you can't give the customer real exercises to do instead of simulations. In your simulated exercises, you need to give customers the feel of the product by having them type information and select items from menus, but you are seldom able to show them the results of their actions. Your words have to bridge the gap between the tutorial and the product.

Softcopy Books

Softcopy books are units of information that are designed to be printed and read like books, and also presented as online information and viewed at the computer screen. Whether you want to write the softcopy or the printed book first, and no matter which one you prefer, you want to use the same source files for both versions of the information to avoid major retagging and revising. If you plan carefully, you might be able to convert the online files to files suitable for printing—or convert the files intended for a book into online documentation.

It's possible to write either the hardcopy or softcopy version of a book first. The first softcopy books were simply printed books that were converted and put online. A conversion tool formatted the source files for online presentation and, with some tools, could add a branch facility that let the customer select an item from the table of contents or the index and jump right to the selected information. More recently, writers have had to find ways to convert information intended to be only online into printed books because some customers require printed versions as well.

Characteristics of softcopy

Originally, the purpose of softcopy books was to put information online so that users could look it up rapidly and wouldn't have to leave their computer screens to hunt for a book. Some early tools for the conversion process were minimal and provided nothing but long files to scroll through. Many customers found these unusable. When tools were improved and keyword search functions were added, however, softcopy books began to live up to their purpose.

Now, with improved branches from the table of contents and the index, softcopy books can present large amounts of information online and provide retrievability aids as well. Today, the main purpose of softcopy books is to provide reminders about information that the user already understands but doesn't want to leave the computer to locate.

Although the usefulness of softcopy books has diminished with the development of other types of online documentation, they're still useful for certain kinds of information and certain kinds of customers. In general, three kinds of information do well in softcopy books: conceptual information, procedures, and lists.

Write the lists of commands and procedures to the programmer audience, omitting everything but the technical details of the commands and steps. Write the conceptual material to the general audience, which might include both highly technical and nontechnical people; you don't need to make the information suitable to the novice because these users are more likely to use the tutorial and to read introductory explanations in hardcopy before venturing into the softcopy.

Conceptual information. Conceptual information can introduce new functions that the customer needs to know about. Conceptual information shouldn't run over one or two screens in length per topic, each topic should be a stand-alone unit, and a table of contents or similar listing should give the user a way to select a topic to read about. If possible, users should be able to install and remove the conceptual material according to their needs.

For a new product, many users prefer to have general explanations in small chunks, online and selectable by topic, rather than search through books for just one thing. However, once users are familiar with the product, they might want to remove the conceptual material to save disk space. Softcopy conceptual material can contain more technical information and greater detail than tutorials can, but it's not the best place for the most highly technical information.

Procedures. Procedures, or steps for accomplishing a task, often work well in softcopy for three reasons: tasks usually have distinct names to enter into the table of contents or other type of listing, the steps for each task can be summed up in one or two screens, and many users prefer the immediacy of refreshing their memories with a quick online search to the necessity of locating the right book and then finding the right procedure in the book.

Some softcopy tools let you display the information in a window, so users can see the steps they need at the same time that they're typing or selecting items in the product screen. In this use of softcopy, you give the steps for each procedure and provide a minimum of other information—no discussions, explanations, or reasons—just enough to get the user going.

The arrangement of the procedures in the table of contents can be either chronological if the entire list of procedures can be viewed at the same time, or alphabetical if the entire list can't be viewed at one time.

Lists. A final use of softcopy books is to display lists of items, such as all the commands available in a certain product or programming language. Online lists of commands serve as quick references to help system users remember information that's easy to forget and sometimes hard or annoying to look up in a book.

Like procedures, lists of commands provide only the bare minimum of information, such as the syntax of the command, its required and optional parameters, and possibly an example of its use. Some softcopy tools support the use of simple diagrams to provide a visual representation of the parameters, somewhat like a flowchart.

Figure 9.3 gives an example of a syntax diagram in which the message parameter on the delete command is optional. If users want to display a message when they delete, they can choose to post either the full text of the message (the txt parameter) or just the number (the num parameter) that identifies the message.

Softcopy design problems

The most important design consideration for softcopy books is the question of double use: Will you need to provide both an online and a printed version of the information? If you don't need to worry about both, you can concentrate on making the softcopy book as useful as possible to the intended audience.

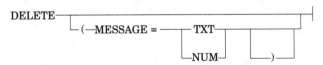

Figure 9.3 Syntax diagram with optional message parameter.

If you must provide both an online and a printed version of the information, you must answer several major questions before you begin.

Tagging one source file.   Can the tagging symbols used in one version also be used in the other version with little or no revision?

This question requires a good deal of thought and investigation. Some softcopy tools supply a what-you-see-is-what-you-get (WYSIWYG, pronounced "wizzy-wig") editor that doesn't require tagging. You just place your cursor where you want to type and start typing. When the information is displayed online, it looks just like what you typed in the editor. However, the code supporting the editor might use various controls that won't permit you to take the same files and just insert the tags needed for the printed version.

Many methods of producing printed manuals require the use of a tagging or mark-up language specific to the computer that prepares your camera-ready copy for the publishing company. Therefore, you end up with two sets of files, which means you'll be making updates and other changes in two places.

Using a conversion tool.   If the same tagging symbols can't be used in both versions of the information, can you or someone else write a conversion tool that automatically changes one set of tags to another set of tags? Sometimes called *filters*, these conversion tools, if they work perfectly, can save a great deal of time and effort. A filter lets you write and maintain only one version of the information. The change to the other version is handled automatically.

The problem, though, is that filters seldom handle everything. For example, nearly all printed books use tables of information that contain several rows and columns, along with headings and subheadings; some currently available online tools, however, can't present tables very well.

While a printed book is formatted and printed, a softcopy book is usually compiled and displayed. So far, compilers for text aren't as sophisticated as formatters for books. Therefore, you might have to design information that works for both versions, even if you have to make compromises you'd rather not make.

Eliminating one version.   If you must use tools that require one source file for the softcopy book and another source file for the printed book, can you eliminate one of the versions without seriously affecting the usability of the product? It's important to decide what you can throw out to avoid duplicating your writing and maintenance.

Which version you eliminate depends on the customer's needs. If most of the intended users prefer online documentation, then get rid of the printed book, and vice versa. One justification for keeping the softcopy version is that many programs provide a way to print screens or files, which would allow customers to print only the parts of the information that they wanted. However, if the information contains error recovery and diagnostics, you want to keep the printed version, since the customer can't get to the online documentation when the computer is down.

Choosing a tool. Which tool should you use for the softcopy book? It's usually beyond the scope of the writer's job to research, buy, and maintain tools, but, if asked, you can voice the concerns mentioned here, as well as any you think of on your own. After being trained to use the tool, you can write the softcopy book in much the same fashion as you would write a printed book.

Help Panels

Help panels are units or nodes of information that pertain to the parts of an interface, such as selection items, entry fields, function keys, and action bars. Help panels might also be provided for the procedures and commands in a product. If the authoring tool you're using supports an index, help panels might include an index to all the help panels, a general introduction to the help facility, and a brief explanation of the function of the product panel from which the help panel can be displayed.

Help panels can sometimes be accessed from error messages that are displayed on the screen. The help panels that have relevance only to those items from which they are accessible are often called *context-sensitive information*. See Fig. 9.4 for an illustration of such a help panel.

Characteristics of help panels

The purpose of help panels is to assist customers right when they need a little help to remember what to type in an entry field, understand which selection item they need, learn what caused an error message, and recover from the error. Since help panels have been available in products for several years, many customers have learned to use and rely on them instead of turning automatically to books. If the help panels are truly helpful, customers like them very much. If the help panels are vague, irrelevant to the situation, erroneous, or incomplete, customers are worse off with them than without them.

You can seldom get away with putting out a product today that doesn't provide help panels. As a writer, you need to make them really helpful so that customers feel encouraged to make use of them.

Help panels can be useful in several ways. They can serve as simple reminders of what customers are already familiar with but have temporarily for-

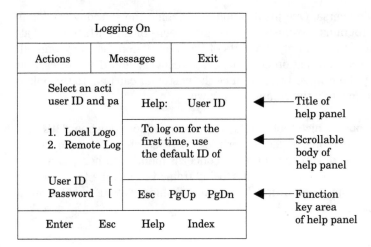

Figure 9.4 Help panel.

gotten. They can also remind customers about the length, format, and permitted characters for an entry field. They can provide definitions for customers coming upon unfamiliar terms. They can supply suggestions for using the functions of a product that customers might not think of on their own.

For error messages, help panels can provide critical information about correcting minor mistakes or about where to get further help for major problems. Since help panels are usually accessed with a single keystroke and contain brief, pertinent information, they can be extremely useful to both experienced and inexperienced customers.

Help panel design problems

Design problems for help panels might be less under the writer's control than those for tutorials and softcopy. You might have some freedom with those types of online documentation, but help panels are usually installed with the code and are required to fit into the general design of the product interface. By the time you start on the project, programmers or designers might already have selected the colors, fonts, shapes, sizes, and locations of pop-up panels, including those in which help panels are displayed; the names and positions on the screens of selection items and entry fields; the tools for creating help panels; and the format of the index to the help panels. These technical people might also have very strong ideas about the content, style, format, and length of the help panels because the help panels really are part of the code.

As with other types of online documentation, you need to find out what the code will support and whether you can get the code changed to accommodate your design. As a writer of help panels, you might become frustrated if the writing itself is important to you. Up to 75% or 80% of your time might go to tracking, uploading, and other nonwriting activities. Help panels also require a more restrictive and less creative style than books.

If you are required to have these technical people review and approve your work, which is nearly always the case, you might find yourself in some heated battles if their decisions aren't the right ones for the help panels. Following are some problems with help panels that programmers and interface designers might not consider.

Naming convention. In a fairly large product, you might find yourself trying to manage 3000 separate help files. The naming convention used for a few dozen or a few hundred product panels might be wholly inadequate for thousands of help panels. For example, in an eight-character naming convention, programmers might take the first five characters to identify the product, leaving only three characters for up to 999 specific panel identifiers. This scheme is too restrictive for help panel identifiers because it gives you no flexibility to use mnemonics or other devices to keep track of a large number of help panels.

Interface changes. Since each programmer might be responsible for only a few dozen product panels or code modules, the product designers might think nothing of changing the name of a selection item or the title of a panel. The programmers might regret taking time to modify a few panels or lines of code, but you have a much more time-consuming task if you have to modify a thousand help panels.

If you think such changes might happen in your project, you should insist on being consulted first. Tools exist that can run a batch job, making simultaneous changes in thousands of separate help files. But you still need to be aware of potential problems. In most help systems, each help panel is in a separate file because the code calls help panels individually when the user presses the function key designated for help. Opening and closing each file, even if done automatically, can take some time. Also, it's possible for an automated procedure to miss changes that a human being would know to make. For example, suppose you have to change the text string `Cap Lock` to `Caps Lock` in several hundred help panels. A case-sensitive automated procedure won't change such variant strings as `Cap lock`, `cap Lock`, `cap lock`. No automated procedure finds and changes misspellings and typos.

If you think you might need to search all the help files for certain words or phrases, a common occurrence, you should obtain a program that opens and closes each help file very rapidly as it searches for the string. A slow tool can take a long time to make such a search.

Multipurpose help panels. Sometimes, in order to cut down on the sheer number of help panels, programmers want to call the same help panel from different points in the product. They might assume that every help panel with the same title is identical. For example, the product might have dozens of entry fields with the title `File Name`, into which the user is to type the name of a file to use. However, the circumstances might be different for each of them, and the help panel should contain slightly different information. You might need to convince the programmers to call individual help panels rather than one generic help panel so that your information can be tailored to each situation the customer gets into.

Duplicate help panels. Sometimes the reverse is true—if several help panels turn out to be identical, there is no point in keeping more than one version of the help. The code can call the same help panel as many times as you need it to. Unless you write, compile, integrate, and test your own help panels, you need to work closely with the programmers to ensure that their help panel look-up table, or other calling scheme, is accurate.

Uploading. If you use an authoring tool to write and integrate help panels into the product, uploading problems don't apply to your situation. If you don't use such a tool, however, you might have to move your help files to the same location to which the programmers send their panels and code for the purpose of being integrated into the product. You might have to make such *code drops* many times during the development process. Ordinarily, you use an editor on the mainframe or on your own computer for writing the help panels, and then send, or *upload*, them to a centralized storage place. You might also have to insert them into some type of database or file from which they'll be copied onto the product diskettes.

You need some extremely fast, extremely reliable programs to upload, insert, and keep track of thousands of help panels. You don't want the upload program to insert extraneous characters into your files, delete any lines, or change certain characters to other characters. You want a tool that automatically inserts hundreds of help panels into a database or file so that you don't have to insert them one by one.

Perhaps most importantly, you want a tool that helps you keep track of the location and status of each help panel.

Developing a template. If you don't use an authoring tool to write help panels, one of your first writing tasks is to develop a template or model to use for help panels so that you won't forget how many letters you can put on a line of text, how many lines you can use (unless the help panels are scrollable and therefore can be as long as you want), whether the title is flush-left or centered, what colors to use, what style of capitalization to use, and other minor but important matters.

A template is necessary because consistency is essential but difficult for even one writer to achieve, let alone a team of writers. Following are some guidelines you might want the help-system writers to adhere to:

- Begin each help panel for a selection item with the same word (such as *select*, *choose*, or *pick*). Continue with a definition of the selection item and the reasons why the customer might want to use it.

- Begin each help panel for an entry field with the same word (such as *type* or *enter*). Continue by giving the length, format, and allowable characters for the entry field. Explain whether the customer needs to obtain the name from someone, such as a system administrator, or whether it can be an individually chosen name.

- Begin each help panel for an error message with the cause of the error, or at least some likely causes. Continue with an explanation of how to correct the error or refer the customer to someone who can help, such as administrative or service personnel.

As you are writing the help panels, keep in mind that each help panel must be a stand-alone unit with no cross-references to other help panels. It's also a good idea not to include references to books because you have to update these references with each new release of the product, since books commonly have release numbers in the titles. You can't assume that the customer has read any of the other help panels, so you have to provide all the pertinent information in each help panel. However, you can't include everything in each help. A good rule of thumb is to supply all the information the user needs to perform the task at hand.

Indexing the help panels. If you aren't using an authoring tool to write help panels, you might have more work, but also more freedom, in developing an index. For example, you need to think about the purpose of the index and what use it might have for the customer.

For example, for a small number of help panels, each with a unique title, you might want to provide an alphabetic list from which the customer can select a help panel. With this scheme, users can display any help panel at will, not just when they're on the right product panel. For a huge number of help panels, many of which have identical titles, you might not want to provide a list on the grounds that it would be unusable. (Think of 1500 help panels for error messages, all entitled Message Help.) Instead, a topical index would be more usable. In this case, you have to write the topics, since you won't already have topical help panels, but such an index is appreciated by the customer.

Hypertext

The latest type of online documentation to be implemented is *hypertext*, an information system that provides branches or links between units of information. Customers can move through the information in any order they please because the links permit unique, nonlinear, associative pathways through the information. In many hypertext systems, a word or phrase that contains a link to another unit of information is highlighted in some way. Several such highlighted words or phrases might be included on each screen, as Fig. 9.5 shows.

Although Fig. 9.5 implies that you start at the "top" and work "down," a better way to think of the nodes is to see them as unique, stand-alone units all on the same level and accessible from several directions. The order in which customers read the units of information, the amount they read, and the path they take through the information varies according to their needs.

Characteristics of hypertext

The two main components of a hypertext system are usually called *nodes* and *links*. Synonyms for nodes include *modules, chunks, articles,* and *segments*; synonyms for links include *launches, jumps, branches,* and *connections*.

A node is the smallest accessible unit of information, and it might range in size from a small paragraph to several screens of information. A link is a programmed connection between two points, usually signaled by some type of highlighting, controlled by a tag, and supported by the code of the hypertext system. Figure 9.6 illustrates hypertext links and nodes.

In addition, most hypertext systems provide a keyword search facility that lets users locate very rapidly the exact information they want. Most hypertext systems also have a feature that records customers' paths through the information by keeping a log, trail, history file, or path record of every node displayed during one use of the hypertext system. Some of the logs are permanent so that customers can reuse the logs after they tailor unique paths through the information.

Another feature of many hypertext systems is a map, graph, table of contents, or picture of the nodes and links in the system so that customers can get an overall view of the available information. Some systems let customers mark the sections of the map that they've displayed so that they can keep track of what they have and have not read.

Three additional features of many hypertext systems are the bookmark, the notepad, and the cut-and-paste facility. The *bookmark* lets customers insert electronic markers into the hypertext system so that they can locate certain information easily. They might want to mark all information relating to a certain topic, or they might want simply to mark the point at which they stopped

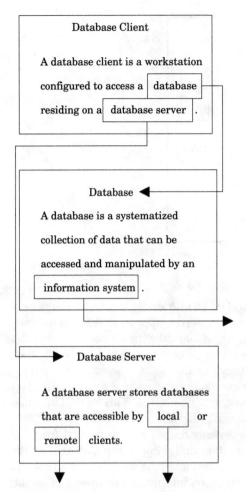

Figure 9.5 Hypertext links from "database client" panel.

reading during their previous use of the system. The *notepad* provides a small area on the screen where customers can make notes in their own words and attach these jottings to specific nodes in the system. The *cut-and-paste facility* lets customers mark blocks of text and copy them to other locations.

Hypertext systems are becoming popular because they provide many useful features. Technical people who have no computer phobias usually enjoy the possibilities of a hypertext system and learn to use it rapidly. However, novice users, and even some technical people, might find hypertext frustrating, disorientating, and difficult to learn at first.

A hypertext system can be frustrating to use if it's not intuitive and well-

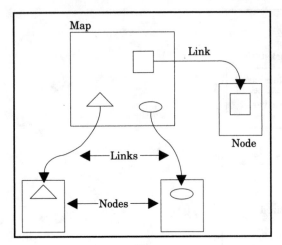

Figure 9.6 Hypertext links and nodes.

designed. It's easy to feel frustrated by an unfriendly system and to get exasperated at having to take a trial-and-error approach. Also, some customers become rather disoriented when they take the wrong path and can't return to where they started. They might worry that they'll get so lost they won't be able to read everything they need.

The learning difficulties some customers experience relate to the fact that a hypertext system takes some getting used to. This kind of information doesn't look like a book and doesn't read like a book. Unlike other types of online documentation, hypertext really has no existence apart from the screen, keyboard or mouse, and system unit. However, hypertext has the advantage of offering fast access to information. Books attempt to control the customer's pace and path through the information by means of layout, headings, transitional devices, and so on; hypertext offers the customer control of the pace and path.

Hypertext design problems

Design problems in writing for a hypertext system center around making the right decisions in several areas.

Accessibility. Will the hypertext information be accessible from within the product panels or will it be separate from the product? This decision is one of the most important ones to make because it strongly influences the remainder of the design considerations.

If customers can enter the hypertext system at any point within the product, you'd be well-advised to treat the nodes almost as if they were extensions of the help panels and make them both self-contained and callable from various locations. If customers have to exit from the product in order to see the hypertext, you can treat the nodes more like units in a softcopy book. This decision might have been made for you already, and you have to work with the tool that was purchased.

Starting environment. Are you starting from the beginning with a new product, or are you changing an existing library of information over to a hypertext system? Both have advantages and disadvantages.

For a new product, you get the adventure of learning a new product, a new tool, and a new way of doing business all at once, and sometimes you end up redoing work others have already done. But if you put a lot of thought into design upfront, you can have the satisfaction of doing the job right.

For an existing product, you get the headache of converting from one medium to another, but at least you'll be familiar with the product and need to learn only the new functions.

Approach. For your particular customers, will a purely associative, nonlinear approach work, or will you need to provide some kind of hierarchy, perhaps in the form of panels that offer selections?

In the nonlinear approach, the only structure customers might see is the map or table of contents from which they choose their first link. Thereafter, they read through some introductory text containing highlighted words and phrases and, from these, link to any node they want. In the hierarchical approach, one or more panels containing selection items can branch customers to increasingly specific information. At the end of this tree-like structure are the actual nodes or articles that the customer wants to read. Novice users sometimes feel more comfortable with the hierarchical approach.

Layers. How many links should a customer have to choose before arriving at information pertaining to specific needs? The nonstructured and the hierarchical approach both have a potential danger: forcing customers into annoyingly circular paths in the nonstructured approach, or forcing customers to make far too many selections before they find the information they want in the hierarchical approach.

As a general rule of thumb for both approaches, remember that most people don't want to move through more than three or four layers or selections before they get to the information they want.

Map. What kind of map or table of contents will you provide to launch customers into the hypertext? Can you arrange everything by tasks, by commands, by order of importance, by type of information, or some similar scheme?

For a very small library of information, these questions might be moot, but for a very large one, they're of the utmost importance. If the product for which you're designing hypertext has only one audience, such as end users, administrators, programmers, or service personnel, your task might be a little easier than if you have several audiences. Even so, you need to design several types of nodes, such as those containing introductory material, those with procedures or steps for tasks, and those with reference information, and make them accessible from the map or table of contents.

Node structure. How will you structure the smallest units of information, the nodes? This decision relates not only to the size of nodes but also to the contents and purpose of the nodes. Sometimes a hypertext system can be thought of as a database of nodes, any of which can be accessed at will from any point external to the database. Using this model, you can think of nodes almost as if they were objects that you pick up and put down as you need them. You might be tempted to restrict each node to a 100-word paragraph with highly specific contents, but if you're converting a 20,000-page library to hypertext, you could wind up with the nightmare of tracking 60,000 to 80,000 nodes. Coming up with a reasonable method of naming, tracking, updating, and linking to such a large number would be challenge enough.

A better plan is to reduce the number of nodes by making each one long enough to cover several aspects of the topic. For example, in all the task-oriented nodes, you might start with a brief explanation of what the task accomplishes, including definitions of major terms, go on to the steps of the task, and conclude with alternate ways to perform the task or shortcuts and expert advice.

Compiling and debugging. In addition to design problems within a hypertext system, you might have a more peripheral, but troublesome, concern: compiling, debugging, and revising the nodes so that all the links work correctly. If the tool you're using requires that you compile the nodes, you might feel more like a programmer than a writer, especially since some hypertext tools offer little help in locating, diagnosing, and correcting errors. One typographical mistake in a link tag or in the head-reference tag of a node can require hours to locate and fix.

Using a programmable editor. Another peripheral concern is which editor to use. If at all possible, use an editor for creating hypertext nodes that lets you program certain function keys with the complete syntax for a tag. With one keystroke, you can display a whole tag and have to insert only the specific identifier to reference a certain node. Also, try to develop a naming convention for the nodes that's at least partially mnemonic so that you can match a node identifier with the right section of the hypertext. For example, if you have a section on configuration, you might use CFG in the identifier of each node pertaining to that section.

As a writer, you might enjoy the novelty of hypertext, but, as with help panels, hypertext demands far more time to track and compile nodes, debug links, and upload for code drops than it does for the actual writing. If you are adapting an existing hardcopy library to hypertext, you might do hardly any writing, depending on the condition of the existing information. You might omit great portions, revise some sections, and decide how to divide parts of the information into stand-alone nodes, sometimes called *chunking the information*. But the only real writing you might do is for new functions being added to the next release.

However, designing and writing for a hypertext system can add valuable skills to your repertoire, increase your interest in the process, place you on the forefront of technical writing, and provide you with expanded career opportunities. Hypertext is certainly worth mastering, since customers are creating more and more demand for it.

10

Reviewing and Testing for Quality

Nobody likes reviews and tests, just as nobody likes to go to the dentist. Nevertheless, virtually all writing shops conduct document reviews, and many also conduct tests, because these activities are the most objective and powerful way of ensuring the quality of a book. It's just that no one wants to spend so much money, time, and energy.

Objections to reviewing and testing publications come from three groups of people:

- Technical people sometimes feel they have so much "real work" to do that they shouldn't spend their time reading books.

- Writers sometimes believe that reviewing is a necessary evil but testing isn't needed. Some might feel intimidated or angered by the reviewing and testing process.

- Managers might not be sure they're getting their money's worth, since reviewing and testing take up resources that could go to other activities.

However, reviewing and testing are useful and reliable methods of ensuring quality. Both methods bring other people than the writers into the process and focus additional expertise on the details of the information. If writers, reviewers, testers, and others agree to follow certain guidelines, the experience can be valuable for all.

Guidelines for Reviewing and Testing

Distributing a book for review or test is usually the first time the document goes out of the writing area—or perhaps out of the writer's hands—so keeping the following four points in mind is important:

- Make every effort to edit and proofread the draft so that reviewers won't waste time on typos and writers won't lose credibility with technical people.

- Make sure that all who read the book are reviewing or testing the writing, not the writer. Although personal attacks upon writers are rare, unhelpful or insensitive comments about a book are more common. For example, a reviewer who writes, "This is wrong" or "This is terrible" can be perceived as criticizing the writer instead of the information. For reviewers to improve the quality of the document, they should identify problem areas as neutrally as possible and then work with the writer to solve the problems.

- All books have minor errors, and some have major ones. Recognize that all books have flaws and defects that the writers just didn't see. Getting too close to the task, writing under serious time constraints, using inadequate source material, misunderstanding technical details, or neglecting to revise as you go along can cause anyone to produce flawed documentation. Writers need to keep an open mind about their own work, being neither too proud nor too humble about it. Some writers find it difficult to accept the fact that their work isn't perfect, but the sooner they do, the sooner they can start incorporating any good ideas they might get from reviewers and testers.

- All books can be revised. Given enough resources, any document can show improvement in quality. Resources include time, tools and equipment, people, and either paper for books or resources for reviewing and testing diskettes for online information. When resources are in short supply, which is usually the case, remember that money spent early in the cycle pays off in decreased costs later in the cycle and in satisfied customers in the marketplace. The more errors you can find and fix before the information goes out to customers, the better.

Deciding Whether to Review or Test

In determining whether to review or test, you should note that printed books can benefit from reviews as well as tests, but online documentation usually benefits more from testing because it's part of the interface and frequently doesn't have a printed version that customers are supposed to see. You can ask reviewers to read a hardcopy version of online information, but unless they also see the relationship between the interface and the information that supports it, they can't always make useful comments. Testing online documentation, however, shouldn't completely replace reviewing. In a well-coded help system, poorly written online information might look all right until you read it. A good hardcopy review can help ensure that the information is written well.

Reviewing and testing have the same goals but different procedures and purposes. *Reviewing*, the more common of the two, means having others read the book, looking for technical errors, definition inaccuracies, omissions, redundancies, ineffective organization, inconsistencies, and confusing passages, as well as such editorial concerns as grammar, spelling, and punctuation. *Testing*, which is becoming increasingly important in today's customer-oriented environment, means having others try to use the documentation to accomplish specific tasks, such as installing a program or replacing an adapter.

Ideally, printed books and online documentation should have both reviews and tests.

Preparing for Reviewing

Having information reviewed is not as simple as it might seem. You can't just distribute a book to reviewers and expect to get anything useful back. Having books reviewed takes planning, negotiation, and paperwork.

Planning for reviewing

The task of planning for reviews includes answering the following questions:

- What do you want the reviewers to look for as they read? Some readers mark typos even if you ask them not to, but not many reviewers notice organizational flaws in long procedures or lists of steps, even if you ask them to.

- At what stage of development should you schedule a review and how many reviews should you have? You might want to consider having chapters reviewed early in the development cycle instead of waiting until you have an entire draft. You might want two or three reviews if you can schedule that many, but more than three aren't usually productive.

- Who should review the book? You should try to get a balance of designers, programmers or engineers, market-oriented people, and editors to review the book or online documentation. You want people who can tell you what's wrong with the book, not what's right with it. Above all, you need people who will take the job seriously and who will give you helpful information.

- How much time should you give reviewers to read the book? Depending on the size and complexity of the material you ask them to review, somewhere between one and three weeks is usually enough.

- Will you hold a meeting in which reviewers discuss and agree upon proposed changes? For major or controversial changes, a meeting is usually mandatory to ensure that all reviewers reach a consensus about proposed changes. A meeting is also advisable after the last distribution of the cycle so that the reviewers can agree on the final contents of the book.

Planning for reviews is sometimes the responsibility of the writers, sometimes the responsibility of planners, team leaders, or managers. The circumstances depend somewhat on the usual way of doing business. Whoever does the planning should get involved with the considerable amount of negotiating that must also be done.

Negotiating for reviewing

The advantages of having documentation reviewed are so great that the potential disadvantages usually receive little attention. Before you start negotiating, however, you should be aware of the following negotiating concerns:

- Reviewing is never free. If a programmer is reviewing a book, he or she is not writing code.

- Reviewing takes time that you and the reviewers might not think you have in a tight schedule.

- Reviewers who mark up information that's beyond their areas of expertise might introduce confusing or erroneous material.

- Reviewers who can't agree on a change might cause political problems, technical inaccuracies, or other difficulties for you.

- Technically oriented reviewers who are unaware of customers' needs might try to insert so much technical jargon that the book is no longer useful for its intended audience.

- Some reviewers might not do a good job, and you might be faced with last-minute changes when other reviewers see errors.

- Reviewers might expect their exact words to go into your book and get offended if you change anything. You should make it clear that you own the book and have final say on the wording, the format, the artwork, the organization, and other matters.

- Some late reviewers might try to insist on changes after your deadline has passed. You should, of course, stop the presses for catastrophic errors, but you should also take the time to verify the changes with other reviewers.

Getting good reviews

With the negotiating concerns in mind, try to get the best reviewers you can get—those who are both technically astute and conscientious about doing a good job. If possible, enlist management support to ensure that reviewers build reviewing time into their job descriptions. You can also do a number of small things to get good reviews from good reviewers:

- Hold a kickoff meeting when your draft is ready to distribute. Getting reviewers in the same room, even if you have to supply donuts, can bring peer pressure into play. If a junior, but important, reviewer sees lead programmers taking their reviewing jobs seriously, he or she is more likely to do the same.

- Provide a brief overview of the book, both in writing and orally, if you hold a kickoff meeting. Now is a good time to demonstrate that you fully understand the technical details of the product and that you have represented them accurately.

- Assign specific sections to the reviewers, if possible, that relate to their areas of expertise. Also make sure that you ask several people to look at the whole book to see whether it presents the product to customers in the most useful, logical way.

- In the unfortunate event that you had to write about a poorly designed or hard-to-use product, explain what you did to compensate for these flaws and suggest ways to improve the product in a future release. Software designers are just as human as anyone else and sometimes make mistakes. Even though your recommendations for improvement might have no influence, you should state them and get them into the minutes of the meeting anyway. Eventually someone might hear you.

- Inform all reviewers that you'll record and distribute minutes of the review meetings to all attendees. The minutes should include all work items assigned to specific attendees and the date by which each work item is to be completed. For example, a reviewer might be asked to research a topic on which there was disagreement or for which information was missing. Making the person and the date a matter of public record provides a way for both the reviewer and the writer to keep track of the work item.

- Ask for a specific type of review, such as a technical review to ensure that the technical content is accurate and complete, an editorial review to ensure conformity to style guidelines and the correctness of the language, a usability review to ensure that the book is easy to use for its intended audience, or a library-oriented review to ensure that a particular book fits well into the library of books for the product.

The form of review comments

You should consider the form in which you'll receive reviewers' critiques or comments and negotiate to get the type you want. If you get telephone calls from reviewers, you should be careful to log the reviewer's name, the date, and a summary of the call so that you have a written record of the suggested change.

Logging and tracking telephone calls can be difficult, so you might ask reviewers to send you written comments as well. However, if a call is the only type of response you receive from certain reviewers, you'll have to record their comments as best you can. An excellent practice is to send a note containing the gist of the call and to ask for confirmation that you have accurately recorded what the reviewer meant.

If all reviewers agree to give you written comments, you can consider what form you'd like them to take. Common forms of written critiques are the following:

- The reviewer's handwritten comments in the margins of the review draft of the book
- Page-by-page lists of errors on separate sheets of paper
- Online comments entered with an online reviewing tool or sent to you as electronic mail

Sometimes a good strategy is to provide reviewers with a log in which they can record their changes. If reviewers want to keep their drafts, which some do, they should be willing to use a log to list errors they find. Asking reviewers to comment using a log has several distinct advantages:

- Gathering all the changes into a master file corresponding to the pages and chapters of your book is easier and more efficient than flipping through a dozen or more reviewers' drafts, looking for all the comments that apply to a particular paragraph.
- Trivial comments might not seem worth entering into a log, so you'll get only the important technical changes that you want.
- A log lets you see contradictory or duplicate comments more quickly than if you have only the marginal notations that reviewers make as they read.

The technical review meeting

A final point to negotiate is the conduct of the review meeting. You should insist that reviewers not waste time on arbitrary wording changes and other minor concerns—otherwise, you risk having a meeting stretch on for days. The main function of a review meeting should be to resolve conflicts among technical comments. There will be disagreements, if not on the details themselves, then on the way you presented these details.

For the review meeting, you can also negotiate some of the following conditions to obtain the best results:

- Set an agenda and stick to it to make sure you cover all of your concerns.
- Limit debate and rebuttal on technical issues to a few minutes per person.
- Discourage conversations about such side issues as future enhancements to the product, schedule changes, and so on once the meeting is underway. You can pick up interesting news either before or after the meeting.
- Help reviewers stay alert and focused on the details of the draft itself. If a

reviewer has been silent for some time, for example, ask a direct, but friendly, question.

Paperwork for reviewing

Successful negotiating might cut down on the amount of paperwork required for a good review, but nothing can quite eliminate it. The paperwork you might prepare when having a book reviewed includes the following:

- A cover letter explaining what the book contains, how it relates to other documentation for the same product, what the reviewers should look for, when they should return their critiques to you, when the review meeting will take place, who will moderate the meeting, who will take the minutes, and who will distribute the minutes.
- A list of reviewers and their addresses and telephone numbers.
- Copies of the critique log.
- Management's agreement for the reviewers to take the time they need to read and mark up the book, attend the meeting, and work with the writer on changes.
- The writer's agreement to incorporate agreed-upon changes into the book.
- Minutes of the meeting, to be distributed to all who attend.

Paperwork might seem unnecessary in a small, friendly environment, but even in the best of circumstances, a written record is much more reliable than people's memories. The main purpose of the minutes is to document the agreements reached at the review meeting on what changes will be made, what changes will not be made, who is responsible for obtaining any answers that were not available at the meeting, and when those answers will be given to the writer.

Sometimes the minutes can include the date when the next draft will be distributed, especially if there are few comments and your schedule is set.

Preparing to Test Printed and Online Information

Having a document reviewed can improve its quality if the technical experts cooperate fully in giving the publication careful and thorough attention. However, reviewing remains an in-house exercise in which even experts sometimes miss errors. A better way to ensure quality is to have both printed and online information tested, preferably by people who did not develop the product.

Testing printed and online information goes beyond reviewing because representative customers are asked to put the document to use in typical day-to-day activities. If the intended audience is data entry people, then these are the people who should be test subjects for the document, not the technical experts who designed and implemented the code or the hardware.

Testing documentation can be far more expensive and time-consuming than reviewing it, but the results can justify the cost in today's competitive market. You really can't guarantee that your customers will be delighted with your printed or online documentation unless you test it.

Tools for testing

Labs, test cases, and test subjects are key tools for testing both printed and online information. The lab doesn't have to be fancy, but it does have to simulate your customer's setting. As nearly as possible, use the same hardware and software that your customer uses. Configure the machines the way your customer does. Place the same demands on your equipment that the customer does. Short of going out to your customer's workplace, try to re-create the real world in your lab.

Similarly, try to understand how your customer will use the new product. Develop scenarios for tasks that your customer actually needs to perform. Use test subjects that closely match your customers in experience.

Sometimes the lab might be your own office and machine, and your test subjects might be anyone who comes into your office with a few minutes to spare. However, the closer you can come to reality, the better.

Test plans and test cases

You need to spend some time on your test cases and test plans. A *test case* is one task, or group of related tasks, for a test subject to perform in a fairly short period of time—two to four hours. A *test plan* lists and describes the test cases and establishes the goals of the tests.

In addition to simulating customers' tasks, you need to bear in mind which aspects of the printed and online information you are testing. For example, you might want to find out how long it takes test subjects to find certain information. They might look in the table of contents or the index, or they might flip through the pages. If you know how most people like to look for information, you can plan to give them the retrieval system they want.

Writing test cases

Writing test cases is a skill well worth developing. A good format to use is the written scenario that

- Outlines the experience level of the test subject
- Describes the setting, including the hardware, software, books, and online information available to the test subject
- States the task to be performed
- Specifies the end point of the test

Create a text file, give it a name, type 10 lines of text in the file, save the file, and then revise it by adding a few more lines to it.

Remove the defective Token-Ring adapter card from the system unit and replace it with a new one.

Configure your system for a 3270 connection to a VM host, using a non-switched line.

Write a series of SQL statements that will extract the names of all employees with 10 years of service from a database named EMPLHIST.

Format your hard file with two partitions and install the new operating system on the primary partition.

Figure 10.1   Test-case tasks.

The test case should not say to start on page 12, or to look up installing in the index. Instead, make a fairly general statement about the exact task you want the test subject to attempt. Some examples of tasks are shown in Fig. 10.1.

Keeping records

As your test subjects begin working, you or a test administrator should watch closely to see how they use the documentation. You should find some means of recording what the test subjects are doing. One of the most reliable recording methods is a video camera focused on the screen and keyboard that a test subject is using. If a test subject talks through the process of reading or flipping through the book and performing a task, you will have a complete record.

For subjects who aren't very talkative, you should probably interrupt with questions to make sure you know why they are reading certain sections, having trouble finding what they need, neglecting to use the publication, and so on. If you can't use a video camera, you can try an audio cassette recorder, provided the test subjects talk enough, or you can resort to watching and taking notes.

You can also ask test subjects to fill out a form at the end of the test that indicates how satisfied they were with certain parts of the printed or online information, such as the organization, the index, the artwork, the steps or procedures, the glossary, the tables and graphs, the page size, the tone and style, and the audience definition.

A simple rating scale of 1 to 5, from most satisfied to least satisfied, is enough for most cases. Soliciting free-form comments as well by providing space for additional comments is also a good idea. Figure 10.2 gives an example of a form for rating documentation.

RATING SCALE

Book or Online Unit:_____

Circle the number from 1 to 5 that best corresponds with your rating of the test topic for this book.

Test Topic	Great	Good	Average	Fair	Poor
Accuracy	1	2	3	4	5
Completeness	1	2	3	4	5
Usefulness	1	2	3	4	5
Clarity of language	1	2	3	4	5
Index	1	2	3	4	5
Artwork	1	2	3	4	5
Retrievability	1	2	3	4	5

Additional Comments:

Figure 10.2 A form for rating documentation.

Test strategy

How many test cases and how many test subjects does it take to find all the errors in a book or online information system? That depends on your requirements and resources. Unless you have a great deal of time and money, or a mandate from management, don't even try to achieve perfection. A better strategy to adopt is to focus on the parts of the documentation that you're least secure about. Good candidates for the most thorough testing include the following:

- The most complex information
- The sections that all readers will use
- The newest material, particularly for a product being updated for a new release
- The sections that received customer complaints in a previous release

Sometimes one test subject will give you enough feedback for you to begin revising the documentation. If three to five test subjects with the right skills can perform the tasks in a reasonable amount of time and have no complaints about the printed or online documentation, you're probably safe to conclude that the information is presented in a useful, logical way for your intended audience. If you have more time and more test subjects, you can use them more effectively than having them repeat the same test over and over. Instead, write two versions of the same material with slightly different organizations, styles, or whatever, and see which version satisfies the test subjects better.

Formal vs. informal test reports

What do you do with the results of a test? Sometimes a formal report is necessary, and sometimes informal feedback is better. Advantages of the formal report include the following:

- It keeps a written history of defects in the documentation.
- It looks official, especially if you include statistics.
- It can be presented to management.
- It can be compared with later test reports to show improvement.
- It can be used to track revisions and to ensure that they get done.

The formal report has some disadvantages, though. It takes time to compile statistics and write the report, and writers are sometimes intimidated to know that defects in their books are the subject of a formal report. Unless you are careful with your observations, measurements, and statistics, the formal report can be a waste of resources.

Advantages of informal feedback, whether written or oral, include the following:

- It's much more immediate, especially if the writer observes the test.
- It can be friendlier if everyone focuses on fixing the defects instead of blaming the writers for doing a bad job.
- It involves fewer people and, usually, fewer conflicts.

Disadvantages of informal feedback are usually limited to the fact that oral feedback can't be used for measuring, tracking, or enforcing revisions. Written feedback, especially hastily jotted notes, might not carry enough weight to ensure a change in deadlines or to get more help for a book with major problems.

If you have any control over the testing process, you should present the test results in the form that best accomplishes the goals that you have for the documentation.

Using test results

How should you use test results? The answer is not as obvious as it might seem. You want the documentation to be as error-free as possible, but you should look at test results from both the manager's and the writer's point of view. You should also take a practical approach to using test results.

The manager's point of view. A manager can both love and hate the results of a test. If testing reveals many errors, a manager might want to penalize the writer in some way. Managers with a punitive attitude toward early drafts need to be educated to the advantages of finding defects before the documentation goes out to customers. They shouldn't castigate the writers, as long as the errors are fixed. Enlightened managers are more interested in getting the writers the help they need to improve the document.

If a manager finds it difficult to support writers whose books contain many errors and who don't do everything perfectly the first time they try it, he or she should try to concentrate on providing a safe environment in which the writer can work on improvement without fear of reprisals.

Early drafts, after all, don't often go out to customers.

The writer's point of view. From the writer's perspective, test results that reveal problems in printed or online information shouldn't be anything to fear. Just as programmers have learned to predict a certain number of defects per thousand lines of code and are glad when they debug that number, writers too can learn to anticipate errors and feel a sense of relief in revising them. Writers can use test results, even disappointing ones, in a positive way.

A practical approach. Another way to look at using test results is to prioritize the errors and make a decision to correct a certain number of errors in certain circumstances. For example, if you need to reorganize 50 pages but have only a day, you can try to negotiate an extension of your deadline, ask for help from other writers, or fix the most important problems to meet your deadline and save the other errors for the next release.

Whatever your choice, you should keep careful written records of what you corrected, what you correct, how much time you had, and why you corrected what you did. In early drafts, you can usually postpone some of the revisions until a later draft.

Even when documentation is almost ready to be manufactured, you might find some minor flaws that you would like to fix but can't. For example, it's probably not worth missing your deadline to fix something that customers probably won't notice, and won't be concerned about if they do notice, such as leaving one space instead of two between a period and the start of the next sentence.

One of the best uses of test results is to analyze patterns of errors, correct the errors, retest the revised information, and demonstrate to all concerned the high quality of the retested information. Then you should work to correct whatever caused the pattern of errors.

Testing Printed Information

Testing printed information differs considerably from testing online information. As the older and more established of the two, testing books is so much faster and easier for most people that this method seems the natural way to test. Hardcopy methods have even been used to test online information, but with less than satisfactory results.

For books, keyboard templates, quick-reference cards, and any other type of printed material, the test consists of watching and recording a test subject's attempts to carry out the test case. Three overriding concerns dominate most hardcopy testing: when to test, whether to involve the writer in the test, and how to merge writing and testing schedules.

Early testing

The question of when to test worries writers in particular because they might never feel the book is ready to send out. Testing an early draft of a book, or even an early draft of a chapter, has both advantages and disadvantages for the writer and for the draft.

For new products or new functions added to existing products, the earlier the book is tested, the better, provided the draft is complete and can stand as a self-contained unit. Early testing of new material provides feedback that you can use immediately, instead of in the next release. You get a sense of whether you're on the right track in time to change course if you have to.

Early testing also has the advantage of revealing coding and design flaws in the software or hardware. Programmers and engineers might not be able to repair all the defects immediately, but you can at least document them and get assurances that they will be fixed in the next release.

The disadvantages of early testing center mainly around concerns about time. If you test too early, the code might change, the interface might be redesigned, or the icons might have to be made acceptable to the international marketplace. Any number of things can change, including the whole purpose of the product. You can usually recycle some of your early material through a redesign, but not all of it.

Another disadvantage of early testing is the pressure that writers might come under to produce a piece of usable information before they understand its relationship to the whole book. Although some writers like to work from the parts up to the whole, many others need to acquire an understanding of the entire product before they can start breaking information out into sections or chapters.

You should strive to test new material as early as you are comfortable doing so.

Mid-cycle testing

Testing a mid-cycle draft of a book has many advantages. By mid-cycle, you've probably written most of the information you planned to include but might not have done the final layout, artwork, indexing, and other tasks. You've probably studied the product long enough to know its technical details. You have likely decided on the structure of the book. Perhaps most important, you have developed close enough rapport with the designers and developers of the product that you don't anticipate major changes. By mid-cycle, you should feel relatively comfortable offering the book for the approval of those who read it and test it. If there are some problems with certain passages, you still have time to reword them, but not time to completely reorganize the book.

The disadvantages of testing at mid-cycle are similar to those of testing early:

- The product might change, causing you major rework when you thought you were ready to polish.

- You might not feel comfortable testing something you haven't gone over dozens of times.

- You might also be concerned that test subjects expect the book to be in final form and might lose respect for you, the product, or your company.

Whoever conducts the test should explain carefully that the book is a work-in-progress and that the purpose of the test is to ensure that the final draft is of the highest quality.

Late testing

Testing late in the cycle, when the book is almost ready to be published, has some use, but not as much as testing earlier. For books in a second or subsequent release of a product, late testing might be all that's needed if the following holds true:

- The major documentation problems were found and fixed in the earlier release.

- The writers are experienced and knowledgeable.

- The new functions added to the product were similar to existing functions and could be documented in a similar way.

Late testing under these conditions can save a lot of time and money.

Skipping the test entirely is rarely a good idea, but you can certainly abbreviate it. You can also use this kind of test to validate corrections you made in earlier releases by retesting sections that generated customer complaints.

The main disadvantage of testing late in the cycle, even for updates to existing books, is that you hardly have time to fix anything. If you really are in the final stages of polishing, you might have to redo your layout if you add or delete a single line.

One real danger of testing heavily revised books late in the cycle is that you might have been too busy documenting new features to look at how the new sections fit into the old structure of the book. Sometimes everyone realizes too late that the book should have been completely reorganized to accommodate the additional features. If this situation occurs, you can either work overtime to fix the book much more rapidly than usual, or you can let it go out as it is, promising yourself that you'll restructure it in the next release.

In trying to decide when to test a book, you'll get the most value out of testing at two stages: early and mid-cycle for new material; mid-cycle and late for revised material. To cut down on expenses, you can conduct shorter, simpler tests with fewer test cases and test subjects than you would normally use. You can still get a great many useful results.

Involving writers in the test

The question of involving writers in tests of their own books depends only a little on the writers themselves; many professional writers can distance themselves from their work enough to participate. Instead, the question depends more on other factors. For example, if your company has a separate test department, the test employees might not want writers to get involved. However, writers who observe the tests for themselves enjoy certain advantages:

- Writers can see with their own eyes, rather than from a second-hand report, how a test subject might struggle to understand a section of the book.

- Writers can observe how well the retrievability aids help the test subject find necessary information for a task.

- Writers can note how soon the book is abandoned.

As long as the writers aren't the only test observers, it's usually a good idea for them to watch at least part of the test. After seeing a test, the writers will not have to be sold on the need for revision.

The disadvantages of involving the writers center around time. In a very tight schedule, a writer might not have the time to observe a test or, in an extremely tight schedule, a writer might know in advance that he or she has no time to incorporate changes found during test.

With management approval and the agreement of everyone who found the errors, a book might occasionally have to be printed when it still contains minor errors. This situation might be better than delaying the shipment of the product, provided that the errors are truly minor and that they will be tracked and corrected in the next release.

Scheduling testing and writing

The job of merging test and writing schedules for a library of books can be formidable and probably should not fall to the individual writers themselves. A planner, lead writer, or manager—someone with a good overall view of the project—should ensure that testing fits into the schedule for producing the library. This person should apply some common-sense ideas to the project:

- Stagger the test dates so that each book gets a fair test at a time during the cycle when testing is appropriate.

- Give experienced writers shorter schedules so that they finish earlier and are available to help less-experienced writers who might run into problems.

- Communicate, communicate, communicate so that everyone on the project knows what's going on.

Testing Online Information

It could be argued that testing books is something of a luxury if reviews and meetings show that the information has worked well, but for online information, testing is a necessity. So much can go wrong other than the words that not testing is unwise.

Testing online information is frequently more expensive, time-consuming, and difficult than testing books, but it must be done to ensure quality. Since online information goes on diskettes alongside the code, or is frequently integrated with the code, your testing effort needs to be coordinated with code tests to some extent: you can't test online information before the code is ready unless you write your own code, or unless your online authoring tool provides programming support.

Two types of online information are normally integrated into the code of the product: help panels and hypertext modules. Two other types of online information, tutorials and softcopy, can be tested separately from the code because the tools used to create these types of information usually provide their own programming support.

Tutorials

Tutorials, also known as *familiarization diskettes*, *exploration programs*, or *introductions*, require careful testing because they are usually written for the novice user, not the expert user. You must develop a feel for screens, terms, and exercises that would puzzle or annoy the new user. By the time you have lived with a tutorial for many months of writing, you might have lost this ability. Keep in mind that the tutorial might be the first thing the new user looks at after purchasing the product, and try to spot anything that would make the experience less than pleasant and informative.

A tutorial isn't usually integrated into the code of the product because users should be able to view it before they start installing and using the product. Since a tutorial usually has its own supporting code, you have to test the code as well as the words. Whether you wrote the code or, more likely, got someone else to write it, you are still responsible for its success. Generally, testing the code requires three steps: running the tutorial, checking the sequence of the panels, and ensuring that the sample exercises work.

Running the tutorial. Running a tutorial is relatively easy to test, but telling test subjects, and then customers, how to run it is somewhat more difficult. The two main schools of thought require placing instructions in a book or placing instructions on the diskette label. You need to spend some time thinking about the typical user's first action after purchasing the product and, if at all possible, observing what they actually do. Does your intended audience turn to the books first or to the diskettes? Most instructions seem to go in books, but there is no reason a diskette label can't contain a few lines, as in Fig. 10.3.

Unless you call enough attention to running the tutorial, the new user might not find the instructions in a book. At any rate, the test case should determine whether a new user can get the tutorial up on the screen and start viewing it.

Checking panel sequence. The next step is checking the sequence of panels, depending on the choices the user makes. Every possible path should be tested to ensure that the code has no infinite loops and that none of the paths cause a dead end from which the user can't go forward. For example, if the first panel offers several different starting points to accommodate users who don't want to see the entire tutorial at one time, you should write test cases that start at each entry point.

If a panel is out of sequence or if a loop or dead end occurs, you have to get the code fixed before the tutorial goes to customers. A code change, of course, necessitates another round of testing to make sure the change didn't cause another error, such as the wrong colors being displayed, the function keys on the panel coming up in the wrong place, or the title being inconsistent with the other panels.

Checking sample exercises. The final step in testing a tutorial is to ensure that the sample exercises work. The tutorial code should simulate the code of the actual product well enough that a user turning from one to the other would not notice significant differences.

To view this tutorial, insert the diskette into the A: drive and turn the system on. When the A: prompt is displayed, type TUTOR.

Figure 10.3 Tutorial instructions on a diskette label.

However, you don't want to make the tutorial code actually perform any functions of the product. It should remain a simulation, but a realistic one so that the user learns about the product and is able to perform relevant tasks after completing the tutorial. The tutorial doesn't need to teach everything about the product—just the beginning steps to help a novice user get comfortable.

Softcopy books

A softcopy book is online information in long files that the user pages through instead of, or in addition to, reading the information in a book. Some softcopy generators also provide a way to print the information for those users who don't like to read online. Also, some softcopy generators provide a search function so that the user can find specific information rapidly and, in some cases, a table of contents to assist users in finding what they need. Depending on the tool you use to format and display the softcopy, you should test its functions thoroughly.

If the tool you use provides a way to print only certain parts of the softcopy, you should test some of the extreme cases—printing one little section near the end, printing several sections but leaving out intervening sections, printing the whole thing, and so on. Whatever the user could possibly do, you need to test at least a representative sample.

For a test of the search function, for example, see what happens when you search for a word that's not present. Is a meaningful error message displayed, or does the program end abnormally, leaving the user waiting? If the latter happens, you must get the code fixed.

To test the table of contents, write a test case that jumps around in the document and goes to different parts of the table of contents. Make sure the code displays what it is supposed to display. It might be impossible to test every possible combination of jumps, but try to design a true test of code stability so that customers won't have any problems as they use the softcopy book.

Help panels

If you use an authoring tool that automates help panel design and creation, you might not need to conduct much more than a cursory test. If you do not have such a tool, the following discussion will help you test manually created help panels.

Help panels are usually integrated into the product interface and must be tested in conjunction with the code. As a writer, you might not control the mechanism that displays the help panels, such as a help panel look-up table. Therefore, if you find errors, such as the wrong help panel being displayed, you might have to negotiate with the programmers to ensure that the errors are fixed.

Test procedure for menu help panels. Menu help panels are those that are accessible from any of the product menus. Menu help panels are usually provided for selection items, entry fields, function keys, and action bar items.

A useful way to test menu help panels is to step through each panel of the product, pressing the help key and noting whether the expected help panel is displayed. For each one that is incorrectly displayed, record the location and identifier of the incorrect help panel so that you can give this information to the programmer responsible for maintaining the help panel look-up table.

Frequently, such a test is the first time anyone sees how the help panels relate to the interface, and surprises are bound to occur. In hardcopy reviews, a help panel might read well, but when viewed online during use, you might find that it gives incomplete information or, worse, incorrect information for the particular situation.

Test procedure for message helps. For message helps, creating all the errors that could occur during use of the product is very difficult and time-consuming. Many test groups settle for ensuring that the look-up table provides an informative help panel for each error message that the code can generate. Test personnel might place all the messages into one file and all the help panels into another and then compare the two files.

However, if you can write realistic test cases that generate errors, you can do a much better job of determining whether the message help panels provide the customer with useful error recovery information. You might be able to determine which error messages are most likely to be displayed and make sure that you test at least those help panels.

Sometimes the programmers can tell you that certain errors have little chance of occurring, and you can skip them or test them last.

Testing the interface. Another task associated with testing help panels is to examine the interface carefully. Look for consistency in the following:

- The use of color on each panel
- The wording and placement of the title on each panel
- The contents and location of the function key area on each panel
- The terminology and language used in each panel

You might also need to watch for grammar problems, inconsistencies, spelling errors, and unacceptable abbreviations because the programmers who code the interface panels might not notice such errors. Getting the programmers to fix language errors might be difficult, but you should try. If you find such errors late in the cycle, you can plan to get them changed in the next release.

Hypertext

The final type of online information is hypertext, which might be integrated into the code of the product like the help panels. Unlike the help panels, however, hypertext provides either hierarchical or user-defined paths through the information. Some hypertext tools provide a combination of paths. Whatever the case, you need to test a large number of paths to ensure that the code doesn't have loops or dead ends.

In a hierarchical system, the task is a little easier because users have to select items from a series of menus before they link to the node they want to read. The menus offer stable reference points, and you can branch out from each selection item in a logical, orderly manner, ensuring that you access each node in each section.

Testing paths in a user-defined system can be much harder because you can't easily predict which location the user will jump to next. Some users like to browse widely through a hypertext database, and others like to get right to the information they need. Your test cases should accommodate both kinds of users. Since many hypertext systems also keep a history file or a list of nodes that the user accesses, you also need to test this file to ensure that it is accurate and that users can repeat their steps through the nodes.

Accessing hypertext.   The question of how to tell users about accessing the hypertext nodes is similar to that of telling them how to use a tutorial: you can put information in a book or online, or both. For a first release of a hypertext system, you probably want to feature it in a separate section of the user's guide, or whatever book you expect users to read first.

Since hypertext is still new to many users, you need to define terms, show the advantages of hypertext, and explain that linking to nodes isn't hard once they get used to it. For second and subsequent releases, you should cut down on the amount of hardcopy explanation and instead rely on a few online help panels or a short tutorial that describes the system to new users and refreshes the memory of experienced users.

Testing hypertext nodes and links.   The real work of testing a hypertext system is both the time-consuming process of stepping through each link to ensure that the correct node is displayed and the trickier process of designing test cases for test subjects. A smart idea is for you to do the stepping through first and then to call in test subjects for the more complicated branches and paths. If the system you're using has a cut-and-paste facility, be sure to include some tests in which users copy snippets of a sample program, drag and drop them into programs of their own, and then successfully run the programs.

Because hypertext is unfamiliar to many of your users, you might have some difficulty predicting their satisfaction with the new way of accessing and using information. However, as long as test subjects can complete their tasks successfully, your test work can provide many benefits.

Conclusions

Reviewing and testing might seem too expensive, too time-consuming, or too hard to accomplish. However, in these market-driven times, it's absolutely necessary at least to review information and, if possible, to test most hardcopy and all online information.

The benefits of testing are assurance of quality and satisfied customers. The dangers of not reviewing or testing are customer complaints, poor sales, and a reputation for low quality that can haunt a company for years. New books, or new information added to existing books, must be reviewed as early in the cycle as possible and then tested later in the cycle to achieve the highest quality. Online information, new or revised, must be tested with the code that runs it so that you can ensure its quality. Reviewing and testing are the best ways to guarantee that your information is of high quality.

Style Guides

Developing and following a style guide is a very practical way to save a lot of time and to achieve uniformity of style. Consistency throughout a book and throughout a product library can help customers by cutting down on their confusion and irritation. For example, if you always tell them to exit, instead of sometimes saying quit, escape, leave, or shut down, you contribute to the clarity of the book and avoid frustrating customers who might wonder if two similar words have any difference.

A style guide can range from a one-page list of rules to the 750-page *Chicago Manual of Style*. Even if you're a one-person writing shop, you still need a guide unless you want to spend a lot of time checking what you said early in the book when you're near the end, or checking earlier help panels when you're writing later ones. Developing a style guide that you can refer to as you go along makes your work easier.

Following are some topics you should include in your style guide:

- Punctuation
- Spelling and acronyms
- Highlighting
- Numbers
- Lists and tables
- Word use and terminology

Punctuation

General punctuation rules might be pretty cut and dried, but you need to spell out exactly how to use each punctuation mark anyway. Following are some suggestions:

- In formal writing, rule out the exclamation point and the dash; these are more appropriate for the informal and middle styles.

- Restrict the use of double and single quotation marks if your books will be translated because other languages use these marks for different purposes.

- Decide whether to place a comma before the *and* when you have items in a series. Will you write *apples, oranges, and bananas* or *apples, oranges and bananas*? Journalists don't use this comma, but most other writers do.

- Decide how to use parentheses, brackets, and curly braces in arithmetic expressions.

- Rule out semicolons unless the writers are thoroughly familiar with semicolon rules.

- Restrict the question mark to rhetorical questions in informal writing.

- When you refer to keyboard characters other than the alphanumeric ones, you should spell out the name and then put the symbol in parentheses. For example, "Use the asterisk (*) to specify a string of any length."

Spelling

Spelling itself doesn't usually pose any problems, but you need to give rules for plurals, hyphenation, and acronyms. Following are some suggested rules:

- Even if an acronym is printed all uppercase, its plural form should have the *s* in lowercase, as in *256 TCPs*.

- Make a number or letter plural by adding *s* unless the result would cause confusion, in which case use's. The plural of *A* is *A's* and the same is true for other vowels. The plural of *0* is *0's* and of *1* is *1's*.

- Hyphenating words at the ends of lines might not be under your control, depending on the word processor or publishing system you use. If you have to produce right-justified copy, you'll probably decide to hyphenate, but you probably won't for ragged right copy. For online information, it's usually better not to hyphenate.

- A common rule for acronyms and abbreviations is to spell them out at their first use and to include the acronym or abbreviation in parentheses, such as *kilobytes (Kb)*.

Highlighting

Highlighting rules should be consistently applied to a library. Following are some items you might need to set off from the regular text, with suggestions for how to highlight them:

- Commands (usually in all caps)
- File names (usually in italics)
- Words and phrases in the interface (usually in boldface)
- New terms at their first use (usually in italics)
- Words and phrases that the user must type (usually set in a different font than the regular text)

Numbers

Rules for numbers can be very simple if you ignore the usual advice to spell out numbers under 10, instead using Arabic numerals for everything. In on-line information, you save room on the screen as well as storage space by using only numerals.

Lists and Tables

Lists and tables have only a few rules:

- Use an ordered list (1, 2, 3,...) only when you present steps that the customer must follow in order. Use a bulleted list when the order isn't important. Elements in a list should, of course, be grammatically parallel.
- Use a table for a visual display of technical reference information, such as Table A.1.

TABLE A.1. An Example of the Visual Display of Technical Information.

Feature	OpSys1	OpSys2	OpSys3
Sessions	1	4	256
Threads	0	12	1024
Windows	1	2	8
Commands	20	48	512
Utilities	4	16	48
Applications	12	40	120

Word Usage and Terminology

Word usage and terminology can occupy a large part of your style guide because you need to create rules for things like the following:

- Avoiding sexist language by using *you* and *they*
- Avoiding culturally dependent examples, such as social security number, to make examples generic
- Selecting stock words and phrases to be repeated throughout the product library, such as "press button 1" or "click the mouse"
- Deciding on the name and acronym for the product
- Providing definitions and possibly a glossary of technical terms
- Listing indexed terms under many different synonyms, such as *start, begin, open,* and *power on*

Rules like these might sometimes feel like a straitjacket, but following a style guide is essential for high-quality computer information. Add any rules that you think will cut down on inconsistency and promote clarity, usability, and attractiveness in your book.

Sample Chapters
from a Design Guide

This appendix is adapted from Chapters 10 through 14 in a design guide for the IBM RISC System/6000 workstation family (courtesy of David McMurray, IBM-Austin). The first four chapters address front matter, back matter, hardcopy, and copyrights as they pertain to the product library; the last section is really a style guide for the product library. (RISC System/6000 is a trademark of the IBM Corporation.)

Chapter 10. Front-Matter Components

This chapter discusses the following front-matter standard components for hardcopy versions of RISC System/6000 publications: front cover, title page, warranty statements, edition notice, trademark information, communications statements, safety notices, about this book (preface), and the table of contents. (Differences in format and content between hardware and software publications are indicated.)

Front cover

Two front covers are available, one for hardware books, as shown in Fig. B.1, and one for software books, as shown in Fig. B.2.

- Use the full official name of the publication on the front cover.

- The form number should appear in the bottom right corner.

Figure B.1 Front cover art for hardware books.

- Edit the form number to reflect the number of the publication.
- Insert a superscript TM on RISC System/6000, but not on the IBM logo itself.
- Hardware technical-reference booklets will use a different style of front cover. NOTE: In simple printouts, the front cover and title page appear to be identical except that the order number is not displayed on the title page. However, the front cover is a thicker stock and the text and artwork are in color.

Warranty statements

Only operator guides contain the two warranty notices, "Warranty Exhibit to IBM Statement of Limited Warranty IBM RISC System/6000 System

Name System Unit" and "Statement of Limited Warranty."

- The Warranty Exhibit appears on the back of the front cover. Remember to change the name of the system unit.
- The Statement of Limited Warranty begins on the first odd page after the front cover.
- The wording for both types of statements is standard.

Title page

- The title page is a duplicate of the front cover, except that the order number does not appear.

Figure B.2 Front cover art for software books.

- The title page always appears on an odd-numbered page.
- Do not display the page number or a footer (although the title page is page i).

Edition notice

- Position the edition notice at the bottom of page ii (this page number is not displayed), which is the even-numbered page following the title page (the reverse side of the title page).
- Use the standard hardware or software edition notice available on the system.
- Insert the title of your book in italics on the first line. Change the date and edition number if necessary.
- In both hardware and software books, do not display footers or page numbers for the edition notice.
- If you are using a trademark page, delete the trademark notes from the edition notice. If you are not using a trademark page, make sure that you list all of the trademarks that occur in your book.
- If your book is in a second or later edition, change the date in the copyright line. (List only the first and current copyright dates, for example, 1989, 1993.)
- Hardware technical-reference booklets do not contain an edition notice (there will be an edition notice for the entire binder that contains the booklets).

For examples of the edition notice for hardware and software publications, see Chapter 13.

Trademark information

To indicate trademarks used in the book:

- If a trademark page is not needed or required, place the trademark notes on the edition notice page below the text of the edition notice and above the copyright line.
- If a trademark page is required, it should appear on the next odd-numbered page after the edition notice. (This is the first page number that is actually displayed.)
- In software books, the odd-page footer for this section should be "Trademarks." In hardware books, the odd-page footer should be "Preface." In both cases, display the page number, and use the short form of the book title as the footer on even-numbered pages.

- The title for this section, "Trademarks and acknowledgments," is a chapter component with a solid ruled line the length of the title and just above the title.

See Chapter 13 for guidelines on trademarks and the content of trademark notes or page.

Communications statements

Only operator, service, installation, set-up guides, and the General Information and Planning Kit should contain the communications statements section. (See Fig. B.3 for an example of the communications statement.)

Communications Statements

The following statement applies to this IBM product. The statement for other IBM products intended for use with this product appears in their accompanying manuals.

Federal Communications Commission (FCC) Statement

Note: This equipment has been tested and found to comply with the limits for a Class A digital device, pursuant to Part 15 of the FCC Rules. These limits are designed to provide reasonable protection against harmful interference when the equipment is operated in a commercial environment. This equipment generates, uses, and can radiate radio frequency energy and, if not installed and used in accordance with the instruction manual, may cause harmful interference to radio communications. Operation of this equipment in a residential area is likely to cause interference in which case users will be required to correct the interference at their own expense.

Properly shielded and grounded cables and connectors must be used in order to meet FCC emission limits. IBM is not responsible for any radio or television interference caused by using other than recommended cables and connectors or by unauthorized changes or modifications to this equipment. Unauthorized changes or modifications could void the user's authority to operate the equipment.

This device complies with Part 15 of the FCC Rules. Operation is subject to the following two conditions: (1) this device may not cause harmful interference, and (2) this device must accept any interference received, including interference that may cause undesired operation.

VCCI Statement

This equipment is Type 1 Data Processing Equipment and is intended for use in commercial and industrial areas. When used in residential area, or areas of proximity, radio and TV reception may be subject to radio interference. VCCI-1.

Avis de conformité aux normes du ministère des Communications du Canada

Cet équipement ne dépasse pas les limites de Classe A d'émission de bruits radioélectriques pour les appareils numériques, telles que prescrites par le Règlement sur le brouillage radioélectrique établi par le ministère des Communications du Canada. L'exploitation faite en milieu résidentiel peut entraîner le brouillage des réceptions radio et télé, ce qui obligerait le propriétaire ou l'opérateur à prendre les dispositions nécessaires pour en éliminer les causes.

Figure B.3 Communications statement.

Safety Notices

Note: For a translation of the following safety notices, refer to the *IBM RISC System/6000™ Translated Safety Information*, Form Number SA23-2652.

Definitions of Safety Notices

A *danger* notice indicates the presence of a hazard that has the potential of causing death or serious personal injury. *Danger* notices appear on the following pages:

3-5
3-17
4-3

A *caution* notice indicates the presence of a hazard that has the potential of causing moderate or minor personal injury. *Caution* notices appear on the following pages:

3-5
3-22

A *warning* notice indicates an action that could cause damage of a program, device, system, or data.

Safety Notice for Installing, Relocating, and Servicing

For safety checks when installing, relocating, or servicing, refer to Chapter 2, "Using the System Unit," and Chapter 3, "Moving the System Unit."

Note: Before connecting or removing any cables to or from the system, be sure to follow the steps specified for installing the system in the installation and service guide for your system device.

Lithium Battery

CAUTION:

A lithium battery can cause fire, explosion, or severe burn. Do not recharge, disassemble, heat above 100 degrees C (212 degrees F), solder directly to the cell, incinerate, or expose cell contents to water. Keep away from children. Replace only with the part number specified for your system. Use of another battery may present a risk of fire or explosion.

The battery connector is polarized; do not attempt to reverse the polarity.

Dispose of the battery according to local regulations.

Figure B.4 Safety notice for hardware book.

For the communications statements section:

- This section should begin on page iii (unless a trademark page is used, in which case it starts on the next odd page).
- The odd-page footer for this section should be "Preface."
- The title for this section, "Communications Statements," is a chapter component with a solid ruled line the length of the title and just above the title.
- Hardware technical-reference booklets do not contain a communications statement section.

Safety notices

Any book that contains danger or caution notices must have a safety-notices section. See Fig. B.4 for an example.

- Begin the section on an odd-numbered page.
- The odd-page footer for this section should be "Preface."

- The title for this section, "Safety Notices," is a chapter component with a solid ruled line the length of the title and just above the title.

- In "Definition of the Safety Notices," list the page numbers or the name of the section in which danger and caution notices occur in the book, or the titles of the sections within which they occur.

- This section ends with an all-caps danger notice that warns the user to unplug the power cable.

- Hardware technical-reference booklets do not contain a safety-notices section.

About this book (preface)

For the about-this-book section:

- Begin this section on an odd-numbered page.

- In hardware books, the odd-page footer for this section should be "Preface"; in software books, "About This Book."

- The title for this section, "About This Book" (or "About This Guide" if the publication is called a guide), is a chapter component (a solid ruled line just above the title and the length of the title).

- In hardware books, use these two headings (head level 1):
  - ~ How to Use This Book
  - ~ Related Publications

- In software books, use these headings (all are head level 2 except where noted):
  - ~ Who Should Use This Book
  - ~ How to Use This Book
  - ~ Overview of Contents (head 3)
  - ~ Highlighting (head 3)
  - ~ Related Publications
  - ~ Ordering Additional Copies of This Book

- In "How to Use This Book," explain the contents, purpose, and intended audience of the book. Provide an overview of the specific chapters and appendixes of the book.

- In "Related Publications," list all books cited within the current book. Include the full title of each book, its order number, and a brief statement about its content and purpose.

- Individual hardware technical-reference booklets do not contain an about-this-book section.

Table of contents

For the table of contents, see Fig. B.5 and note the following:

- Begin this section on an odd-numbered page.

- For hardware books, the odd-page footer for this section should be "Preface"; for software books, "Contents." The even-page footer should be the short title of the book.

- In hardware books, the title of this section is "Table of Contents"; in software books, "Contents." In both cases, it is a chapter component with a solid ruled line the length of the title and just above the title.

- Within the table of contents, titles of chapters and appendixes should be bold.

- Head 1's, the first level of heading after the chapter heading, should use the same left margin as the chapter heading; each lower level of headings indents an additional 1 pica.

- If the book is specifically divided into chapters, include the word *chapter* and the chapter number in the table-of-contents entry.

- If the book is divided into parts, use a chapter component for the name and number of the part; do not use leader dots or indicate page numbers. Use an Arabic number rather than Roman for the part number.

- In software books using encyclopedia-style organization, arrange sections alphabetically (for example, "Accounting," "AIXwindows Desktop," "Backup," and so on).

- Within sections of software books using encyclopedia-style organization, present concepts first, procedures second, examples last. Arrange concept articles or procedure articles from general to specific or from most to least common.

Table of Contents

Part 1. Emulators

Figure B.5 Excerpt from a table of contents.

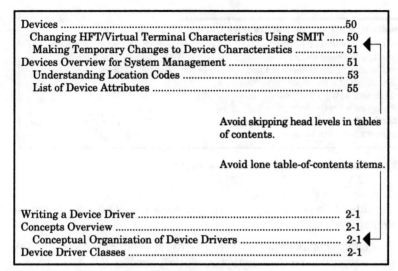

Avoid skipping head levels in tables of contents.

Avoid lone table-of-contents items.

Figure B.6 Common problems in tables of contents.

- The table of contents need not include detail below the second level of headings.

- Individual hardware technical-reference booklets each contain their own table of contents, called "Contents" (an Interleaf chapter component), located on the reverse side of the cover, on an even-numbered page.

- In the table of contents, avoid skipping heading levels and creating lone entries, as illustrated in Fig. B.6.

Chapter 11. Back-Matter Components

This chapter describes the following standard back-matter elements of hardcopy versions of RISC System /6000 publications: appendix, glossary, index, reader's comment form, and the back cover. (Differences between format and content of hardware and software publications are indicated.)

Appendices

For appendices included in the book, note the following:

- Begin each appendix on an odd-numbered page.

- For the odd-numbered-page footer, use the word *Appendix* and the letter identifying the appendix followed by the title of the appendix. For example, "Appendix B. Template Documents."

- Use the letter identifying the appendix in the page numbering. For example, page numbers in Appendix B would read B-1, B-2, B-3.

Appendix B. InfoExplorer for Graphics Interface

If you are a new user of the InfoExplorer program, you should read the information about the following tasks in the sequence shown. These tasks contain information you need to accomplish some of the tasks shown in the other help articles.

• Scrolling through an Article on this page.
• Selecting a Hypertext Link on page B-2.
• Selecting a Button on page B-2.

Starting InfoExplorer

There are two ways to start . . .

Figure B.7 Heading style for the first page of an appendix.

■ Use the title of the book (or a shortened version of it) as the footer on even-numbered pages.

■ Use the chapter component for the title of the appendix (a solid ruled line just above the title and the length of the title). See Fig. B.7.

■ Do not use a table of contents for appendices. Begin the body text of the appendix immediately after the heading.

■ If there is only one appendix, call it "Appendix," not "Appendix A."

Glossary

For the glossary, note the following:

■ Begin the glossary on an odd-numbered page.

■ Use the chapter component for the title, "Glossary."

■ Number the pages of the glossary with the prefix "X."

■ Use "Glossary" as the footer on odd-numbered pages in the glossary.

■ For phrasing, formatting, cross-referencing, and highlighting glossary entries, see Chapter 21 of *IBM Style Guideline*. In particular, keep these guidelines in mind:

~ Use the *Dictionary of Computing* as the primary source of definitions.

~ Insert an acknowledgment of definitions taken from other sources as explained in *IBM Style Guideline*, page 135. See Fig. B.8.

~ In cross-references, use the standard phrases, *synonymous with, synonym for, contrast with, see,* and *see also* as defined in *IBM Style Guideline*, page 139.

~ Italicize the cross-referenced term.

~ For abbreviations, provide only the spelled-out form of the term. Put the definition with the spelled-out form of the term.

~ Place special characters (those beginning with numbers or symbols) at the beginning of the glossary, and before words beginning with *a*.

Index

The following contains highlights of, exceptions to, and elaborations on the *Information Development Guideline: Indexing*. Refer to that publication for a complete discussion of assembling a topic and subject index.

Types of entries. Index entries fall into the following four categories:

- Topic: Points to a substantive discussion of a subject. Does not point to pages that merely mention the term or subject.

- Restriction: Points to a safety notice.

- Definition: Points to the definition of an important term.

- Text Reference: Points to a reference to another document in cases where the reader needs to know that a particular subject is not covered in the publication being indexed.

Synonyms and cross-references. Include any synonymous or deprecated terms that a reader would be likely to search for. In entries for deprecated

---

Master Glossary

This glossary provides definitions of specialized terms used in the hardware and software information for the RISC System/6000 system. Terms that are defined in nontechnical dictionaries and that have no special meaning in information processing are not defined in this glossary.

This glossary includes terms and definitions from the following publications:

ISO Vocabulary—Information Processing, developed by the International Organization for Standardization, Technical Committee 97, Subcommittee 1, as well as definitions from draft international standards, draft proposals, and working papers in development by the ISO/TC97/SC1 vocabulary subcommittee.

CCITT Eighth Plenary Assembly Red Book, Terms and Definitions and working documents published by the International Telegraph and Telephone Consultative Committee of the International Telecommunication Union, Geneva, 1985.

American National Dictionary for Information Processing Systems, copyright 1982 by the Computer and Business Equipment Manufacturers Association (CBEMA). Copies can be purchased from the American National Standards Institute, 1430 Broadway, New York, New York 10018.

Figure B.8 Glossary acknowledgments of sources.

or synonymous terms, use a *see* reference to point to the preferred term and do not give a page reference (see page 10 for an exception), as in the following:

system administrator
See root user.

See also references point to related terms and subjects, as in the following:

BIND password 3-4
See also node verification.

Sequence of alphabetic entries. The index begins with the alphabetic section. Entries are grouped alphabetically beneath individual letter headings (A, B, C), which are level 2 headings.

Since the *Indexing Guideline* was written, IBM has changed the alphabetizing standard from word-by-word to letter-by-letter, so ignore the various subtleties of the word-by-word system detailed in the *Indexing Guideline*. In letter-by-letter alphabetization, as described in *The Chicago Manual of Style* 18.43 and 18.92, alphabetize until the first punctuation mark, and then stop. A slash or a hyphen between two words is not considered a punctuation mark. For example, both input-output and input/output are considered one word. (The slash in root user authority/superuser authority is between more than two words, so this entry would be alphabetized only to the slash.)

Sequence of numbers and special characters. Entries that begin with a number appear below the alphabetic section of the index under the heading "Numeric" (head level 2). (Treat a Roman numeral as its Arabic equivalent; for example, VII would be treated like 7.) Automatic indexing systems arrange numbers character-by-character, so 773 would appear before 9. The *Indexing Guideline* allows this order, but if a writer or indexer thinks that nonnumeric order would confuse the user, the entries should be arranged in numeric order.

Numeric entries should also appear in the alphabetic section of the index as though they were spelled out.

Entries that begin with a special character, such as a $ (dollar sign), follow the numeric entries under the heading "Special Characters" (head level 2). Indexing systems automatically arrange these entries.

Word order within entries. Arrange each entry to feature the most important word, but include in the index any combination a user would be likely to search for. For example, include all of the following as entries:

magnetic tape storage

storage, magnetic tape
tape storage, magnetic

General format of entries.   For all entries, comply with the following guidelines:

- Capitalize entries as they appear in the text.

- Do not use special highlighting rules in index entries. For example, although they are bold in text, commands should not be bold in index entries.

- In entries that are nouns or gerunds, the singular form is preferred to the plural, unless the plural is the more prevalent form (like *bacteria*).

Phrasing of entries.   Phrase primary entries as nouns or gerunds, never as adjectives, verbs, or adverbs.

The phrasing of secondary (and all lower-level) entries does not need to be restricted to noun and gerund phrasing and can be in any of the following forms:

- Noun or adjective subentries can modify their primary entry as in the following:

  ~command
    ~ geometric
    ~ mathematical
    ~ utility

- When the relationship between noun subentries and their primary entry is unclear, use prepositions, as in the following:

  ~ data set
    ~ format of
    ~ storage of
    ~ tables in

- In some cases, however, using prepositions in this way becomes confusing, as in the following:

  ~ parameters
    ~ format of input of
    ~ format of output of

In such cases, delete the extra preposition if the user can determine the relation between the primary and secondary entry without it. Ideally, a list of subentries would use only one of these grammatical forms, but often this is not possible.

- Mixing different forms is acceptable, as in the following:

  ~ commands

~ mathematical
~ storage of
~ use of output

Punctuation of entries.   Only the comma and parentheses are used to punctuate index entries. Commas perform the following two functions:

■ Commas separate page references (11-8, 12-6).

■ Commas signify that words have been taken out of grammatical order, as in the following:

~ input, format of
~ input, use of

Parentheses perform the following two functions:

■ Parentheses are used to enclose the spelled-out version of an abbreviation or acronym or they enclose the abbreviation or acronym for a spelled-out entry, as in the following:

~ reduced instruction set computer (RISC)

■ Parentheses can also be used in place of a *see* reference when the preferred term has only one or two page references and no subentries. Instead of the following:

reboot
  See restart.
.

.

.

restart 18-3

use parentheses to indicate the preferred term and also give the page reference as in the following:

reboot (restart) 18-3
.

.

.

restart 18-3

Page references within entries.   Use the following guidelines when creating page references:

■ No entry should have more than two page references. Create subentries if this limit is exceeded for any particular entry. If an entry has subentries, the primary entry should have no page references.

- Indicating a page range for a topic is acceptable, but using only the first page of the range is preferred. Use an en dash (–) not a hyphen (-) to indicate a range. This is especially important in books using the double-enumeration system of page numbering, for example, 2–4-2–6.

Indexing guidelines specific to the RISC System/6000 library. In addition to the preceding, be aware of the following when writing a guideline for a RISC System/6000 publication:

- Use an index for all customer books with more than nine pages.

- Service manuals and technical-reference manuals do not require an index.

- Begin the index on an odd-numbered page.

- Use the chapter component for the title, "Index."

- If a glossary is used, continue numbering the pages consecutively with the prefix "X."

- Use "Index" as the footer on odd-numbered pages in the index.

- Do not use an index in hardware technical-reference booklets or problem determination guidelines (MAPs).

Reader's comment form

The reader-comment form is a template document (Fig. B.9). Make sure the title and order number on this form match those of the book. The reverse side of the form should be the return-mail envelope (not included in hardware-technical-reference booklets).

Back cover

The back cover is also a template document (Fig. B.10). Make sure the order number and copyright date are correct.

Chapter 12.   Other Hardcopy Elements

This chapter describes the following standard elements for the body text of hardcopy RISC System/6000 publications: parts, chapters and chapter tables of contents, body text, footers, headers, page numbers, cross-references, widows and orphans, artwork and tables, special format for technical reference, and translation considerations. (Differences between format and content of hardware and software publications are indicated.)

Parts

If the book is divided into parts, begin each part page on an odd-numbered page (which is blank on the reverse side).

Reader's Comment Form

Title of Publication

SA23-0000-00

Please use this form only to identify errors or to request changes in publications. Your comments assist us in improving our publications. Direct any requests for additional publications, technical questions about IBM systems, changes in IBM programming support, and so on, to your IBM representative or to your IBM-approved remarketer. You may use this form to communicate your comments about this publication, its organization, or subject matter, with the understanding that IBM may use or distribute whatever information you supply in any way it believes appropriate without incurring any obligation to you.

☐ If your comment does not need a reply (for example, pointing out a typing error), check this box and do not include your name and address below. If your comment is applicable, we will include it in the next revision of the manual.

☐ If you would like a reply, check this box. Be sure to print your name and address below.

Page	Comments

Please contact your IBM representative or your IBM-approved remarketer to request additional publications.

Please print

Date _____
Your Name _____
Company Name _____
Mailing Address _____
_____
_____
Phone No.   ( ) _____
Area Code

No postage necessary if mailed in the U.S.A.

Figure B.9 Reader's comment form for all publications.

- Parts are numbered with Arabic numerals, for example, "Part 2. Getting Started."
- Use a chapter component (a solid ruled line just above the title and the length of the title) for the title on the part page.
- Do not display page numbers on the part page. The footer on the odd-numbered page of a part page contains the title of that part of the book,

Figure B.10 Sample back cover.

including "Part" and the part number, for example, "Part 1. Emulators." The even-page footer is the shortened book title.

Chapter tables of contents

For the chapter and the chapter table of contents see Fig. B.11 and note the following:

- Place the chapter table of contents, which is the first page of the chapter, on the first odd-numbered page.

- Use a chapter component to show the title of the chapter.
- Use the heading "Chapter Contents" over the chapter table of contents (but do not include "Chapter Contents" as an entry).
- List all headings used in the chapter.
- Use the chapter name for the odd-page footer (but exclude the word chapter and the number of the chapter from this footer).

Body text

For the main text of the chapter:

- Use head 1's for the first-level headings. Head 1's use a solid ruled line from left to right margin.
- The body text of the chapter begins on the page following the chapter table of contents (an even-numbered page unless the chapter table of contents is more than one page long).
- Make the name heading indicate as specifically as possible the content or purpose of the article for softcopy users who need more detail to find their way in the information. For example:

  ~ **Too general heading:** Configuring Profiles
  ~ **Revision:** Configuring SNA Profiles

  However, to avoid repetition in the headings in hardcopy publications, make the repetitious element in the heading softcopy only. For example:

  ~ **Softcopy heading:** Using ASCII to EBCDIC Translation in em7
  ~ **Hardcopy heading:** Using ASCII to EBCDIC Translation

NOTE: Place the softcopy-only element at the end of the heading to prevent softcopy-build problems.

Chapter 1. System Unit Description

Chapter Contents
Typical Office Arrangement 1-2
System Unit 1-2
    Fixed-Disk Drives 1-3
    System Unit Features 1-4
External Device Connectors 1-6

Figure B.11 Chapter table of contents.

Footers

For footers in main-text pages of hardware publications:

- Use the chapter name for the odd-page footer, but exclude the word chapter and the number of the chapter from this footer. The chapter number is evident in the pagination.

- Use the title of the book for the even-page footer (if necessary, this title can be shortened).

- Use a hyphen (-), not an en dash (–) or em dash (—), in the page number.

- For footer style in front and back matter, see Chapters 10 and 11.

   For footers in software publications:

- Make the even-page footer the short title of the book: for example, "General Concepts and Procedures" rather than "AIX Version 3 for RISC System/6000 General Concepts and Procedures."

- Make the odd-page footer the title of the chapter; do not include the word *chapter* and the number of the chapter in this footer: in other words, "System Management Task for Communications" rather than "Chapter 1. System Management Tasks for Communications."

- In books using encyclopedia-style organization, use the topic name (for example, "Devices," "Problem Solving," or "Text Formatting") as the footer.

- Do not place any footers on the title page or edition notice.

- For other front-matter pages, use "Trademark" as the odd-page footer for the trademarks and acknowledgments page, "About This Book" for the about-this-book section, and "Contents" for the table of contents. (The even-page footer for all these pages should be the short title of the book.)

Headers

Do not use headers in hardware publications. For headers in software publications:

- Use headers only in reference-type information.

- Make the header the name of the language entity (for example, command, subroutine, function) but do not include the generic name: Use "Islv" rather than "Islv Command" in Fig. B.12.

- In books using encyclopedia-style organization, use encyclopedia-style headers. In the example in Fig. B.13, the Reverse Video On command starts the page and the Select Drawing Bitmap command ends the page.

- Headers should be placed on the right margin on odd-numbered pages and on the left margin on even-numbered pages.

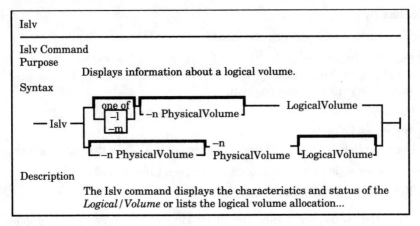

Figure B.12 Header style in commands-reference information.

Page numbers

For page numbers:

- Odd-numbered pages are right-hand pages. Even-numbered pages are left-hand pages.

- Use lowercase Roman numerals for front matter.

- Do not display the page number on the front or back covers, edition notice page, or the reader-comment form.

- Use the double-enumeration page numbering system; for example, 1-1, 1-2, 2-1, 2-2, 2-3, 2-4. (A few books, such as *General Concepts and Procedures*, do not use this pagination style in the main text; however, back-matter components such as appendices and indexes do.)

- Number pages in appendices using the appendix letter as the prefix; for example, A-1, A-2, B-1, and C-4. As in chapters, start the page number at 1 for each appendix.

- Number pages in the glossary and index consecutively with the prefix X-, beginning with X-1.

- In hardware books, use a regular hyphen (-), not an en dash (–) or an em dash (—) between the chapter number and the page number. In software books, use the en dash (–).

Cross-references (hardcopy)

Follow these guidelines for creating cross-references within hardcopy to books, chapters, appendices, other book components, sections, figures, and tables.

- To help readers understand why they should refer to the cross-referenced information, provide some idea of the topic, purpose, or contents of that information.

- Exact titles of books, either complete or shortened, should be italicized. Exact names of parts of books, chapters, sections within chapters, and appendices should be enclosed in double quotation marks. (To get a true opening double-quotation mark, press and hold the Alt key and then type the double-quotation mark.)

- For standard book components such as the preface, table of contents, index, and glossary, use initial caps and no quotation marks.

- Do not use highlighting guidelines when items such as commands occur in cross-references to headings or titles:

  ~ **Problem:** See "Using the exit Command" for information on . . .
  ~ **Revision:** See "Using the exit Command" for information on . . .

- Add the article *the* before book titles if doing so prevents awkward writing style. Do not include the article as part of the formal title of the book; do not italicize or capitalize it. For example, "see the *CD-ROM Technical Reference*."

- Use titles of books, chapters, sections, or articles only as titles. Note the following:

  ~ **Problem:** Do the "Installation Procedures."
  ~ **Revision:** Follow the steps in "Installation Procedures."

- In a cross-reference to a chapter, use the chapter number. In softcopy, for information without chapter numbers or with chapter numbers that are

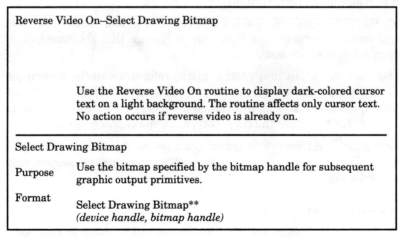

Reverse Video On–Select Drawing Bitmap

Use the Reverse Video On routine to display dark-colored cursor text on a light background. The routine affects only cursor text. No action occurs if reverse video is already on.

Select Drawing Bitmap

Purpose   Use the bitmap specified by the bitmap handle for subsequent graphic output primitives.

Format
Select Drawing Bitmap**
(device handle, bitmap handle)

Figure B.13   Encyclopedia-style headers.

appended at hardcopy-build time, use the title or the subject matter of the information for the cross-reference. For example:

~ **Chapter reference:** See Chapter 5 for information on em78 file transfers.

~ **Title reference:** See "em78 File Transfers" on page 142.

~ **Subject matter reference:** See the information on em78 file transfers.

- Include the page number in a cross-reference to the same document if the system can keep track of page numbers. Never include a page number in a reference to another document.

- Cite the exact name of a book, part, chapter, or section in a cross reference if your system can keep track of the name, and if it would help the reader understand the topic or purpose of the cross-reference.

- In text, use shortened titles for publications whose official name is listed in the related publications section. All publications referred to in the book should be listed.

- In running text, use the short form of the title in cross-references to other publications.

- References to external publications should take the form of a full bibliographic reference as described in Chapter 16 of *The Chicago Manual of Style*. Bibliographic references include the author, editor, or organization responsible for the publication, the name of the publication, the city where the publisher is located, the publisher, and the publication date. The following example applies for a book with multiple authors:

~ Merk, Jane S.; Fogg, Ida J.; and Snowe, C. Q. *Meteorologists Handbook*. Chicago: Amati Press, 1988.

- If you shorten the title of a publication, continue to italicize it. For example, *General Concepts and Procedures*. Ensure that shortened titles used in references are distinctive.

- Do not italicize or put in quotation marks references to the content of books, parts, chapters, sections, or articles. In this example, you would not use quotation marks on installation procedures even though there is a book by that title: "see the chapter on installation procedures."

- Do not italicize references to generic categories of books: for example, "see the operator guide for the specific RISC System/6000 system unit you purchased."

Widows and orphans

Follow these guidelines in controlling widows and orphans in hardcopy text:

- A heading should never occur at the bottom of a page with fewer than two lines following on that page. Instead, force the heading to the next page. Exception: If the following page contains a full-page figure, the head can be widowed. In this case, place at least a one-line introduction to the figure after the heading.

- Never place a single line of text (for example, the first line of a paragraph) at the end of a page.

- Never place a single line of text at the top of a page before another component, or on the page by itself. Place at least two lines before the component, or on the page if no component follows.

- Avoid placing a single list item on a page, especially if the page does not face the rest of the list items. Exception: A very long list item that takes up most or all of a page can remain an orphan.

- The introduction to an example, figure, or table should occur on the same page as the example, figure, or table. Exception: If an example, figure, or table takes up an entire page and cannot be broken into two pages, it can remain an orphan. In this case, at least try to place the introduction on a facing page.

Special format for hardware technical reference

For hardware technical-reference booklets:

- Major headings within the booklets should be head 1's.

- When reasonable, head 1's should begin a new page (for example, if the head 1 were otherwise going to appear in the bottom third of the page).

- Simple pagination style should be used (1, 2, 3, rather than 1-1, 1-2, 1-3).

- Main text of a booklet should begin on page 3.

- Both even- and odd-page footers should carry the title of the booklet.

- For front-matter elements of these booklets, see the chapter on front matter.

Translation considerations

Although some of the following may no longer be of concern in softcopy, consider the following physical factors before writing or revising information:

- Provide adequate expansion space for translation, especially where the English text is short. (For details, see your translation planner or your site National Language coordinator.)

- For pages in hardcopy documentation, consider 15% of each page to be white space. When laying out a page, allow for expansion space whenever text is enclosed within such things as line artwork, artwork boxes, and grid lines.

- Consider the following chart for calculating the expansion space needed. The principle in allowing expansion space is as follows: the shorter the text of the English version, the more expansion space should be allowed for the translated version, as the following chart shows.

- Leave sufficient space for monetary values. Some countries use seemingly large values for small transactions.

- Do not use abbreviations to save space. Using abbreviations does not save space because the expansion space must be calculated based on complete words. See Table B.1.

Chapter 13. Copyright and Trademark Guidelines

The following information explains legal requirements for copyrights and trademarks in RISC System/6000 softcopy and hardcopy.

General guidelines

The following items apply to copyrights and trademarks in general:

- If you suspect certain product or service names in your information may be trademarked, contact the owner of the trademarks list (currently, the coordinating editor).

- Do not make references to UNIX without a qualifying noun like one of the following: a UNIX operating system or a UNIX System V. Never refer to the UNIX system (according to AT&T directives).

- Because of world-trade considerations, do not refer to any trademarks as registered other than IBM. IBM should be the only trademark listed as registered.

TABLE B.1   Guidelines for Calculating Expansion Space for Translation.

English Length	Additional Space
Up to 10 characters	100-200%
11-20 characters	81-100%
21-30 characters	61-80%
31-50 characters	41-60%
51-70 characters	31-40%
Over 70 characters	30%

- In copyright and trademark notes, write out words like Corporation unless the organization requires the abbreviation. Do not use abbreviations like Corp., Co., and Inc., unless specifically required.

- Do not use trademarked names as nouns; use them only as adjectives followed by an appropriate qualifying noun: for example, write Micro Channel architecture or Micro Channel bus, not Micro Channel by itself as a noun. (A traditional exception to this guideline is the trademark IBM; it routinely appears in IBM publications without the qualifying noun Corporation.)

- Be careful about capitalization, spelling, and abbreviations in product and organization names: use the exact style required by the organization that owns a trademark or copyright.

- Observe the conventions for trademarks given in *Information Development Guideline: Style*, sections 7.121 through 7.121.2.

- Sometimes contracts with vendors stipulate certain style and wording for trademark notices. Check with the IBM owner of the contract.

- If you simply use the name of a company, for example, "Intel" or "Motorola," but not one of its products, there is no need to trademark.

- Listing trademarks is a courtesy to other companies, not a legal requirement.

Copyrights and trademarks in softcopy publications

Use the following guidelines for indicating copyright and trademark information in softcopy:

- Do not provide trademark notes or links to the trademark article in individual softcopy articles where trademarks occur. The Welcome to InfoExplorer window provides a link to an article containing trademark notes on IBM and non-IBM product names. This window is displayed when users first access softcopy. Trademark information is also available from a pull-down menu at any point within softcopy.

- Do not provide copyright information or links to the copyright article in individual softcopy articles where copyrights apply. The Welcome to InfoExplorer window (Fig. B.14) provides a link to an article containing copyright notices for other organizations or companies that have copyright to portions of the documentation. Copyright information is also available from a pull-down menu at any point within softcopy.

- The softcopy copyright article must list all copyrights that apply to softcopy information as a whole. The softcopy trademark article must list all trademarks that apply to softcopy information as a whole.

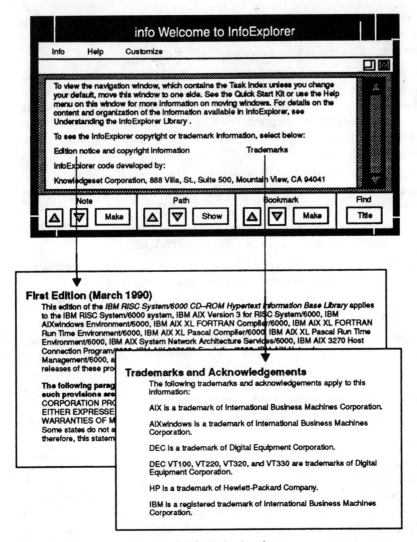

Figure B.14 Copyright and trademark information in softcopy.

Copyrights and trademarks in hardcopy publications

Indicate copyrights and trademarks in hardcopy publications as explained in the following.

Copyright information in hardcopy publications. Use the following guide-lines for copyright information in hardcopy publications:

■ In hardcopy, copyright information appears at the bottom of the edition notice.

- Make sure that the date or dates in the copyright information available on the system are correct. If there are more than three copyright dates, use the first-edition date and the current-edition date.
- If you use the edition notice available on the system, be sure to cut the trademark items that do not apply to your information.

See Figs. B.15 and B.16 for demonstrations of the placement of copyright information on the edition notice. For details on the format of copyright information and of the edition notice itself, see Chapter 10 on front matter.

Trademarks in hardcopy publications. Use the general guidelines in this chapter for deciding when and how to cite trademarks in your information.

First Edition (January 1990)

This edition notice applies to the *IBM RISC System/6000 POWERserver and POWERstation Translated Safety Information.*

The following paragraph does not apply to the United Kingdom or any country where such provisions are inconsistent with local law: INTERNATIONAL BUSINESS MACHINES CORPORATION PROVIDES THIS PUBLICATION "AS IS" WITHOUT WARRANTY OF ANY KIND, EITHER EXPRESS OR IMPLIED, INCLUDING, BUT NOT LIMITED TO, THE IMPLIED WARRANTIES OF MERCHANTABILITY OR FITNESS FOR A PARTICULAR PURPOSE. Some states do not allow disclaimer of express or implied warranties in certain transactions; therefore, this statement may not apply to you.

This publication could include technical inaccuracies or typographical errors. Changes are periodically made to the information herein; these changes will be incorporated in new editions of the publication. IBM may make improvements and/or changes in the product(s) and /or the program(s) described in this publication at any time.

It is possible that this publication may contain reference to, or information about, IBM products (machines and programs), programming, or services that are not announced in your country. Such references or information must not be construed to mean that IBM intends to announce such IBM products, programming, or services in your country.

Requests for copies of this publication and for techincal information about IBM products should be made to your IBM Authorized Dealer or your IBM Marketing Representative.

IBM is a registered trademark of International Business Machines Corporation.

IBM RISC System/6000 is a trademark of International Business Machines Corporation.

© Copyright International Business Machines Corporation 1990. All rights reserved.

Note to US Government Users—Documentation and programs related to restricted rights— Use, duplication, or disclosure is subject to the restrictions set forth in GSA ADP Schedule Contract with IBM Corporation.

Figure B.15 Edition notice for hardware books.

First Edition (March 1990)

This edition of the *AIX General Concepts and Procedures for IBM RISC System/6000* applies to *Version Number 3* of the *IBM AIX for RISC System/6000, IBM AIXwindows Environment/6000,* and *IBM AIX Personal Computer Simulation/6000* licensed programs and to all subsequent releases of these products until otherwise indicated in new releases or technical newsletters.

The following paragraph does not apply to the United Kingdom or any country where such provisions are inconsistent with local law: INTERNATIONAL BUSINESS MACHINES CORPORATION PROVIDES THIS MANUAL "AS IS" WITHOUT WARRANTY OF ANY KIND, EITHER EXPRESSED OR IMPLIED, INCLUDING, BUT NOT LIMITED TO, THE IMPLIED WARRANTIES OF MERCHANTABILITY AND FITNESS FOR A PARTICULAR PURPOSE. Some states do not allow disclaimer of express or implied warranties in certain transactions; therefore, this statement may not apply to you.

This publication could include technical inaccuracies or typographical errors. Changes are periodically made to the information herein; these changes will be incorporated in new editions of the publication. IBM may make improvements and/or changes in the product(s) and/or the program(s) described in this publication at any time.

It is possible that this publication may contain reference to, or information about, IBM products (machines and programs), programming, or services that are not announced in your country. Such references or information must not be construed to mean that IBM intends to announce such IBM products, programming, or services in your country. Any reference to an IBM licensed program in this publication is not intended to state or imply that you can use only IBM's licensed program. You can use any functionally equivalent program instead.

Requests for copies of this publication and for technical information about IBM products should be made to your IBM Authorized Dealer or your IBM Marketing Representative.

A reader's comment form is provided at the back of this publication. If the form has been removed, address comments to IBM Corporation, Department 997, 11400 Burnet Road, Austin, Texas 78758-3493. IBM may use or distribute whatever information you supply in any way it believes appropriate without incurring any obligation to you.

© KnowledgeSet Corporation, Mountainview, California, 1990.

© Copyright Adobe Systems, Inc., 1984, 1987

© Copyright INTERACTIVE Systems Corporation 1984. All rights reserved.

© Copyright 1989, Open Software Foundation, Inc. All rights reserved.

© Copyright 1987, 1988, 1989, Hewlett-Packard Company. All rights reserved.

© IBM RISC System/6000 is a trademark of International Business Machines Corporation.

© Copyright International Business Machines Corporation 1987, 1990. All rights reserved.

Notice to U.S. Government Users— Documentation Related to Restricted Rights—Use, duplication or disclosure is subject to restrictions set forth in GSA ADP Schedule Contract with IBM Corporation.

Figure B.16 Edition notice for software books.

For details on the format of trademark notices in the edition notice or on the trademark page, see Chapter 10 on front matter components. In hardcopy, trademarks can be presented in two ways—on the edition-notice page or on a separate trademark page.

- If fewer than four trademarks are used in a book, list the notes for those trademarks on the edition-notice page just above the copyright line.

- If more than four trademarks are used in the book, list them alphabetically on a separate trademark page, just after the edition notice.

See Fig. B.17 for examples of trademark notes on a separate trademark page.

Chapter 14. Writing Style, Usage, and Terminology

This chapter contains guidelines on common sentence style problems, concise writing techniques, punctuation (for commas, semicolons, colons, hyphens, dashes, apostrophes, and slashes), sentence structure problems (parallelism, dangling modifiers, and misplaced modifiers), grammar and usage problems, acronyms and abbreviations and symbols, translation considerations, numbers, terminology, and claims.

Sentence-style problems

Problems involving sentence style have little or nothing to do with correct grammar and usage. The sentence-style problems discussed in the following sections cause writing to be less clear, less direct, and less concise. For a thorough treatment of sentence-style questions with plenty of examples and exercises, see Joseph M. Williams, *Style: Ten Lessons in Clarity and Grace, 2nd ed.*(Glenview: Scott, Foresman, 1985).

Active and passive voice. Whenever possible, use the active voice in preference to the passive. For example, "The user selected the session to be deactivated." Not: "The session was selected to be deactivated by the user." (In some cases, the active voice is not practical. For example, it is preferable to write "The information is displayed" as opposed to "The system displays the information.")

Weak passive voice: Before any of the following procedures are done, the power to the system unit and connected devices should be turned off.

Revised for active voice: Before doing any of the following procedures, turn off the power to the system unit and connected devices.

Weak passive voice: Any cables that have been unplugged from the rear of the system unit must be labeled.

Trademarks and Acknowledgments

The following trademarks and acknowledgments apply to this information:

AIX is a trademark of International Business Machines Corporation.

AIXwindows is a trademark of International Business Machines Corporation.

DEC is a trademark of Digital Equipment Corporation.

DEC VT100, VT220, VT320, and VT330 are trademarks of Digital Equipment Corporation.

HP is a trademark of Hewlett Packard Inc.

IBM is a registered trademark of International Business Machines Corporation.

INed is a trademark of INTERACTIVE Systems Corporation.

InfoExplorer is a trademark of International Business Machines Corporation.

InfoTrainer is a trademark of International Business Machines Corporation.

Network Computing System is a trademark of Apollo Computer, Inc.

Personal Computer AT and AT are trademarks of International Business Machines Corporation.

Personal System/2 and PS/2 are trademarks of International Business Machines Corporation.

POSIX is a trademark of the Institute of Electrical and Electronic Engineers (IEEE).

PostScript is a trademark of Adobe Systems Incorporated.

RISC System/6000 is a trademark of International Business Machines Corporation.

RT is a trademark of International Business Machines Corporation.

Sun OS and NFS are trademarks of Sun Microsystems, Inc.

UNIX was developed and licensed by AT&T and is a registered trademark of AT&T Corporation.

Note to Users

The term "network information service (NIS)" is now used to refer to the service formerly known as "Yellow Pages." The functionality remains the same; only the name has changed. The name "Yellow Pages" is a registered trademark in the United Kingdom of British Telecommunications pic, and may not be used without permission.

Legal Notice to Users Issued by Sun Microsystems, Inc.

"Yellow Pages" is a registered trademark in the United Kingdom of British Telecommunications pic, and may also be a trademark of various telephone companies around the world. Sun will be revising future versions of software and documentation to remove references to "Yellow Pages."

Figure B.17 Trademarks and acknowlegments for hardware books.

Revised for active voice: Label any cables you unplug from the rear of the system unit.

Negative impressions.   Avoid language that imparts blame to the user or to the system and its creators. Find positive ways to tell users that they may have made a mistake.

Find positive language to explain system problems; avoid the impression that the system is poorly designed.

Negative impression: Failure to assign parameter values correctly may cause the system to crash.

Revision: Incorrectly assigned parameter values may cause system problems.

Negative impression: The subroutine failed because you overloaded the system.

Revision: The subroutine did not succeed because the system was overloaded.

Weak *be* verb phrasing.   Watch for sentences that make weak use of the verb *to be* and that can be written using an active verb. Quite often, sentences like these contain a form of the be verb followed by a prepositional phrase and can be improved by changing one of the nouns in the sentence into the active verb. (Do not, however, change nouns into nonstandard verbs.)

Weak *be* verb: The creation of both options is a new shared library text image.

Revision: Both options create a new shared library text image.

Weak *be* verb: The report from the shlib command is to indicate any discrepancies between the previous key and the new key.

Revision: The shlib command reports any discrepancies between the previous key and the new key.

Unnecessary expletives.   Expletives (in this sense) are forms of *it is* or *there are*. When used unnecessarily, they cause sentences to be unclear and wordy.

Unnecessary expletive: There are several flags in the print command that let you control how the files print.

Revision: Several flags in the print command let you control how the files print.

Unnecessary expletive: This chapter explains that there are files systems stored on the AIX fixed disk.

Revision: This chapter discusses the file systems stored on the AIX fixed disk.

Unnecessary expletive: When you first log in to the system, it is your login directory in which you are working.

Revision: When you first log in to the system, you are working in your login directory.

Redundant phrasing. The following is a partial list of typical phrases that are wordy, accompanied by their shorter, more concise alternatives. (Much of this section is based on Williams' *Style*.)

Redundant Phrases	Concise Versions
the reason for, for the reason	because, since, why
that, due to the fact that, in light of the fact that, considering the fact	
despite the fact that, regardless	although, even though
of the fact that, notwithstanding the fact that	
in the event that, if it should happen that, under circumstances which	if
as regards, in reference to, with regard to, concerning the matter of, where *xx* is concerned	about
it is crucial that, it is necessary that, there is a need/necessity for, it is important that, cannot be avoided	must, should
is able to, has the capability to, has the capacity for, has the ability to, is capable of	can

Meaningless modifiers. Words such as *basically, practically, virtually, generally, particular, certain, very, really,* and *various* are often used needlessly.

Needless modifiers: For all intents and purposes, American industrial productivity generally depends on certain factors that are really more psychological in kind than of any given technological aspect.
Revision: American industrial productivity depends more on psychology than on technology.

Redundant categories. When a specific word implies the category to which it belongs, both words need not be stated.

Redundant categories: The educational process and athletic activities are the responsibility of county governmental systems.
Revision: Education and athletics are the responsibility of county governments.

Unnecessarily varied or complex tenses. Often, tenses other than the simple present are used needlessly. Unnecessary use of the future tense is one of the most common misuses. Complex tenses such as the past perfect or present perfect continuous are seldom required.

Unnecessarily complex tense: Using the cat command will display the file on the monitor.
Revision: Using the cat command displays the file on the monitor.

Complex tense: It may be months before anyone notices that an important file has been damaged or is missing.
Revision: It may be months before anyone notices that an important file is damaged or missing.

Etc. and so on. Avoid *etc., and so on,* and *and so forth* by using the words *such as,* as in the following example, ". . . discusses storage media such as diskettes, fixed disks, and compact discs." The *such as* implies *and so on* and *and so forth.*

Sentence length. Avoid overly long sentences. While the 17-word-per-sentence average can certainly be exceeded at times, watch out for sentences significantly over that average and for text in which sentence after sentence exceeds that average.

Sentence order. Be careful about the sequencing of information within an individual sentence: Do not write "Drain the oil after you have placed the pan beneath the car." Instead, write "After placing the pan beneath the car, drain the oil."

Concise writing techniques

The strategies presented in this section illustrate ways of making information more concise. Please use them carefully; in some cases, these techniques can make sentences harder to read, much colder, and impersonal in tone. Try these techniques; if they reduce word count without harming the clarity or tone of your writing, use the revisions that result.

Convert declaratives to imperatives. Whenever possible, convert declarative-mood sentences to the imperative mood.

Declarative: With this command you can back up each file or only those files that have changed since a previous backup.
Imperative: Use this command to back up each file or only those files that have changed since a previous backup.

Declarative: It is a good policy to check the integrity of a file system . . .
Imperative: Check the integrity of a file system . . .

Change clauses to phrases. Watch for situations in which a clause can be converted to a shorter phrase.

Clause: Only you can determine the best backup policy for your system, but the following general guidelines should help.
Phrase: To determine the best backup policy for your system, follow these guidelines.

Clause: Think through each of these possible ways that information can be lost, and design a backup policy that would enable you to recover your system after any of them.
Phrase: With these possibilities in mind, design a backup policy to enable recovery after any of them.

Longer phrase: Files can change while they are being backed up.
Shorter phrase: Files can change during a backup.

Longer phrase: . . . a policy developed for a system on which many files are changed daily.
Shorter phrase: . . . a policy for a system on which many files are changed daily.

Delete understood nouns following adjectives. Watch for situations in which a generic noun following an adjective (that could easily be used as a noun) can be deleted and the adjective can be converted into a noun.

Adjective noun phrase: Files can change during a backup procedure.
Revised phrase: Files can change during a backup.

Delete adjectives implicit in nouns. Watch for adjectives implied in the nouns that they modify.

Original phrasing: This chapter gives a broad overview of the IBM RT system and . . .

Revised phrasing: This chapter gives an overview of the IBM RT system, and . . .

Original phrasing: You can read the current chapter for a quick summary of the system or as an introduction to the functions that are explained in the later chapters.

Revised phrasing: You can read this chapter for a summary of the system or as an introduction to the functions explained in the later chapters.

Delete adverbs implicit in verbs. Watch for adverbs that are implicit in verbs. In the example that follows, anything that works, by definition, works well.

Adverb: A policy that works well for one user . . .

Deleted: A policy that works for one user . . .

Pull information in separate sentences into series. Watch for situations in which you can extract information from several sentences and combine it into a series.

Original phrasing: You especially need to watch for invalid memory locations if you use absolute branch instructions. Watch for invalid locations also if you use an .org pseudo-op without an absolute operand. This can also become a problem if the .direct pseudo-op is used.

Revised phrasing: You especially need to watch for invalid memory locations if you use absolute branch instructions, an .org pseudo-op without an absolute operand, or the .pseudo-op.

Avoid fussy overspecification and unnecessary precision. Watch for situations in which more detail is provided than the situation warrants.

Fussy: It may be months before you or some other user of your system notices that an important file has been damaged or is missing.

Revised: It may be months before anyone notices that an important file is damaged or missing.

Subordinate one component of compound sentences. Watch for compound sentences in which one of the two halves can be changed into a dependent clause or phrase.

Compound version: Only you can determine the best backup policy for your system, but the following general guidelines should help.

Subordinated version: To determine the best backup policy for your system, follow these guidelines.

Combine sentences to delete obvious or repeated information. Watch for sentences that unnecessarily repeat information from preceding sentences.

Separate: Your system should not be in use when you make your backups. If you back up a file system while it is in use, files can change while they are being backed up. The backup copy of a file backed up while in use would not be accurate.
Combined: Your system should not be in use when you make your backups because files that are changed during a backup are not accurate.

Use pronouns when the antecedents are clear. Avoid being overly cautious in situations in which you could use a pronoun instead of repeating the noun or noun phrase.

Repeated words: If you want to log out of the system, but leave the system running for other users . . .
Pronouns: If you want to log out of the system, but leave it running for others . . .

Use ellipsis when possible. Watch for situations in which you can omit understood words through ellipsis.

Original phrasing: The RT microprocessor comes in two versions. Models 10, 15, 20, 25, and A25 are shipped with the standard 032 Microprocessor. Models 115, 125, and B25 are shipped with an Advanced Processor Card (APC).
Revised phrasing: The RT microprocessor comes in two versions. Models 10, 15, 20, 25, and A25 are shipped with the standard 032 Microprocessor; and models 115, 125, and B25 with an Advanced Processor Card (APC).

Terminology. Terms used in this discussion of concise-writing techniques are defined as follows:

- **pronoun** Words such as *it, they,* and *them* that stand for a noun or noun phrase.
- **antecedent** A word to which a pronoun refers. For example, in the excerpt ". . . these instructions. Their op code is used to . . . ," the pronoun is *their*, the antecedent, *instructions*.
- **ellipsis** Cutting obvious or understood words from text, for example, in the sentence "The day was Sunday; the time, 17:30," the second was has been deleted through ellipsis.

- **declarative** A type of sentence that makes a statement but does not ask a question or give a command, for example, "The user then presses the Enter key."

- **imperative** A type of sentence that gives a direct command, for example, "Press the Enter key."

- **subordination** Reducing a sentence to a dependent clause or phrase and embedding it in another sentence.

- **coordination** Joining two or more elements (words, phrases, clauses) in a sentence with a conjunction such as *and, or, not,* or *but.*

- **phrase** Word groups such as prepositional phrases, infinitive phrases, noun phrases, appositives, and participial phrases.

- **clause** Word groups such as noun, adjective, and adverb clauses.

- **independent clause** A clause that is a complete sentence.

Punctuation

The following sections discuss rules and common problems involving commas, semicolons, colons, hyphens, dashes, apostrophes, slashes, quotation marks, and periods.

Commas. Keep in mind the following rules for commas:

- Use a comma after an introductory element in a sentence. For example, "If the system unit is on, press the Enter key."

- Use a comma between two complete sentences joined by a conjunction (*and, or, nor, but, yet, for, whereas*). Use this rule for compound imperative sentences also: "Go to the system prompt ($), and then type e . or type e $HOME."

- Do not use a comma between short compound sentences joined by a compound conjunction. For example, "Wait 2 minutes and press the Enter key." The comma is unnecessary.

- Do not use a comma to join two sentences lacking a conjunction between them. Use a compound conjunction or a semicolon. In this example, "Connect the power cord to the system unit, then plug it into a properly grounded electrical outlet," the comma should be replaced with a semicolon, or the conjunction *and* should be inserted after the comma.

- In a series of three or more items, use a comma before the conjunction. For example, "The system also has a display, printer, and keyboard."

- Use commas for nonrestrictive elements but not for restrictive elements, as in the following:
  - ~ This book is intended for RT users who create, enter, or edit files on the AIX system.
  - ~ The Advanced Processor Card, which is shipped with Models 125 and B25, includes a fast processor, 4Mb of fast memory, and a built-in floating-point accelerator.

Semicolons. Keep in mind the following rules for semicolons:

- Avoid or at least minimize the use of semicolons, particularly in compound sentences.
- Use semicolons between items in a series when the items are long and complex or contain internal punctuation.
  - ~ The modules perform these functions: define the vector tab system queue area, and buffer; provide access to the data; and place the processing unit in extended mode.
- Use a semicolon between two parts of a compound sentence, as follows:
  - ~ The address operator is commonly used in accessing the pointer; you can use it to reference the address of an object.
- The following words should be preceded by a semicolon when used transitionally between clauses of a compound sentence: *then, however, thus, hence, indeed, accordingly, besides,* and *therefore.*

Colons. Keep in mind the following rules for colons:

- In vertical lists, place a colon after the lead-in wording unless another sentence intervenes between the lead-in wording and the list. If a sentence intervenes, both the lead-in sentence and the intervening sentence end with periods, as in the following example:

  The search order for commands that you enter is as follows. The external commands reside in the /usr/dos/bin directory.
  - ~ The directory /user/dos/bin
  - ~ The working directory
  - ~ Each directory in the dos path.

- For in-sentence lists and enumerations, place a colon after the lead-in wording if it is a complete sentence. For example:
  - ~ The system has three operating modes: entry mode, verification mode, and correction mode.

  If there is no break in continuity between it and the listed items, use no punctuation. For example:

~ The system's three operating modes are entry mode, verification mode, and correction mode.

■ Use only one space after the colon when it occurs before in-sentence lists and enumerations.

■ The terms *as follows* and *the following* require a colon if followed directly by the items or if the introducing clause is incomplete without such items.

> The steps are as follows:
> 1. Turn off the system unit.
> 2. Turn the brightness control fully clockwise.
> 3. Wait about 1 minute.

Hyphens. Keep in mind the following rules for hyphens:

■ In Interleaf, create the hyphen by pressing the Alt and dash (-) keys. Pressing the dash (-) key without the Alt key produces an en dash.

■ Do not use a hyphen with prefixes (for example, write nonnumerical) unless the unhyphenated version creates confusion with another word. For example, use re-sent rather than resent.

■ Use a hyphen with a prefix if the root is an acronym, numeral, or proper name; for example, non-IBM, pre-1980, or non-English.

■ Ignore the rule about not hyphenating trademarked words. For example, non-IBM and UNIX-based are acceptable.

■ Use a hyphen between units forming a compound adjective that modifies a noun. For example, deep-blue color.

■ Hyphenate compounds when they occur after a linking verb. For example, "This adapter is memory-mapped."

■ An adverb ending in *ly* is not joined with a hyphen to the adjective that it qualifies. For example, "highly developed intelligence."

■ When representing key sequences, link the individual keys in the order pressed with a hyphen, not a plus sign. For example, "the Ctrl-Alt-Delete key sequence."

■ Use a hyphen, not an en dash, for double-enumerated page numbers and for double-enumerated figure numbers; for example, page 3-12 and Fig. 4-2.

Dashes. Keep in mind the following rules for dashes:

■ Use the em dash (—) for situations such as those described in *The Chicago Manual of Style*, 5.82. To create the dash, press the Alt and plus sign (+) keys.

- In regular text, use the word *to* or *through* instead of the en dash. For example, write "bits 6 through 12" rather than "bits 6–12."

- Disregard the discussion of 2- and 3-em dashes in sections 5.95 and 5.96 of *The Chicago Manual of Style* (13th edition).

Apostrophes for contractions and possessives. Avoid using contractions. Do not use apostrophes to show plural of letters, numbers, or symbols: 3s, Rs, 1960s, #s. The only exception to this rule is that 0's and 1's are used to avoid confusion.

Slashes for conjunctions. Do not use a slash to represent any combination of *and* and *or*. Avoid using the conjunction *and/or* (*Style*, page 146). A phrase such as "3278 console/keyboard" can mean "3278 console and keyboard"; or it can mean "3278 console, keyboard, or both." Normally, such precision with *and/or* is not necessary.

Single- and double-quotation marks. Keep in mind these guidelines for quotation marks:

- Do not use single- or double-quotation marks for emphasis.

- Use double-quotation marks for unusual usage of words, but keep this to a minimum.

- In running text, use double-quotation marks around references to concept and procedure articles. For example:

  ~ For more information on logical volumes, see "Understanding Logical Volumes."

- In the suggested-reading section, however, do not use double-quotation marks.

- Use double-quotation marks on cross-references to other sections within an article. For example:

  ~ see "Syntax."

  If possible, however, avoid the necessity of quotation marks by writing

  ~ see the syntax section

- Do not use quotation marks for references to standard hardcopy book components. For example:

  ~ see Appendix A or see the Index.

Periods. Use only one space after the period (or other end-punctuation mark, question mark, exclamation point) at the end of a sentence.

Sentence-structure problems

Problems with sentence structure involve the way clauses and phrases are put together or arranged in sentences.

Parallelism. Parallelism means using similar types of grammatical phrasing for items in a series. These types include the following:

- **Clause** A group of related words that contains both a subject and a predicate. A dependent clause is not a sentence, but functions as a noun, adjective, or adverb within a sentence.

- **Participial phrase** A verb, adjective, or adverbial phrase that contains a participle and any modifiers, objects, or complements. The participle in the phrase is the verb form ending in *-ing*, *-d*, or *-ed* that is used as a verb, adjective, or adverb.

- **Infinitive phrase** The word *to* plus a verb and any related modifiers, subjects, objects, or complements that function as noun, adjective, or adverbial phrase.

- **Noun phrases** A group of related words that contains a noun and its modifiers and functions as a noun within a sentence. When two or more items are in a series, use only one of these types of grammatical phrasing; do not mix them. Here are some examples of sentences lacking parallelism and their revisions;

    ~ **Incorrect:** To delete the current message and you want to display the next message, enter d. (infinitive phrase and noun clause)

    ~ **Correct:** To delete the current message and to display the next message, enter d. (two infinitive phrases)

    ~ **Incorrect:** Enter the df command to determine the total number of disk blocks, number of disk blocks free, and how many are used. (two noun phrases and a noun clause)

    ~ **Correct:** Enter the df command to determine the total number of disk blocks, number of disk blocks free, and number of disk blocks used. (three noun phrases)

Dangling modifiers. Watch for dangling modifiers. For example, "Checking the error message, the cause of the problem should be clear" sounds as if cause is doing the checking rather than the user. The following revisions solve this problem: "Checking the error message, the user can find the cause of the problem" or "Checking the error message should enable the user to find the cause of the problem." In dangling-modifier sentences, the actor (the person, animal, or thing doing the action) is either absent from the sentence or not located next to the modifier.

Dangling modifier: To reach IBM 6150 system units more easily, extension cables are commercially available.

Revision: You can use commercially available extension cables to reach IBM 6150 system units more easily.

Dangling modifier: Before doing any of these procedures, the power to the system unit and all connected devices should be turned off.

Revision: Before doing any of these procedures, turn off the power to the system unit and all connected devices.

Dangling modifier: If connected, you should unplug the display power cable and system unit power cable.

Dangling modifier: If connected, unplug the display power cable and system unit power cable.

Revision: If connected, the display power cable and system unit power cable should be unplugged.

Misplaced modifiers. Watch for misplaced modifiers. For example, "If the panel only requires one table, it must be a root table." Only is out of place in the sentence. The sentence should read: "If the panel requires only one table . . ." Other words such as *almost, even, hardly, nearly, merely,* and *just* cause the same kinds of misplaced-modifier problems. The following examples show how moving a modifier around in a sentence can change the meaning:

The corporation executive just died, with his wing-tips on.
The corporation executive died with just his wing-tips on.
Just the corporation executive died with his wing-tips on.

A similar problem can occur with clauses and phrases. In the problem-modifier version of this example, it is not clear which action secures the adapter—installing or removing the screw:

Misplaced-modifier problem: Install the screw you removed in step 2 to secure the adapter.

Revision: To secure the adapter, install the screw you removed in step 2.

Grammar and usage problems

Grammar and usage problems often involve rules that seem arbitrary but because of common usage have become the norm.

Antecedents.   Check to make sure that the antecedent of a pronoun is clear. For example: "The system unit runs a power-on self-test each time it is switched on." Does *it* refer to the system unit or to the power-on self-test?

Person.   Keep the person consistent. Notice the change of person from second person *you* to third person *customers* in the following paragraph:

Problem: You can obtain information for ordering additional keys by writing to the address listed on the key tag. Customers outside the U.S. and Puerto Rico should contact their place of purchase for information on ordering additional keys.

Revision: You can obtain information for ordering additional keys by writing to the address listed on the key tag. If you live outside the U.S. and

Puerto Rico, contact your place of purchase for information on ordering additional keys.

Personal pronouns. Do not use *he, his, him, she, her,* or *hers* unless the antecedent is obviously male or female. Many terms, such as customer engineer, programmer, and student, commonly used in IBM manuals, clearly do not fit solely in the masculine category.

One way to avoid this problem, though not always workable, is to use the plural pronouns *they, them,* and *their,* and then rephrase. Instead of, "A customer engineer should be well-trained on the machines he services," say: "Customer engineers should be well-trained on the machines they service."

Plurals. Avoid using *(s)* for ambiguous plurals. Where possible, make the noun plural.

Prefixes. Keep in mind the following rules for prefixes:

- Do not use a hyphen with prefixes unless confusion with some other word is created or unless a double vowel or double consonant results.

- If using a prefix creates a double vowel, reword so that the prefix is not needed. For example, use, "Enter the command again," instead of, "Reenter the command."

That and which (restrictives and nonrestrictives). *Which* introduces a nonrestrictive modifier and is preceded by a comma. The information *which* introduces is not essential to the meaning of the sentence: it simply provides additional information; the information could be deleted without changing the meaning. *That* introduces a restrictive clause and should not be preceded by a comma. The information *that* introduces is essential to the meaning of the sentence; you could not delete it from the sentence without altering the meaning.

For example, the following sentence is imprecise: "A valid key is a key which is recognized by the host session." The fact that the key is recognized by the host session is important to the sentence since it is a definition. Substitute *that* for *which* in the sentence.

For a summary of the usage of *which* and *that*, see *Style*, 5.33.1.

Verb tense. Keep in mind the following rules for tense:

- Keep the tense consistent throughout the book (usually in the present tense).

- Avoid the future tense. For example, "The cable connectors fit only one way," not, "The cable connectors will fit only one way."

- Avoid unnecessarily complex tenses such as past perfect conditional continuous (for example, would have been running).

Acronyms, abbreviations, and symbols. Generally avoid acronyms unless the acronym is better-known than its spelled-out version or unless using the acronym significantly economizes on words.

The RISC System/6000 glossary will contain most of the agreed-upon abbreviations and symbols. In particular, however, keep the following problems in mind:

- Use A for ampere and mA for milliampere.
- Use Hz for hertz, MHz for megahertz, and kHz for kilohertz.
- Write CD-ROM with a hyphen.
- Make AC and DC uppercase.
- Use V ac and V dc (space after the V) for volts alternating current and volts direct current.
- Do not use K and M for kilobytes and megabytes, unless it is part of a product name. Instead:
  - ~ Use K-byte and M-byte and K-bit and M-bit for adjectives (for example, 256K-byte memory). Typographically, do not insert a space between the value and the symbol.
  - ~ Use K byte and M byte and K bit and M bit for nouns (for example, 256K bytes of memory). Do not insert a space between the value and the symbol.
  - ~ Use Kb and Mb for kilobits and megabits, KB and MB for kilobytes and megabytes.
- Do not use Latin abbreviations such as i.e., et al., e.g., etc.
- Typographically, put a space between the value and the symbol, for example, 8 Hz, not 8Hz. (K bytes and M bytes are an exception to this rule: write 256K bytes or 256K-byte, according to the rule stated previously.)
- The name of a key is the letter, symbol, or abbreviation printed on the keytop, with the same cap style. For example, the Esc key, the Enter key, the A key. For keys without printed names, use headline caps for the conventional name: for example, the Spacebar key, the Left Arrow key.
- Generally do not use symbols in place of words in running text. For example, in the following, substitute the word *equals* for the equals sign: "if x = z, do the following." (This guideline is often suspended in hardware technical-reference books.)

In addition, be aware of these translation-related abbreviation problems:

- Use only standard abbreviations and explain them all in an abbreviation list. Explain all the abbreviations in the abbreviation list in the product glossary provided to the translator.
- Avoid the United States symbol for pound or number (#). (Ignore this rule in programming context when the symbol is used as a prompt or comment indicator.)
- Avoid using the raised period to indicate multiplication.
- Avoid using a.m. and p.m. when specifying time. Use the 24-hour clock representation.

Number. See Chapter 8 in Style for the general policy on treatment of numbers. Spell out the numbers zero through nine, and use numerals for the number 10 and above except in the following cases:

- Use numerals for the numbers zero through nine when the number:
  - ~ Represents a unit of measure or a unit of storage size
  - ~ Identifies a particular item or unit
  - ~ Represents a specific value
  - ~ Is part of a compound adjective and represents a unit of measure or storage size, identifies a particular item or unit, or represents a specific value
  - ~ Is side-by-side with a spelled-out number and should be displayed as a numeral for clarity
  - ~ Is a part of a series of numbers, any one of which is 10 or above and is expressed as a numeral
  - ~ Is part of a mixed number (a combination of a whole number with a fraction)
  - ~ Is displayed with an abbreviation or a symbol.
- Spell out the numbers 10 and above when the number:
  - ~ Is the first word in a sentence
  - ~ Is side-by-side with a numeral and should be spelled out for clarity.

Translation considerations

Keep in mind the following guidelines for translation:

- Do not use humor. Most humor is temporal and local, not universal. (M. Harper points out that the British apparently fail to see much humor in *Far Side* cartoons; K. Glover adds that many U.S. citizens miss the humor in Monty Python.)

- Avoid slang, jargon, and colloquialisms.

- Do not use personification.

- Do not express dates in all-number form. In many countries, the expression 10/2/81 means 10th February 1981, while in the United States it means October 2nd 1981. To avoid ambiguity, always give the month in alphabetic form. If it is necessary to abbreviate, use the first three letters of the month name, for example 10 Feb 1981 or 2 Oct 81.

- Use dual-dimensioning except where international convention dictates otherwise, for example: tire sizes, water pipes, nails, and film. Always list metric dimensions first, for example 2.54 cm (1 in.).

- Avoid references to holidays that are exclusive to one country.

- When writing metric measurements along with other measurements, be sure the context makes the meaning clear. To readers in the United States and the United Kingdom, 4,791 means almost five thousand. In many other countries, where the period and the comma are often used in reverse positions, 4,791 means almost five. (For numbers with five or more digits, use spaces rather than commas: for example, 13 456 123.)

Terminology

The following contains discussion and guidelines on terminology in the following areas: general guidelines, translation considerations, general terms, hardware terms, criteria for new terms, sources and standards, ambiguous words, terms to avoid, specific vocabulary problems, and product names. See style guide for specific terminology questions, including specific terms to avoid or to use only with certain limitations.

RISC System/6000 documentation should:

- Convey information to the reader through language that is easily understood and terms that do not need formal definition.

- Contain uniform and consistent terminology derived from an internal word list.

- Communicate clearly and simply so that glossaries can be kept to a minimal length.

- Attempt to find more suitable terms for UNIX terminology such as master, slave, barf, and kill unless technical problems would be created by doing so. If avoiding such terms, which have become industry-wide standards, would cause problems, continue using these terms.

Keep the following translation guidelines for terminology in mind:

- Use general or nontechnical terms consistent with the definitions found in general dictionaries, such as Webster's New Collegiate Dictionary.

- Make sure that specialized terminology is based on national or international terminology standards, recognized dictionaries, or approved glossaries. Any term not listed and defined in a general or technical dictionary must be defined in the RISC System/6000 product-specific glossary.

- Assist designers and developers with assigning names and terms to parts of the product with which the user comes into contact. These parts include items such as keys, switches, knobs, command names, error messages, system messages, and screen titles.

- Use each term consistently throughout the document or library, even if it causes repetition. Translators generally assume that two different words refer to two different concepts and strive to translate accordingly.

- When using phrases (groups of two or more words acting as a grammatical unit), be sure that they have only one meaning and that they are used consistently. For example, the phrase program definition has been used with the meanings "definition of the program" and "definition by the program."

- Limit phrases to three words. It is hard to determine which word modifies what in a string such as "wrap fault locating terminator plug." If longer phrases must be used, use hyphens and commas: for example, "dressy, wide, patent-leather belt."

- Be careful with the following terms that often cause translation difficulties:

  ~ *as*. Use this word in the sense of *while*, not *because*.

  ~ *if, whether, whether or not*. Do not use the word *if* when it means *whether*. Further, use *whether* instead of the phrase *whether or not*, because *whether* implies *or not*, as in the following: "The program returns a value that indicates whether (not *if*, or *whether or not*) the value was sent."

  ~ *only, merely, just, mainly, simply*. Be careful where these words are placed in the sentence. A sentence can have several different meanings if you move one of these words.

  ~ *since*. Use this word to refer to the passage of time ("since last week"), not in the sense of *because*. To avoid misunderstanding, use the word *because* when that is the intended meaning.

  ~ *so*. Use *so* by itself to introduce a clause of result, as in the following: "The register is empty, so there is no information to retrieve." Use *so* followed by *that* to introduce a clause of purpose, as in the following: "Compact the files so that they occupy less space."

  ~ *when, if*. Use the word *when* only if the event described is inevitable.

Use the word *if* if the event depends on some other event.

~ *while*. Use this term in the sense of during the time that, not in the sense of *although*.

~ Avoid using a word as a noun and as a verb. It makes translation more difficult, and even in English, creates confusion for the reader. For example, in an article discussing functions (as in the delete function), do not use function as a verb, as in the following, ". . . the operand functions with INed permissions. . ." This could refer either to functions that have INed permissions or to operands functioning with INed permissions. Likewise, in all documents, avoid using read as a noun, as in the following: "The disk drive beeps when the read finishes." Instead, make read an adjective by inserting operation after it.

Other terminology guidelines include the following:

- The RISC System/6000 product glossary contains the precise spelling and treatment of announced IBM products and certain non-IBM products. Guidelines will be made available for handling unannounced product names.

- Do not describe machinery in human terms. Do not use phrases normally applied to human activity. For example, do not write, "The system is telling you. . ." or its inverse, "By pressing this key, you are telling the system. . .."

- Avoid slang, colloquialisms, or words with double meanings.

- Avoid words or terms from languages other than English.

- For the sake of brevity, write "Enter x"; it means the same as "Type x and press the Enter key."

Claims

Avoid claims about product performance that may not be substantiated. As opposed to writing that a certain utility improves performance, state that it may improve performance or that it is designed to improve performance.

Index